Alexis de Tocqueville, the First Social Scientist

This book proposes a new interpretation of Alexis de Tocqueville that views him first and foremost as a social scientist rather than as a political theorist. Drawing on his earlier work on the explanation of social behavior, Jon Elster argues that Tocqueville's main claim to our attention today rests on the large number of exportable causal mechanisms to be found in his work, many of which are still worthy of further exploration. Elster proposes a novel reading of *Democracy in America* in which the key explanatory variable is the rapid economic and political turnover rather than equality of wealth at any given point in time. He also offers a reading of *The Ancien régime and the Revolution* as grounded in the psychological relations among the peasantry, the bourgeoisie, and the nobility. Consistently going beyond exegetical commentary, Elster argues that Tocqueville is eminently worth reading today for his substantive and methodological insights.

Jon Elster currently holds the position of Professor at the Chaire de Rationalité et Sciences Sociales, Collège de France. He previously held teaching positions at the University of Oslo, University of Chicago, and Columbia University. He is a member of the American Academy of Arts and Sciences, Academie Europeae, and the Norwegian Academy of Science. He is also Corresponding Fellow of the British Academy and Doctor honoris causa of the Universities of Valencia, Stockholm, and Trondheim. His numerous books include *Explaining Social Behavior: More Nuts and Bolts for the Social Sciences* (2007), *Closing the Books: Transitional Justice in Historical Perspective* (2004), and *Alchemies of the Mind* (1999).

D1479310

Alexis de Tocqueville, the First Social Scientist

JON ELSTER
Collège de France

LIBRARY
FRANKLIN PIERCE UNIVERSITY
RINDGE, NH 03461

CAMBRIDGE
UNIVERSITY PRESS

CAMBRIDGE UNIVERSITY PRESS

Cambridge, New York, Melbourne, Madrid, Cape Town, Singapore, São Paulo, Delhi

Cambridge University Press
32 Avenue of the Americas, New York, NY 10013-2473, USA

www.cambridge.org
Information on this title: www.cambridge.org/9780521740074

© Jon Elster 2009

This publication is in copyright. Subject to statutory exception
and to the provisions of relevant collective licensing agreements,
no reproduction of any part may take place without the written
permission of Cambridge University Press.

First published 2009

Printed in the United States of America

A catalog record for this publication is available from the British Library.

Library of Congress Cataloging in Publication Data

Elster, Jon, 1940–
Alexis de Tocqueville : the first social scientist / Jon Elster.
        p.   cm.
Includes bibliographical references and index.
ISBN 978-0-521-51844-4 (hardback) – ISBN 978-0-521-74007-4 (pbk.)
1. Tocqueville, Alexis de, 1805–1859. 2. Social scientists – France – Biography.
3. Social sciences – Philosophy. 4. Social sciences – France – History. I. Title.
H59.T53E47 2009
300.92 – dc22   2008036545
[B]

ISBN 978-0-521-51844-4 hardback
ISBN 978-0-521-74007-4 paperback

Cambridge University Press has no responsibility for the persistence or accuracy of URLS for external or third-party Internet Web sites referred to in this publication and does not guarantee that any content on such Web sites is, or will remain, accurate or appropriate. Information regarding prices, travel timetables, and other factual information given in this work are correct at the time of first printing, but Cambridge University Press does not guarantee the accuracy of such information thereafter.

Contents

Preface		*page* vii
A Note on the Texts		ix
	Introduction	1
1	Preference Formation	11
2	Belief Formation	27
3	Self-Interest and Individualism	47
4	Passions	59
5	Desires, Opportunities, Capacities	79
6	Patterns of Social Causality	94
7	Equality and Mobility	114
8	Democratic Government	133
9	Revolution	150
	Conclusion	181
References		193
Index		199

Preface

I first read Tocqueville almost fifty years ago, as part of my French studies at the university. As I was largely ignorant of social science and of history, I was unable to benefit from him. When I returned to *Democracy in America* fifteen years later, having spent most of the intervening years learning those disciplines, I had an experience I have only had with two other books, Thomas Schelling's *Strategy of Conflict* and Paul Veyne's *Le pain et le cirque*. The work put me in such a state of intellectual and nervous excitement that I could not sit still, but had to get up from my chair and walk about from time to time.

When I tried to penetrate more fully into the work, its brilliance began to seem more blinding than illuminating. As I explain in the Introduction and document throughout the book, Tocqueville's unsystematic, not to say incoherent, analyses detract from the value of *Democracy in America* as a guide to either democracy or America. On further reflection, however, I was able to understand why my initial impression was justified. Instead of assuming that Tocqueville was a political theorist or an observer of American society, I began reading him as a social scientist. *Democracy in America* is filled to the brim – indeed, sometimes overflowing – with small and medium-sized causal mechanisms and highly sophisticated methodological insights that, although they do not add up to the grand theory to which he aspired, have lasting value. Even today, it seems to me, they are not as fully explored and utilized as they ought to be.

Although this reassessment put me in a different camp from virtually all writers on Tocqueville, it was not a solitary work. From the very beginning it was an enterprise carried out jointly with Stephen Holmes. In two footnotes I point to specific points on which he shaped my reading of *Democracy in America* and of the *Recollections*, but the importance of our collaboration is both much greater and more diffuse. On several occasions we taught Tocqueville together to our students at the University of Chicago. We also sat down, in Oslo, Paris, or Chicago, side by side, and read the main texts page by page, paragraph by paragraph. In so doing we hammered out an overall understanding of Tocqueville as a social scientist, as well as our interpretations of specific passages and arguments. Often, I cannot tell whether this or that idea originated with him or with me. Many conclusions were such a natural outcome of our exchanges that they seemed almost unauthored. While Steve ought to receive a great deal of credit for whatever is valuable in this book, it should go without saying that he is not responsible for any of its shortcomings.

The book grew out of a course I taught at Columbia University in 2007. As with many of my earlier books, the interaction with my students was essential for sharpening the argument and clearing up confusions. Two of their specific contributions are acknowledged in the footnotes. I also thank Diego Gambetta, Peter Stone, and several anonymous referees for their valuable comments on the manuscript. In addition, I am indebted to discussions with Arthur Goldhammer, Hélène Landemore, and Bernard Manin for the meaning of some particularly dense passages in the French texts. Finally I thank Stéphanie Novak for her painstaking checking of the passages I cite from Tocqueville.

A Note on the Texts

I cite *Democracy in America* (*DA*) from Arthur Goldhammer's translation for the Library of America (2004). In a few cases, I have made minor tacit emendations to that text. On one occasion I also cite a text that is included in the Lawrence translation, *Democracy in America*, New York: Anchor Books 1969. I cite from the drafts of the work by referring to the edition in Tocqueville, *Oeuvres* (Pléiade), vol. II, Paris: Gallimard 1992, abbreviated as *O II*. Translations from the drafts are mine.

There is no good English translation of the *Ancien régime* (*AR*). In my article "Tocqueville in English," *Archives Européennes de Sociologie* 40 (1999), 148–55, I point to severe flaws in the two existing translations.[1] The texts cited here are translated by Arthur Goldhammer, who is preparing a new translation of the work to be published by Cambridge University Press. The page references are to the edition of *AR* in Tocqueville, *Oeuvres* (Pléiade), vol. III, Paris: Gallimard 2004. Goldhammer has also translated the passages I cite from Tocqueville's notes for the projected second volume of the *Ancien régime*. I cite most of these by referring to the same edition as *O III*. For a few passages from these notes that are not included in the Pléiade edition, I refer to vol. 2 of the edition of the *Ancien régime* in the *Oeuvres Complètes*, Paris: Gallimard 1954, as *OC II-2*. I refer to vol. 2 of his *Ecrits*

---

[1] The new Penguin translation by Gerald Bevan appeared after the manuscript to the present book had been sent to the publisher.

et discours politiques, Paris: Gallimard 1985, also in the *Oeuvres Complètes,* as *OC III-2.*

I cite Tocqueville's 1836 article for the *Edinburgh Review* on "Political and social condition of France" by referring to *O III,* as above.

R refers to the *Recollections*, New Brunswick, NJ: Transaction Publishers 1987.

L refers to the *Lettres choisies*, Paris: Gallimard 2003. Translations are mine.

ER refers to *The European Revolution and Correspondence with Gobineau,* Gloucester, Mass.: Peter Smith 1968.

Introduction

The title of this book places me in a minority position on two separate counts.

Most scholars of Tocqueville think he was a great political theorist, and pay little attention to him as a social scientist. They view his main concern as normative, not as explanatory. Although I intend to show that he was an important social scientist, it is of course harder to prove the negative statement that he was not a major political thinker. Indeed, I am not going to make a systematic argument to that effect. I may mention, as one indicator, that in the index to John Rawls's *A Theory of Justice* there are twenty references to John Stuart Mill, but not a single one to Tocqueville. A more direct refutation of any claim on his behalf to be a great political thinker is given by the hugely incoherent structure of the work on which any such claim would have to rest, *Democracy in America*. I believe the bulk of the present book will make it clear beyond doubt that in that work, at least, Tocqueville was not a systematic thinker. Although he asserts in the Introduction to the book that a new world needs "a new political science," he does not provide it. His work on the ancien régime, while much more coherent and systematic, is a profound work of historical sociology but not of political theory. Yet, to repeat, my claim that he was not an important political theorist is strictly subsidiary to my positive argument.

Most social scientists, if they have read Tocqueville, probably do not think he is up to their standards. They may applaud his ambition, but deny that it was matched by any actual achievements. I do not have any hard evidence to prove this statement, but a long acquaintance with the social sciences tells me that he is much less of a household name than Marx, Durkheim, or Weber. In the index to James Coleman's *Foundations of Social Theory*, these receive respectively eight, nine, and sixteen references, Tocqueville only one. The reason, I suspect, is that for contemporary social science what counts as "an achievement" is determined by a certain view of science as resting on lawlike theories and aiming at sharp predictions.

I have argued against this view in various places, most recently in *Explaining Social Behavior*, and I shall not restate my objections here. The only point I want to emphasize concerns my proposal to substitute *mechanisms* for *laws*. The spillover and compensation effects that I discuss in Chapter 1 are mechanisms, not general laws. As laws, they could not both be true; as mechanisms, they may both be applicable, albeit in different situations. The statement that "a man facing danger rarely remains as he was: he will either rise well above his habitual level or sink well below it," further considered in Chapter 4, is hardly a law, but it is not an empty statement either, since *tertium datur*. The proposition that when A favors B over C, the reaction of C is one of envy toward B rather than of hatred toward A is one premise of Tocqueville's analysis of the French Revolution (Ch. 9). In my view, it is a mechanism rather than a law: a child that is not offered the ice cream her sister received may react to the injustice of her parents rather than against the better fortune of her sibling.

It would be misleading to leave the impression that Tocqueville is completely ignored by contemporary social scientists. The "Tocqueville paradox" that I consider in Chapter 9 – revolutions occur when conditions get better, not when they are getting worse – has had a considerable influence on theories of revolutions. It is also generally acknowledged that the equally paradoxical idea of "pluralistic ignorance" that was launched by Floyd Allport in 1924 had a direct precursor in Tocqueville's theory of conformism (Ch. 2). I shall try to persuade the reader that Tocqueville has other insights worth discovering or rediscovering.

The main obstacles to this rehabilitation are Tocqueville's constant ambiguity, vagueness of language, tendency to speculative flights of fancy, and self-contradictions. These flaws are abundantly found in

Democracy in America and, to a much lesser extent, in the generally more sober and coherent *Ancien régime*.

Consider first the ambiguities. It has often been noted that when Tocqueville refers to "democracy" he sometimes means "France," sometimes "America," and sometimes "democracies in general." In any given passage, the reader has to reconstruct the intended meaning. It is also well known that he uses the term "democracy" to denote both democratic government and the social state of equality. It is less generally recognized – but a central thesis of the present book – that the term "equality" itself is highly ambiguous. Sometimes it means equality of fortune at a given moment in time, sometimes rapid changes of fortune over time. This dynamic sense of equality is the main independent variable for many of the most important phenomena in the book, notably the absence of organized classes and hence of class struggle in the United States. Another ambiguity to which I repeatedly draw attention is his tendency to use "hatred" and "envy" as if they were one and the same emotion. They are not: the action tendency of hatred is to destroy the hated person; that of envy is to destroy the envied object, not its possessor.[1] In the analysis of a revolution that began by destroying privileges, and ended by killing the privileged, this distinction is obviously important. Finally, there is his regular tendency to describe a given phenomenon first as a glass that is half full and then as one that is half empty.

Consider next vagueness of language. Tocqueville is sometimes guilty of one of the most frustrating defects in a writer, that of *not being clear enough to be wrong*. At one point below I ask myself whether there is a contradiction between two passages, and answer that one of them is "too vague to be in flat-out contradiction with anything." There is also a frustrating vagueness in the chapters on "How Americans combat individualism with free institutions" and "How Americans combat individualism with the doctrine of self-interest properly understood," as if these were conscious collective efforts to defeat a generally recognized problem. Some of this language may be innocent rhetoric, but sometimes Tocqueville gives the impression that he is transforming cause–effect relations into means–end

---

[1] If we are to avoid tautology, we cannot *identify* these emotions by their effects; rather, we have to look at the beliefs that trigger them.

relations. This tendency is closely related to functional explanation, about which more shortly.

Consider further the speculative tendencies. The reader of *Democracy in America* is struck by the contrast between the concrete and down-to-earth nature of the first volume and the highly speculative, almost sophomoric character of many parts of the second. Most of us are liable from time to time to speak before we think; Tocqueville often seems to have thought before he looked (Sainte-Beuve). James Bryce, who had a deep knowledge of the United States as well as of Tocqueville's work, characterized the second volume as "a series of ingenious and finespun abstract speculations . . . which . . . will appear to most readers overfanciful, overconfident in their effort to construct a general theory applicable to the infinitely diversified facts of human society, and occasionally monotonous in their repetition of distinctions without differences and generalities too vague, perhaps too hollow, for practical use."[2] The most blatant instances, perhaps, occur in his speculative explanations of various religious phenomena. As I say in Chapter 2, in these analyses, he is applying what may be called the first law of pseudo-science: "Everything is a little bit like everything else."

Consider finally the contradictions. In an earlier book that contained two chapters on Tocqueville, I wrote that "There is no point beating about the bush: There is no other great thinker who contradicts himself so often and on such central questions."[3] I now think I overdid it somewhat, by lack of exegetical charity and ingenuity. As I discuss at various places below, some of the prima facie contradictions may be rescued or explained away. Many, however, cannot. In particular, the authority of public opinion is both asserted and denied (Ch. 2), as is the capacity of democratic citizens to be motivated by the long-term consequences of their present choices (Ch. 1 and Ch. 3). On these core issues of the work *we simply do not know what he thought.* In my earlier study I noted other minor inconsistencies that, I believe, are also beyond rescue. From the perspective of the present book, however,

---

[2] Bryce (1901), p. 326. In his review of the second volume, John Stuart Mill remained utterly silent about these speculative ideas, a fact I tend to interpret as indicating similar disapproval on his part. His robust common sense must have told him that they were nonsense, and his friendship with and general admiration for Tocqueville prevented him from saying so. This is of course mere guesswork on my part.

[3] Elster (1993), p. 112.

contradiction is less troublesome than ambiguity, vagueness, and speculation. Each of two contradicting claims may have explanatory usefulness if both are downgraded from lawlike statements to statements
about mechanisms.

In defense of his contradictions, we might also suggest, tentatively,
that they were a side effect of his intense concentration on the matter at
hand, which sometimes caused him to forget what he had written a few
pages earlier. When generalizing recklessly from a few examples, he
also pushed the implications farther and deeper than he might otherwise have done. In a somewhat Tocquevillian phrase (see *R*, pp. 144,
215), he might have probed less deeply had he been more concerned
with consistency. This idea is obviously not a point to be stressed, but to
be taken for what it is: a suggestion.

There is another obstacle to understanding Tocqueville for which he
should not really be blamed, but which nevertheless may be partly
responsible for the unjustified neglect of his views. It seems to me
certain beyond doubt that Tocqueville deployed his "models" or
"mechanisms" in a fully conscious way. I find it impossible to explain
the consistent appeal to the spillover effect and to the desire-opportunity mechanism in *Democracy in America*, or the repeated invocation
of the patterns "destroyed by success" and "saved by danger" in the
Recollections, without assuming that he worked from abstract and
general models. But perhaps out of a combination of the historian's
arrogance and the aristocrat's arrogance he disdained spelling them
out.[4] He seems to have preferred to hide the scaffolding and pretend
that he was simply telling a story, putting one foot ahead of another,
with the occasional maxim or epigram thrown in. Anything else would
have smacked of pedantry and of the abstract eighteenth-century
rationalism that he detested. Like Stendhal, he wrote for the happy
few. That was his privilege, but perhaps posterity's loss.

The main task of this book is to argue for the relevance of Tocqueville for social science in the twenty-first century. It may be useful to
frame some of the more general issues by comparing him with some of
his contemporaries. I believe there may exist a consensus that the three

---

[4] Several readers of the manuscript objected to this claim, which I certainly cannot prove
to be true. It is based on a long acquaintance with Tocqueville's prickly and intensely
private personality and, as I note in the text, his dislike of pedantry.

most important thinkers on social and political matters in the second
third of the nineteenth century were Marx, John Stuart Mill, and
Tocqueville. The comparison between Marx and Tocqueville is espe-
cially instructive. One could also use organicist thinkers such as Hegel,
Spencer, and Durkheim as a foil to bring out what is distinctive about
Tocqueville.

Painting with very broad strokes, the dominant and in my view
deeply pernicious features of nineteenth-century social thought
were holism, organicism, functionalism, and teleology. In complex
ways that I cannot discuss here, these closely interrelated approaches
were partly a legacy of theology and partly a result of the influence of
biology on the analysis of society. They led to all sorts of absurd
arguments and conclusions, many of them deserving a prominent place
in the cabinet of horrors in the history of science. With a few exceptions, Tocqueville was innocent of these sins. Among his contemporaries, only John Stuart Mill had a cleaner record in this respect.

By holism I mean the denial of methodological individualism,
and the claim that supraindividual entities – be they "social facts"
(Durkheim), classes (Marx), or Reason (Hegel) – have independent
explanatory power. An important example is the tendency to ignore
the free-rider problem in collective action, and to assume that cooperation will be forthcoming simply because it is better for all if all cooperate than if none does. Tocqueville was no sort of a holist. As we
shall see, he was very much aware of the free-rider problem, and argued
that either social norms or selective incentives may contribute to overcoming it. His frequent references to "mores" as explanatory variables
do not presuppose that these are anything over and above (shared)
individual attitudes. Moreover, Tocqueville was not only a resolute
methodological individualist, but also, I argue in Chapter 8, an ethical
individualist.

By organicism I mean the tendency to look at societies as analogous
to biological organisms, with an implicit or explicit assumption of
stability and self-regulation. In nineteenth-century sociology and in
more recent cybernetic theories of society, this approach has led to
a great deal of nonsense. Again, Tocqueville can be exculpated on this
count. I argue in Chapter 5 that he thought America in his time was in
(what I shall call) a state of equilibrium, but he did not claim that this
was the natural state of all societies. On the contrary, he argued that

prerevolutionary France was progressively hollowed out and destabilized as a society over a period of three or four hundred years.

By functionalism I mean the explanation of phenomena by their
beneficial effects for something (e.g., social cohesion) or someone
(e.g., the capitalist class) rather than by their causes. If we observe that
a group engages in successful collective action, we might explain it by
its beneficial consequences for the collectivity rather than by the
motives and beliefs of the individual participants. If we observe norms
of vendetta and blood feuds in a backward society, we might explain
them by the fact that they keep the population down at a sustainable
level. Although Tocqueville never proposes any functionalist argument
with that degree of crudeness, he does appeal to this mode of explanation on two important points. He believed that social norms and codes
of honor exist because they satisfy the needs of the group whose
behavior they govern (Ch. 4). More importantly, a key argument in
the *Ancien régime* arguably rests on a confusion between accidental
third-party benefits of social conflict and explanatory benefits (Ch. 9).
These are rare instances, however. As shown by his analyses of religion,
he was fully aware of the existence of *nonexplanatory benefits* of social
practices.

By teleology I mean the idea that history has a *sense*, both a meaning
and a direction. It is related to holism, but one can be a nonteleological
holist. It is also related to functionalism, in the way wholesale trade is
related to retail. One can be a functionalist on this or that specific issue,
without being committed to large historical claims. The Introduction to
Democracy in America may on a first reading seem to constitute a
teleological argument for the irresistible and inevitable progress of
equality in the modern world. I argue in Chapter 2, however, that shorn
of its rhetorical style the reasoning is perfectly acceptable and valid.
Chapter I.5 of the *AR* also has a bit of teleological flavor, but
harmlessly so.

In the ways I have indicated, Marx and Tocqueville are at opposite
poles. Except for the rare lapse into functionalism, Tocqueville looks
for *microfoundations* where Marx looks for aggregate evolutionary
patterns. (They have in common, however, ethical individualism.) Yet
while opposite, they were also connected. We know that Marx read
Tocqueville, and that he was probably influenced by his ideas about
classes (or their absence) in America (Ch. 7). In Tocqueville's notes

from his travels in Germany in 1854, we find a tantalizing reference to the young Hegelians through whom "German philosophy left its elusive spirituality to fall into political affairs (*la matière et les affaires*) with a licentiousness never seen even in France" (*O III*, p. 1097). Although he did not read any German philosophy firsthand, it is possible that his secondhand source, Saint-René Taillandier, referred to Marx.[5]

It is also possible, although supported by no evidence, that Marx and Tocqueville brushed shoulders in Paris in February 1848, where Tocqueville was at the center of events and Marx had a brief stopover on his travel from Bruxelles to Germany. More importantly, they both wrote on the February Revolution, Marx from the point of view of its importance for world history and Tocqueville from the perspective of the unintended consequences of human action (Ch. 9). Nevertheless, they agreed to a considerable extent about the causes of the revolution, both citing the immense contempt into which the July monarchy had fallen. We even find in Marx a variation on the Tocquevillian theme "destroyed by success" (Ch. 9). In a comment on the political crisis in 1851, Marx writes that "Instead of letting itself be intimidated by the executive power with the prospect of fresh disturbances, [the national assembly] ought rather to have allowed the class struggle a little elbow room, so as to keep the executive power dependent on it. But it did not feel equal to the task of playing with fire."[6] Marx's powers of analysis were as strong as those of Tocqueville – at least when he did not succumb to the *search for meaning*. As I remark in Chapter 9, for Tocqueville the events of 1848 were mostly sound and fury; for Marx, even small details tended to acquire world-historical significance.

In the rest of this book I make occasional references to Tocqueville's contemporaries or predecessors. Yet the main task I set myself is to

---

[5] This writer does not cite Marx by name, but refers (Taillandier 1853, vol. I, p. 292) to the creation in January 1842 of the journal, *Rheinische Zeitung*. Marx wrote in this journal and soon became its editor. Puzzlingly, Taillandier cites it as the *Neue Rheinische Zeitung*, which was the name of the journal that Marx was to edit during the 1848 Revolution. It is at least possible that Taillandier was aware of Marx's contributions to both journals and that his reading of them may have colored his exposition of the young Hegelians that Tocqueville relied on. This being said, Arnold Ruge and Max Stirner play a much more important role in Taillandier's discussions of this school.

[6] Marx (1852), p. 162. As we shall see in Ch. 9, Tocqueville used the very same metaphor – tempering the fire without extinguishing it.

elucidate the structure of his arguments, their validity, and their relevance for us today. For that purpose I deliberately chose to limit the scope of the scholarly apparatus compared to what would have been appropriate for a book with a more historical focus. I rely mainly on what for me are the four primary texts: the published versions of *Democracy in America*, the *Ancien régime*, and the *Recollections*, as well as the remarkable notes for the planned second volume of the *Ancien régime*.[7] I shall also on occasion refer to the draft manuscripts of *Democracy in America*, not to reconstruct the evolution of Tocqueville's thinking, but to cite formulations that may be more poignant or striking than what we find in the published work. I decided, however, to ignore Tocqueville's other published or unpublished writings. Although I cite occasionally from his voluminous correspondence, it is mainly to add relief to ideas found in the primary works. Finally, the reader will find virtually no references to the vast secondary literature on Tocqueville, partly because the bulk of the commentaries have focused on other issues than those I discuss and partly because responding to them would have broken the flow of the argument.

Among the four texts (just mentioned) on which I draw, *Democracy in America* and the *Ancien régime* are obviously the most important. Of these the former is by a wide margin the one I cite most frequently. This may come as a surprise to readers who share Dicey's opinion that the *Ancien régime* is "by far the most powerful and the most mature of [Tocqueville's] works."[8] It is certainly more mature (or coherent) than the exuberantly inconsistent earlier work, but not, I think, more powerful. In *Democracy in America* we encounter an enormously creative sociological imagination that generates a steady stream of *exportable causal mechanisms* whose importance Dicey did not fully appreciate. Although the later work is also rich in this respect, it is in the nature of a work of history that the proportion of theory to fact will be lower.

If I can demonstrate that Tocqueville's work does indeed contain exportable mechanisms, I shall have shown him to be a social scientist and perhaps an important one. Readers will ask themselves, however, how I can substantiate the claim that he was the *first* social scientist.

---

[7] I draw extensively on these notes in Ch. 9. Although they are fragments of an incomplete project, they are often extremely insightful.

[8] Dicey (1915), p. 233.

Readers of the manuscript – and some who just came across the title of the book – have argued that others have a stronger claim to that distinction: Montesquieu, Hume, Adam Smith, Condorcet, or Bentham. Not all of these founding figures did, however, share Tocqueville's obsession with causality. In the writings of those who did offer causal analyses, notably Montesquieu and Adam Smith, I do not find the same density of mechanisms. This is obviously a matter of judgment. Nothing is really at stake, except the appropriateness of a catchy title. I return briefly to this question in the Conclusion.

I

Preference Formation

INTRODUCTION

Contemporary social science has little to say about mechanisms of preference formation and preference change. In the case of beliefs, rational-choice theory, theories of motivated belief formation, and theories of conformism offer plausible accounts of how they emerge. As we shall see in the next chapter, Tocqueville anticipated some of these analyses. In the case of preferences, however, modern social science offers less to anticipate. When asked, "What does economics have to say about intrapersonal and interpersonal mechanisms of preference formation," Kenneth Arrow replied, "The short answer is nothing."[1] The other social sciences do not have much more to say.[2] Yet I believe they all have something to learn from Tocqueville.

Preferences are either *formal* or *substantive*. The latter are ordinary garden-variety preferences, such as preferring apples to oranges or Billie Holiday to Ella Fitzgerald. The former include notably *attitudes toward risk* and *time preferences*, which interact with substantive preferences to generate behavior. Tocqueville addresses the formation of both kinds of preferences.

---

[1] Arrow (2006), p. 975. The "long answer" cites peer pressure as a possible mechanism (see Ch. 2).

[2] In their introduction to an edited volume, Lichtenstein and Slovic (2006) enumerate five main theories of "preference construction." I think it is fair to say, however, that they address relatively minor – although often interesting – aspects of the issue.

Generally speaking, we may try to understand the formation either of stable and enduring preferences or of ephemeral and transient ones. The latter are not necessarily less important than the former, since actions taken on the basis of a short-lived preference may be impossible to undo when preferences return to their original state.[3] In the present chapter I consider Tocqueville's views on the formation of stable preferences, the discussion of temporary preference changes being postponed until Chapter 4.

Also quite generally speaking, we may explain preference formation either in terms of extra-mental phenomena or in terms of other mental states. The former question is postponed until Chapter 5. The latter I take up in the present chapter.

SPILLOVER, COMPENSATION, SATIATION

In *DA* Tocqueville often proposes to *explain preferences in terms of other preferences*. To this end, he relies on three mechanisms that I shall refer to as the *spillover effect*, the *compensation effect*, and the *satiation effect*. The first relies on *habit formation*, the two others on *need satisfaction*. Needless to say, he never names or identifies these mechanisms: they have to be extracted from passages scattered throughout the work. Yet I believe that the textual evidence demonstrates that he relies consistently on these effects, especially on the first.

Before I proceed, some background may be useful. Folk psychology and, until recently, scientific psychology tend to assume a great deal of cross-situational consistency of character traits and dispositions, including preferences. It has been argued, for instance, that people discount the future at the same rate whether they are dealing with financial investments or health decisions. Some people are prudent across the board, while others "live in the moment."[4] It has also been claimed that some individuals have an "altruistic personality" that manifests itself in other-regarding preferences in a large variety of situations.[5] Also, the

---

[3] An example is provided by "lobster-trap phenomena," as when young men and women join a guerilla movement in a moment of enthusiasm only to find out later that it is impossible to get out when their emotions are back to normal.

[4] Posner (2000).

[5] Monroe, Barton, and Klingemann (1990).

alleged "authoritarian personality" is supposed to generate "consistency of behavior in widely varying situations."[6]

In recent years, psychologists have proposed compelling arguments against the consistency assumption.[7] Also, individual studies have cast doubts on the cross-situational consistency of some of the traits I listed above. There is little correlation, for instance, between how people discount the future in financial decisions and in health decisions.[8] Studies of rescuers of Jews have found that what distinguished them from non-rescuers was not their altruistic personality, but the more accidental fact of *being asked* to help.[9] Although I do not know of similar studies of the "authoritarian personality," we shall see that Tocqueville's ideas cast doubt on the idea of a consistently *authority-seeking* personality.

Let me now define the three mechanisms I listed a few paragraphs above. The spillover effect says that if a person follows a certain pattern of behavior P in one sphere of his life, X, he will also follow P in sphere Y. The compensation effect says that if he does not follow P in X, he will do so in Y. The satiation effect says that if he does follow P in X, he will not do so in Y. Whereas the spillover effect tends to generate consistency, the other mechanisms tend to produce different preferences in different walks of life.

As a preliminary to the analysis of these mechanisms, let me first cite an interesting passage from Tocqueville's notes for the unpublished second volume of his work on the French Revolution:

It would seem that civilized people, when restrained from political action, should turn with that much more interest to the literary pleasures. Yet nothing of the sort happens. Literature remains as insensitive and fruitless as politics. Those who believe that by making people withdraw from greater objects they will devote more energy to those activities that are still allowed to them treat the human mind along false and mechanical laws. In a steam engine or a hydraulic machine smaller wheels will turn smoother and quicker as power to them is diverted from the larger wheels. But such mechanical rules do not apply to the human spirit. Almost all of the great works of the human mind were

[6] Adorno et al. (1950), p. 6.
[7] Mischel (1968); Ross and Nisbett (1991); Doris (2002).
[8] Chapman (1996).
[9] Varese and Yaish (2000).

produced during centuries of liberty. It does not seem true that the spirit of literature and of the arts is recharged or that they attain high perfection when liberty is destroyed. (*ER*, p. 168)

The immediate continuation of this passage is important for the light it sheds on Tocqueville's theory of political transitions that will concern us in Chapter 6. For now, I only want to draw attention to Tocqueville's objections to the "hydraulic" *theory* of the mind. In my opinion, his objections do not commit him to a denial of hydraulic *mechanisms*. Two passages I shall cite shortly strongly do in fact suggest some kind of hydraulic mechanism in the relation between political and religious authority.

The three effects operate to generate consistency or diversity of preferences across *spheres of activity*.[10] Broadly speaking, we may distinguish among the following spheres: religion, literature and the arts, politics, warfare, and "civil society" or "private life" (including economic relations and the family). Occasionally, Tocqueville also refers to spillover effects inside one of these spheres.[11] Although the three mechanisms are much more frequently cited in *DA* than in *AR*, Tocqueville also makes important use of them in the latter work.

The spillover effect can often be identified by the verbs Tocqueville uses to describe it, *transporter* (and more rarely *passer, se continuer,* or *se propager*), usually translated as "carry over," "transfer," or "pass on." (When he uses different language, identifying the effect can be more controversial.) By definition, the process involves two spheres: the origin of the preference in question and its destination. I shall first discuss how *risk attitudes* and *time preferences* spill over from one sphere to another, and then consider some other important applications of the spillover effect.

---

[10] I use the term "preference" to render what Tocqueville denotes variously as "habit," "instinct," "passion," and "taste." The relations among these dispositional terms are complex, and it is hard to tell whether Tocqueville uses them with systematic nuances of meaning. In one letter, for instance, he claims to "love liberty by taste, equality by instinct" (*L*, p. 331) and in another to "always have loved liberty by instinct" (*L*, p. 353).

[11] E.g., "Americans carry the spirit of trade over into agriculture" (*DA*, p. 647) or "Each citizen of the United States takes the interest aroused by his little republic [state] and carries it over into love of the common fatherland" (p. 184; translation modified). As we shall see in Ch. 2, he also applies the idea of the spillover effect to belief formation.

In *DA* Tocqueville repeatedly emphasizes that the Americans are risk-takers. An eloquent statement is the following explanation of the lack of stigma associated with bankruptcies:

The audacity of their industrial undertakings is the primary reason for their rapid progress, their strength, and their grandeur. For Americans, industry is like a vast lottery, in which a small number of men lose daily but the state wins constantly. Such a people should therefore look favorably on boldness in industry and honor it. Now, any bold undertaking risks the fortune of the person who attempts it and of those who place their trust in him. Americans, who make a kind of virtue of commercial recklessness, cannot in any case stigmatize the reckless. (*DA*, p. 731)[12]

From industry, the spirit of risk-taking and risk-loving spills over into warfare:

Men in democracies naturally feel a passionate desire to acquire quickly and enjoy easily the goods they desire. Most adore risk [*le hasard*] and fear death far less than toil. It is in this spirit that they pursue commerce and industry; and this same spirit, when they carry it to the battlefield, makes them willing to risk their lives in order to assure themselves in an instant of the spoils of victory. No form of grandeur satisfies the imagination of a democratic people more fully than military grandeur, which is spectacular and sudden and obtained without effort, merely by risking one's life. (*DA*, p. 775)

Why, we might ask, do the Americans love risk in commerce and industry? Tocqueville answers that "Those who live amid democratic instability have the image of chance constantly before their eye, and eventually they come to love all undertakings in which chance plays a role" (*DA*, p. 646). For them, emigration "has become a game of chance, which they love as much for the emotions it stirs as for the profit it brings" (*DA*, p. 326). Or again, "An American experiences all of life as a game of chance, a time of revolution, a day of battle" (*DA*, p. 466). The causes and effects of democratic instability will concern us in Chapter 7. For now, we should note that Tocqueville here appeals to

---

[12] In the first volume of *Democracy in America*, Tocqueville had offered an explanation that does not have this functionalist slant: "In the United States, there are no laws regarding fraudulent bankruptcies. Is this perhaps because there are no bankruptcies? No, on the contrary, it is because there are a good many. In the mind of the majority, the fear of being prosecuted as a bankrupt outweighs the fear of being ruined by the bankruptcy of others" (*DA*, p. 257). This is a simple expected-utility argument.

the extra-mental fact of instability to explain the mental attitude of risk-taking. (In the Conclusion I note that the converse causal relation may also apply.) In technical language, a mean-preserving increase in the variance of possible outcomes is associated with a preference change from the less risky option to the more risky.

The idea can be illustrated by assuming that in each of two societies, farmers face the choice between two crops with the same expected yield but different variance. Let me write > for the preference relation and let each expression between parentheses represent a lottery with a 50 percent chance of each yield being realized.

Society A	Society B
$(3, 5) > (2, 6)$	$(1, 7) > (2, 6)$

In society B, the fact that both available crop options are highly risky induces a preference for the more risky one. To my knowledge, contemporary economics and psychology have nothing to say about this particular form of *amor fati*.

Consider next the origin and effects of time preferences. Tocqueville claims that democracies tend to induce a short time horizon:

When everyone is constantly seeking to change places, and all are free to enter a vast competitive arena, and riches are accumulated and dissipated in the blink of an eye under the tumultuous conditions of democracy, the mind becomes acquainted with the idea of sudden and easy fortune and of great wealth easily won and lost, as well as with the image of chance in all its forms. The instability of the social state encourages the natural instability of human desires. Amid these perpetual fluctuations of fate, the present looms large; it hides the future, which fades from view, and men no longer wish to think beyond tomorrow. (*DA*, p. 640)

Here Tocqueville does not claim that democracy causes a "pure time preference" for immediate reward over delayed reward. The argument seems rather to be that the pervasive role of chance or risk causes people to disregard uncertain future rewards: "It seems pointless to think about a future that is so hard to predict ahead of time" (*O II*, p. 1128). We shall see several examples of this tendency. Elsewhere, however, he seems to argue that democracy does induce pure time preference: "Most people who live in ages of equality . . . want to achieve great success instantaneously, but without great effort" (*DA*, p. 498). Or again, what "makes it hard for men in democratic ages to commit themselves to ambitious undertakings is the amount of time they expect to have to devote to preparation" (*DA*, p. 740). And finally, "Since [men who live in democratic centuries] ordinarily aspire only to facile and immediate pleasures, they hasten impetuously after the object of each of their desires. The slightest delay plunges them into despair" (*DA*, p. 826). The causal link between democracy and pure time preference remains unclear, however.

The last-quoted passage continues with a reference to the spillover effect: "This temperament, which they carry over in political life, makes them impatient of forms [procedural formalities] that continually slow or halt the realization of their designs." Religions may, however, serve as an antidote to these tendencies:

In centuries of faith, people locate the ultimate purpose of life after life. Hence the men who live in such times naturally and in a sense involuntarily become accustomed to contemplating, for years on end, a fixed objective toward which they advance steadily, and by imperceptible degrees they learn to repress a thousand fleeting desires the better to gratify the one great and permanent desire that torments them. When these same men turn their attention to earthly matters, the same habits reassert themselves. . . . Religions inculcate the general habit of acting with an eye to the future. In so doing, they contribute as much to the happiness of this world as to the felicity of the other. (*DA*, p. 639)

What happens when religion loses its grip on the minds? In "centuries of disbelief" we will observe the tendency described above (in the passage quoted from *DA*, p. 640). In this case, the remedy lies in politics. Even though the role of chance and rapid fluctuations can never be banished from the *economic* sphere, in a democracy

[those] who govern must do all they can to banish chance from the world of *politics*. . . . In times of skepticism and equality . . . one must take care to ensure that the favor of the people or the prince, which chance may confer or withhold, does not take the place of knowledge or service. It is desirable that every advance should be seen as the fruit of some effort, so that greatness is not too easily acquired and ambition is obliged to set its sights on a goal for a long time before achieving it. (*DA*, p. 641; my italics)

By a spillover effect, the habit of long-term planning in secular matters may even recreate religion:

When men are used to predicting long in advance what will happen to them here below and to thriving on their hopes for the future, it becomes difficult for them always to confine their thoughts within life's exact boundaries, and they are quite prepared to transcend those limits and cast an eye on what lies beyond. . . . Thus the means that allow men, up to a point, to do without religion are perhaps in the end the only means left of bringing the human race back to faith. (*DA*, p. 641)

Tocqueville further asserts the existence in America of a spillover effect from private to public life, whereas in Europe the influence runs in the opposite direction: "In Europe, we often take ideas and habits from private life with us into public life.[13] . . . By contrast, Americans almost always carry the habits of public life over into private life. With them, the idea of the jury turns up in games played in school, and parliamentary forms influence even banquet arrangements" (*DA*, p. 352).

Even in America, however, the causal chain may run from private to public life. Among "the factors that encourage economy in the American government," Tocqueville distinguishes the institutions of democracy from the habits of commerce: the frugal "habits of private life carry over into public life" (*DA*, pp. 245–46). More generally, "The passions that move Americans most deeply are commercial rather than political, or perhaps it would be better to say that Americans take habits formed in trade and carry them over into the world of politics" (p. 329).

The most important spillover effect, however, seems to go from politics to economics. In the chapter of the first volume of *DA* on "the real advantages to American society of democratic government," Tocqueville makes the striking claim that these benefits are to be found only in the side effects or by-products of democracy and not at all in the process of political decision making:

The ceaseless agitation that democratic government introduces into politics then spreads to civil society. I am not sure that in the end this is not the greatest benefit of democratic government, so that I praise it far more for what it causes to be done than for what it does. There is no denying that the people often manage public affairs very badly. But they could not take part in public affairs at all without broadening their ideas and abandoning set ways of thinking. . . .

---

[13] See also *DA*, p. 336: "In Europe, virtually all social disorders are born at home, close to the hearth and not far from the marriage bed. It is at home that men become scornful of natural ties and permissible pleasures and acquire a taste for disorder."

Democracy will often abandon its projects before harvesting their fruits, or it will embark on dangerous adventures. In the long run, however, it achieves more than despotism. It does each thing less well, but it does more things. . . . Democracy does not give the people the most skillful government, but what it does even the most skillful government is powerless to achieve: it spreads throughout society a restless activity, a superabundant strength, an energy that never exists without it, and which, if circumstances are even slightly favorable, can accomplish miracles. These are its true advantages. (*DA*, pp. 279–81)

Democracy, in other words, is to be valued not for what it *does* (badly) in the political sphere, but for what it *causes to be done* (well) in the economic sphere. Or, as Tocqueville asserts succinctly in the drafts: "democratic government is not good but a source of social activity" (*O II*, p. 991). In the second volume of *DA*, Tocqueville spells out this argument as follows, in the chapter on civil and political associations:

It is through political associations that Americans of all walks of life, all casts of mind, and all ages daily acquire a general taste for association and familiarize themselves with its use. Large numbers of people thus see and speak to one another, come to a common understanding, and inspire one another in all sorts of joint ventures. Later, they take the lessons they learn this way and carry them over into civil life, where they put them to a thousand uses. (*DA*, p. 608)

The compensation effect cannot be identified by a specific terminology. Rather, it has to be reconstructed from the logic of the argument. Imputing it is therefore, inevitably, a more fragile or risky enterprise. The effect is also cited much less frequently than the spillover effect. Yet I believe that its existence and importance are undeniable.

The compensation effect arises when needs that are denied an outlet in one sphere of activity seek satisfaction in another. Let me offer some illustrations from an important book on the history of dueling by François Billacois. (I cite further illustrations in the Conclusion.) He suggests that the relation between violence on the stage and revenge behavior in sixteenth-century England and France was governed by the compensation effect: "At a time when France was a prey to duels and collective revenge, its theatre gave only a minor place to the theme of revenge; in England, which escaped these convulsions of social sensibility, the theatre was dominated until 1620 by the theme of vengeance, by the Revenge Tragedy. Can this simply be coincidence?"[14] In his discussion of the relation between duels and warfare, Billacois observes that contemporaries argued in terms of both the spillover and the compensation effects: "Many observers thought that the Wars of Religion 'engendered these particular disorders,' or at least that 'it is from the heart of our civil wars that our duels have taken their vigor, so well do these two evils go together.' But others judged it to be the end of the civil, and indeed international, hostilities under Henri IV that produced so large a number of quarrels, these being the only 'way by which young men believe that they can gain greater praise in times of peace.' "[15] A similar relation obtained between dueling and competitive scholarly activities. For young aristocrats, "intellectual combats and mimed confrontations may have fulfilled a function of sublimation and diverted the aggression of young gentlemen away from bloody fights."

The most striking instance of the compensation effect in Tocqueville arises from his claim that we are subject to two contradictory needs. Toward the end of the second volume of *DA*, he asserts that "Our contemporaries are constantly wracked by two warring passions: they feel the desire to be led and the desire to remain free. Unable to destroy either of these contrary instincts, they seek to satisfy both at once" (*DA*, p. 819). He goes on to claim that the citizens resolve the tension by subjecting themselves to a power that they have themselves freely elected. In the first volume, however, he had offered what I take to be a more profound solution to the same dilemma, in his analysis of the relation between religion and politics.

The slogan of the anarchists was "Ni Dieu ni maître." Religious freedom and political freedom went hand in hand, the one reinforcing the other. Tocqueville himself was not alien to this idea. Relying on the spillover effect, he wrote that

Men who live in ages of equality are . . . not inclined to locate the intellectual authority to which they submit outside and above mankind. Usually they seek

---

[14] Billacois (1990), p. 31. To explain the paucity of duels in Spain, he similarly argues that in Castilian society the duel and the bullfight "could be a substitute for one another" (*ibid.*, p. 38).

[15] *Ibid.*, p. 79. His own view is that while foreign wars reduce the number of duels, civil wars stimulate them (*ibid.*, pp. 80-81).

the sources of truth in themselves or in their fellow men. This is sufficient, perhaps, to prove that no new religion can be established in such ages, and that any attempt to do so would be not just impious but ridiculous and un-reasonable. We may anticipate that democratic peoples will not find it easy to believe in divine missions, that they will be quick to mock new prophets, and that they will want to locate the principal arbiter of their beliefs within the limits of mankind and not beyond. (*DA*, p. 490)

Yet paraphrasing T. S. Eliot, we may ask whether humankind can bear that much freedom. Tocqueville, who asked precisely that question, offered a negative answer:

When no authority exists in matters of religion, any more than in political matters, men soon become frightened in the face of unlimited independence. With everything in a perpetual state of agitation, they become anxious and fatigued. With the world of the intellect in universal flux, they want every-thing in the material realm, at least, to be firm and stable, and, unable to resume their former beliefs, they subject themselves to a master. For my part, I doubt that man can ever tolerate both complete religious independence and total political liberty, and I am inclined to think that *if he has no faith, he must serve, and if he is free, he must believe.* (*DA*, p. 503; my italics)[16]

On this analysis, the two "contrary instincts" are satisfied in differ-ent spheres. In democracies, Tocqueville argues, men seek religion as an outlet for their need for authority. In despotic regimes, they seek irre-ligion as an outlet for their need for freedom: " Even in our own time we find men who believe they can redeem their servility to the pettiest of officials by their insolence toward God and who, even as they have abandoned all that was freest, noblest, and proudest in the doctrines of the Revolution, still boast of remaining true to its spirit by rejecting religion" (*AR*, p. 57).

---

[16] The most eloquent statement of this idea occurs in an 1844 draft of a speech in parliament, in which he refers to "my fundamental idea, which is the reconciliation of religion and liberty, the idea that it was a mistake to separate them, and that our new society can function only at that price. . . . After this carnage of all authority in the social world, in the hierarchy, in the family, in the political world, one cannot subsist without an *authority* in the intellectual and moral world; if it is lacking there, one will have to find it somewhere I do not want to go, in a new hierarchy or in a great political power. One would need soldiers and prisons if faith is abolished" (*OC III-2*, p. 551). For another important statement of the compensation effect, see the letter to Kergolay (*L*, pp. 588–90), who, for his part, argued for a spillover effect.

In aristocratic societies, Tocqueville tells us, the compensation effect induces religion by a different mechanism, close to Marx's idea of religion as the "opium of the people." On this account, what causes religion is not the need for authority but the need for *happiness*: "In nations where the aristocracy dominates society... the people eventually become accustomed to poverty as the rich do to opulence. . . . The poor man's imagination is diverted toward the other world. Though gripped by the miseries of real life, it escapes their hold and seeks its satisfaction elsewhere" (*DA*, p. 618).

Another important instance of the compensation effect arises in the relation between politics and literature in prerevolutionary France. Because of the lack of political freedom under the old regime, "political life was forcibly channeled into literature, and writers, taking it upon themselves to direct public opinion, for a while held the place that party leaders ordinarily occupy in free countries" (*AR*, p. 172). Later, "When [the nation] finally had to act, it carried over [*transporta*] into politics all the habits of literature" (*AR*, p. 177): this is the spillover effect.

An important feature of this argument is the concatenation of the two mechanisms, compensation effect and spillover effect. Because the ban on concrete criticism of the government prevented writers from engaging directly with political matters, they turned to abstract theorizing that the government was willing to tolerate.[17] Later, when they had the opportunity to go into politics, they retained this disastrous propensity to propose general schemes that took no account of facts on the ground.[18]

The satiation effect (which might also be called "the crowding-out effect") can be illustrated by the relation between economic and political democracy. According to some writers, one argument for participation in the workplace is that it prepares the mind for broader political involvements.[19] Yet this spillover effect is sure to be attenuated by the sheer fact that *participation takes time*. "The trouble with socialism," Oscar Wilde is reported to have said, "is that it takes up too many evenings."

An observation by Tocqueville rests on a related argument: "Private life in democratic times is so active, so agitated, so filled with

---

[17] "[The government] rather readily tolerated attacks on the fundamental principles on which society then rested, and even discussion of God himself, provided that one refrained from comment on the most insignificant of its agents" (*AR*, p. 106).

[18] For an example of literally ignoring the facts on the ground, see *AR*, p. 189.

[19] See Adman (2008) for a survey and an empirically based criticism.

desires and labor that individuals have virtually no energy or leisure left for political life" (*DA*, p. 793). Here, too, we are dealing with a concatenation of mechanisms. People are often reluctant to enter into civil associations, since most of them "require members to risk a portion of their property. Industrial and commercial companies are all like this" (*DA*, p. 605). Through the spillover effect from political associations "they learn to subject their will to the will of all and to subordinate their individual efforts to the joint venture. . . . Political associations can therefore be looked upon as vast free schools to which all citizens come to learn the general theory of associations" (*DA*, pp. 605–6). Yet the very success of civil associations undermines, by the satiation effect, the political associations from which they sprang. For Tocqueville, this is a disastrous consequence. He points out that the governments of democratic societies, while wary of potentially subversive political associations, "feel a natural benevolence toward civil associations, because they can see readily that these, far from encouraging citizens to take an interest in public affairs, serve to distract them" (*DA*, p. 607). Once the school of politics has taught the citizens the habit of associations, they become so busy with their commercial affairs that they have no time for politics.

The absorption of Americans with their business affairs also enters into the explanation of the infrequency of adultery: "The tumultuous life of constant worry that equality brings to men . . . discourages love by depriving them of the leisure to indulge in it" (*DA*, p. 702). Similarly, "democratic peoples have neither the leisure nor the desire to seek out new opinions. Even when they come to doubt the opinions they have, they hold on to them nevertheless because it would take too much time and require too much study to change them" (*DA*, p. 757). As we shall see in the next chapter, because Americans lack leisure for study and reflection, they are led to take a shortcut by adopting general, all-purpose ideas rather than following William Blake's dictum: "Art and science cannot exist but in minutely organised particulars."

MOTIVATED MOTIVATIONS

At the outset of this chapter I referred to the idea of motivated belief formation. In a couple of passages Tocqueville hints at the important idea of *motivated formation of motivations*. The idea is not as paradoxical as it may sound.[20] In any society, there is a normative hierarchy of motivations. We approve or disapprove of people not only for what they do, but also for their motives. We might applaud somebody who keeps on a diet for health reasons, but ridicule a person who acts in exactly the same way out of vanity. We might applaud a whistle-blower if we believe he is motivated by the public interest, but change our mind if we learn that he only acted out of greed or malice. Knowing this, people have an incentive to present themselves to others *and to themselves* as being animated by a high rather than a low motivation. In aristocratic societies, this second-order motivation may cause people to present their self-interested actions as based on *honor*:

In aristocracies, what is held in contempt is not precisely work but work for profit. Work is glorious when inspired by ambition or pure virtue. Under aristocracy, however, it is a frequent occurrence that the man who works for honor is not insensible to the lure of gain. But these two desires are joined only in the uttermost depths of his soul. He takes great pains to hide from all eyes the place where the two are wed. He is apt to hide it from himself. (*DA*, p. 642)

In America, more surprisingly, the normative hierarchy may cause people to present their altruistic actions as based on *self-interest*:

Americans . . . are pleased to explain nearly all their actions in terms of self-interest properly understood. They will obligingly demonstrate how enlightened love of themselves regularly leads them to help one another out and makes them ready and willing to sacrifice a portion of their time and wealth for the good of the state. On this point I believe that they often fail to do themselves justice, for one sometimes sees citizens of the United States, like citizens of other countries, yielding to the disinterested, spontaneous impulses that are part of man's nature. But Americans seldom admit that they give in to enthusiasms of this kind. (*DA*, p. 611)

In a letter from 1831 that implicitly contrasts America with Montesquieu's idea that republics are based on virtue, he writes that "the

---

[20] See Elster (1999), Ch. 5 and Elster (2007a), Ch. 4 for fuller analyses.

particular interest manifests itself visibly and announces itself as a *social theory*. This is a far cry from the ancient republics" (*L*, p. 185; my italics).[21]

A few pages later Tocqueville appeals to people's *interest in the afterlife* to make the same argument: "I have met zealous Christians who regularly forgot themselves so as to work more ardently for the happiness of all, and I have heard them claim that they did so only to be worthy of the blessings of the other world. But I cannot help thinking that they are deluding themselves" (*DA*, p. 614). He might have added that according to most varieties of Christian theology, the effort would be self-defeating. Trying to purchase a place in heaven by good deeds would be to force the hand of God, who is not likely to let that happen.

We may ask whether this "norm of self-interest"[22] and the code of honor in aristocratic societies make any difference for *behavior*, or whether they merely provide ex post rationalizations for actions undertaken on other grounds. I believe the norms can make a difference simply because they cannot be switched on and off at will. When honor points in one direction and material interest in another, the latter may have to yield.

We may also ask, however, whether Tocqueville does not exaggerate when he claims that Americans are reluctant to admit to being disinterested. There may indeed be societies in which a concern for the common good is the object of general disapproval. It has been claimed, for instance, that in southern Italy the norms of "amoral familism" have this effect.[23] Whether this claim is true or not, a similar claim about the United States stretches the imagination. In the late eighteenth century, American elites propagated what amounted to a cult of disinterestedness.[24] It is reasonable to think that they still set the tone half a century later. In fact, Tocqueville himself asserts that they did:

---

[21] In the drafts for *DA*, Tocqueville adopts a more nuanced position: "Americans do not constitute a virtuous people, and nevertheless they are free. This fact does not absolutely prove that virtue is not essential to the existence of republics, as Montesquieu thought it was. . . . In America it is not virtue that is great but temptations that are small, which amounts to the same thing. It is not that disinterestedness is great, but that interest is enlightened, which also amounts almost to the same thing" (*O II*, p. 1035).
[22] Miller (1999).
[23] Banfield (1958).
[24] Wood (1987).

As soon as common affairs are dealt with in common, each man sees that he is not as independent of his fellow men as he initially imagined and that, in order to obtain their support, he must often lend them his cooperation. When the public governs, no one is unaware of the value of the public's good will, and everyone tries to court it by winning the esteem and affection of the people among whom he is obliged to live. Several of the passions that chill and divide hearts are then obliged to withdraw into the recesses of the soul and hide there. Pride dissimulates; contempt dares not rear its head. Egoism is afraid of itself. (*DA*, pp. 590–91)

Hence we see Tocqueville both affirming the norm of self-interest among the Americans and claiming that they were afraid of admitting to act out of self-interest. No doubt some of the individuals he met corresponded to the first profile and others to the second. In one context, the latter occurred to him; and when he came to discuss phenomena where he could make explanatory use of the former he had, as I suggested in the Introduction, forgotten his earlier argument.

2

Belief Formation

We have "beliefs" about many kinds of issues. There are factual beliefs (regarding, for example, the number of piano tuners in Philadelphia), causal beliefs (regarding, for example, the impact of minimal wage legislation on unemployment), religious beliefs (regarding, for example, the existence of the afterlife), and political beliefs (regarding, for example, whether affirmative action is acceptable). Except for the last-mentioned (which is more a preference than a belief), all these beliefs presuppose that there is *a fact of the matter*, some feature of the universe by virtue of which the belief, if true, is true. All beliefs, also the last mentioned, can serve as premises for action. Some, however, mainly serve as consolation for misery. As we saw in Chapter 1, this is how Tocqueville explained why the mass of the people in aristocratic societies believed in the afterlife.[1]

How do people come to have the beliefs they have? One answer, mainly relevant for factual and causal beliefs, is that people form *rational beliefs* in order to achieve their aims as well as possible. The process involves both the optimal gathering of information and the correct processing of information. Another answer, which may apply to all sorts of beliefs, is that they are subject to *motivated belief*

---

[1] Even in that case, they may serve as a premise for *inaction*. This was Marx's view.

formation: people gravitate toward the beliefs they would like to be true.[2] In many cases, these two processes yield different results. If I am a rational smoker, I will realize the health dangers of smoking. If I would like to believe that these dangers can be ignored, because I want to keep smoking, I will form a different conclusion. In Freud's terminology, the two processes are governed by, respectively, "the reality principle" and "the pleasure principle." A third answer – it is actually a *set* of answers – is that belief formation is governed by *heuristics and biases* – cognitive shortcuts that can lead us wildly astray while not having any motivational foundation.[3] They do, for instance, cause non-smokers to form exaggerated ideas about the dangers of smoking. A fourth answer is that belief formation is *ideological* – people form beliefs that reflect and perhaps perpetuate the economic and political system under which they live. Paul Veyne argued, for instance, that the Romans were subject to a *cognitive illusion*: since luxury created jobs and the *princeps* created order, a society without luxury or emperor would sink into unemployment or chaos, as if no alternative arrangements were feasible.[4]

Tocqueville addresses all these varieties of belief and of belief formation. Although his main concern is with political and religious beliefs, he has intriguing things to say about how people in different societies form causal beliefs. Some of his general comments on belief formation presumably also apply to factual beliefs. His remarks on the shallow nature of democratic societies may leave the impression that they leave little scope for rational belief formation, but we shall see that his view is more complex. He certainly allowed great scope for motivated belief formation, notably in his analyses of conformism and in his discussion of wishful thinking. As we shall see in Chapter 6, he also allowed for the possibility that people can get it wrong even when motivations do not enter into the belief formation process. Finally, he devoted much attention to ideological belief formation.

---

[2] See for instance Kunda (1990). In addition to standard forms of wishful thinking, based on a desire that the world be in such or such a way, motivated beliefs may also be due to sheer "pride" (*DA*, p. 213): we stick to our beliefs because they are *ours*.

[3] See for instance the papers collected in Gilovich, Griffin, and Kahneman, eds. (2002). Although the idea of "bias" is often assumed to involve motivation (as in "self-serving bias"), in the present sense it is more like an optical illusion.

[4] Veyne (1976), pp. 149–50, 554 ff.

BELIEFS FROM AUTHORITY

The first three chapters of the second volume of *DA* deal exclusively with belief formation in democratic societies. They are, in my opinion, hopelessly confused. The contradiction between Chapter 1 and Chapter 2 is especially striking. Tocqueville first asserts that "in most activities of the mind the American relies solely on the unaided effort of his own individual reason" (*DA*, p. 483), but then goes on to claim that "In ages of equality . . . , the disposition to believe in the mass increases, and the world comes increasingly under the sway of public opinion" (*DA*, p. 491). As we shall see shortly, the theme of belief formation by conformism is more consistent with what Tocqueville writes elsewhere.

Whatever the confusions of these chapters, it may be useful to discuss one idea from Chapter 2, namely, that most of our opinions are accepted on the *authority of others*: "If man were forced to prove for himself all the truths of which he daily avails himself, his work would never end" (*DA*, p. 489). This true, if trite, statement is asserted for all mankind, not only for the citizens of democratic societies. What distinguishes the latter is the nature of the authority on which they rely. By a process of successive eliminations, Tocqueville concludes that since democrats cannot rely on religion or on "the superior reason of a man or class," they must fall back on public opinion.[5] He suggests, moreover, both a *cognitive* and a *motivational* explanation for the tendency to believe that the majority opinion is right.

On the one hand, "it seems unlikely to them that, everyone being equally enlightened, truth should not lie with the greater number" (*DA*, p. 491). This could indeed be a principle of rational belief formation. If the opinions of the citizens are formed independently of one another and each of them is more likely to be right than wrong, Condorcet's Jury Theorem states that the likelihood of the majority being right increases with its size. Yet Tocqueville explicitly denies that the

---

[5] Later, however, he asserts a different fallback position: "I showed earlier how equality of conditions leads each man to seek the truth for himself. It is easy to see that such a method subtly encourages the mind to formulate general ideas. If I repudiate traditions of class, profession, and family and throw off the weight of precedent in order to seek my way by the light of reason alone, I will tend to base my opinions on the very nature of man, which inevitably leads me . . . to large numbers of very general notions" (*DA*, p. 497).

independence condition is satisfied. Perhaps, however, each citizen wrongly believes that all others have reached their opinions by independent consideration of the evidence, and hence (implicitly relying on the Jury Theorem) is inclined to trust the majority. The seemingly paradoxical reference to the "powerful pressure that the mind of all exerts on the intelligence of each" (*DA*, p. 491) can be understood along these lines. That would be a case of "pluralistic ignorance," a phenomenon to be discussed shortly. The mechanism would at most explain, however, how the majority opinion maintains itself over time, not how it emerges.

On the other hand, the citizen follows the majority because "there is no more inveterate habit of man than to recognize superior wisdom in his oppressor" (*DA*, p. 492).[6] Instead of this hyperbolic language, we might perhaps say that people have a need to be like others. Even having a private opinion that differs from the majority opinion is uncomfortable. In democracies, "men resemble one another, and what is more, they suffer in a sense from not resembling one another" (*DA*, p. 780 n. 1). In addition, as I discuss later, they may suffer from the sanctions that others impose on deviants. It is important to note, however, that motivated conformism can arise merely by observing what others do and say even when one is not observed by them.

RATIONAL BELIEFS AND GENERAL IDEAS

Neither the cognitive nor the motivational mechanism is likely to help democratic citizens arrive at *rational* beliefs. Elsewhere, however, Tocqueville is more charitable. When dealing with practical questions, as distinct from political or religious matters, democrats are perfectly capable of achieving rationality, a statement that is not contradicted by the fact that they often get it wrong. In the standard theory of

---

[6] In his discussion of slavery in America, Tocqueville also cites the tendency to recognize the wisdom of one's oppressor: "Shall I call it God's blessing or a final curse of his wrath, this disposition of the soul that renders man insensible to extreme misery and, indeed, often inspires in him a sort of depraved taste for the cause of his misfortunes? Plunged into this abyss of woe, the Negro scarcely feels his affliction. Violence made him a slave, but habituation to servitude has given him the thoughts and ambitions of one. He admires his tyrants even more than he hates them and finds his joy and his pride in servile imitation of his oppressors" (*DA*, pp. 366–67).

rational choice, in fact, the aim of belief formation is not to arrive at the truth, but to guide action. Because the collection and processing of information require not only material resources but also time, which might have been spent on other activities, a rational agent will often choose to act on beliefs that he knows to be poorly grounded and suspects may be false. According to Tocqueville, this is especially true of those who live in democratic societies:

Not only is meditation difficult for men who live in democratic societies, but they are inclined by nature to hold it in relatively low esteem. The democratic social state and institutions encourage most people to be constantly active, and the habits of mind appropriate to action are not always appropriate to thought. The man who acts is often forced to settle for approximations, because he would never achieve his goals if he insisted on perfection in every detail. . . . All things considered, it is less risky for him to invoke a few false principles than to waste time trying to show that all his principles are true. (*DA*, p. 524)

Practical and politico-religious beliefs differ in this regard. In a very confusing and, I suspect, confused way, Tocqueville offers two separate arguments concerning the role of *general ideas* in these domains. In one passage he asserts that the habit of reasoning in terms of general ideas arises from the fact of equality and then permeates all domains of belief by virtue of a spillover effect:

[A] person who lives in a democratic country sees around him only people more or less like himself, so he cannot think of any segment of humanity without enlarging and expanding his thought until it embraces the whole of mankind. Any truth applicable to himself seems applicable in the same way to all his fellow citizens and fellow human beings. Having become accustomed to using general ideas in *the field of studies that takes up the better part of his time and interests him most*, [the person who lives in a democratic country] carries the habit over [*transporte*] into other fields, and in this way the need to discover common rules everywhere, to subsume large numbers of objects under a single form, and to explain a set of facts by adducing a single cause becomes an ardent and often blind passion of the human intellect. (*DA*, p. 496)

A few pages later, he offers an account that is better in line with the rational-belief analysis:

People who live in democratic countries are very avid for general ideas because they have relatively little leisure and such ideas make it unnecessary to waste time delving into particular cases. This is true, but only with respect to *matters that do not occupy their minds on a regular and necessary basis.* Merchants will eagerly seize upon any general ideas one may wish to lay before them concerning philosophy, politics, science, and the arts, and they will not examine these ideas very closely. But they will not entertain ideas having to do with business until they have examined them, and will accept them only tentatively. (*DA*, pp. 499–500)

The two phrases I have italicized, in which Tocqueville defines the field of application of general ideas, seem hard to reconcile with one another, but perhaps the first is too vague to be in flat-out contradiction with anything. If asked which argument is more convincing, I'd certainly opt for the second. The cautious merchant, who knows that mistakes can have serious consequences, will not base his professional decisions on vague and general ideas. But on Sundays he may be happy to speculate about the nature of the universe and the future of mankind in ways that offer him satisfaction at little cost. The satisfaction, to be sure, is spurious. The intellectual pang derived from subsuming a phenomenon under a general concept is intrinsically less gratifying than the pang you get from explaining it in terms of its causes, but it is also easier to achieve. If one doesn't know any better, it is easy to confuse it with the real thing.

In fact, Tocqueville argues, in democracies low-cost speculation is also common in professional intellectuals. In Chapter 1 I cited a passage in which he asserts that "Most people who live in ages of equality . . . want to achieve great success instantaneously, but without great effort" (*DA*, p. 498). "This taste for easy success and instant gratification," he writes, "can be seen in intellectual pursuits as well as other areas of life" (*ibid.*). "General ideas pack a lot into a small volume, so to speak, and yield a great deal in a short period of time" (*ibid.*).

This argument applies more specifically to *historians* in democratic societies. Tocqueville makes a twofold distinction between democratic and aristocratic societies, one concerning the regimes themselves and one concerning the historians who live in the one or the other. On the one hand, he makes the (unverifiable) claim that "General facts explain more things in democratic centuries than in aristocratic ones, and particular influences explain less" (*DA*, p. 570). Yet this is not the only reason why historians in democratic societies (when writing about these societies) attach more importance to general causes. In addition, they emphasize general causes (even when writing about other societies) because of the tendency of democratic intellectuals to take shortcuts. "[The] exaggerated system of general causes . . . is also an admirable source of consolation for mediocre historians. It invariably provides them with a few grand explanations useful for quickly extricating themselves from any difficulties they encounter in their works, and it favors weak or lazy minds by allowing them to garner a reputation for profundity" (*ibid.*).[7]

It is worthwhile to pause at this point, to ask whether Tocqueville himself, in the Introduction to *DA*, was not guilty of excessive reliance on general ideas. As I noted in the Introduction to the present book, this text has a very different tenor from all his other writings. If for "democracy" we substitute "freedom" and for "God" substitute "reason," the following passage could have been taken from Hegel (whom Tocqueville knew only after he wrote *DA* and then only secondhand):

Everywhere a diversity of historical incident has redounded to democracy's benefit. Everyone played a part: those who strove to ensure democracy's success as well as those who never dreamt of serving it; those who fought for it as well as those who declared themselves its enemies. Driven pell-mell down a single path, some in spite of themselves, others unwittingly – blind instruments in the hands of God. (*DA*, p. 6)

Shorn of rhetorical excesses, the Introduction has in fact a simple analytical structure. First note that by "democracy" Tocqueville here really means "equality." He believed that equality could take one of two forms, depending on whether it allied itself with freedom or with despotism. When Tocqueville asserts that the progress of democracy is "irresistible" (*DA*, pp. 7, 14), he did not refer to political democracy – equality-cum-liberty. Rather, he intended to assert that the age of the feudal monarchy, based on natural hierarchies, was gone forever. The assertion is not based on any kind of teleology, but on political psychology. Hierarchies, once broken, cannot be put back together again. They are the product of slow gradual developments by virtue of which their authority comes to appear as natural and

---

[7] See also the reference in *R*, p. 62 to "writers who find these sublime theories to feed their vanity and lighten their labours."

unquestionable. If broken by revolution, they cannot be restored by a counterrevolution because they no longer have the same grip on people's minds.[8] Although *tradition* can be a live force, the deliberate attempt to restore it, *traditionalism*, is sterile.[9] Hence, "People who think of reviving the monarchy of Henri IV or Louis XIV seem to me quite blind. . . . I am inclined to believe that soon there will no longer be room in Europe for anything but democratic liberty or the tyranny of the Caesars" (*DA*, p. 363).

Next, precisely because there are these *two* possible developments, Tocqueville was able to escape the problem of fatalism. The strongest objection he has to historians who live in democratic times is that they "not only deny certain citizens the power to act on the fate of the people but also deny peoples themselves the ability to shape their own destiny. . . . If this doctrine of fatality . . . were to spread from writers to readers . . . it would soon paralyze the new societies and reduce Christians to Turks" (*DA*, p. 572). For Tocqueville, by contrast, the irreversible progress of equality was consistent with the possibility of *choice*: "The change . . . is already so powerful that it cannot be stopped yet not so rapid that there is no hope of altering its direction" (*DA*, p. 7).[10]

Tocqueville claimed that the French political culture in the eighteenth century (or in his own time)[11] was even more obsessed with general ideas than the Americans. The main explanation was that "our political constitution still prevented us from correcting those [very general] ideas through experience and gradually discovering their inadequacies" (*DA*, p. 499), as the Americans were able to do. This

---

[8] In a draft manuscript for *DA*, Tocqueville asserts that "the authority that rests on instinctive respect is absolute as long as nobody contests its right; it is reduced to almost nothing the day it becomes an object of discussion" (*O II*, p. 1001). As Marc Bloch (1961, Chapter VI) pointed out, when French court officials offered documented proof of successful healings of scrofula by the King's touch, the effect would be to undermine rather than strengthen the belief in his powers.

[9] Weil (1971).

[10] It was more difficult for Marx to escape the fatalist paradox. By stating that the advent of communism was inevitable, he weakened the incentive for the individual to contribute to bringing it about.

[11] "Every morning, upon awakening, I find that somebody has just discovered some general and eternal law I had never heard of before" (*DA*, p. 495).

idea is more fully spelled out in the work on the French Revolution. As a result of the spillover effect:

The spirit that guided [the French Revolution] was precisely the same as that which caused so many books to be written on government in the abstract. The same fondness for general theories, complete systems of legislation, and exact symmetry in the law; the same contempt for existing facts; the same confidence in theory; the same taste for the original, ingenious, and novel in institutions; the same urge to remake the entire constitution in accordance with the rules of logic and a unified plan, rather than seek to amend its faulty parts. A terrifying spectacle! For what is meritorious in a writer is sometimes a flaw in a statesman, and the same qualities that have often given rise to great literature can also lead to great revolutions. (*AR*, p. 177)

By contrast, the English "show much less aptitude and taste for generalization of ideas than their American progeny" (*DA*, p. 497), mainly because "their aristocratic habits caused them to cling to highly particular [ideas]" (*ibid.*). Even today, in the twenty-first century, the English may seem more resistant to certain high-flying forms of abstract nonsense than the French and the Americans. This statement is of course itself a dangerous generalization. In this domain, as in many others, there is more variation within than across countries. A strength of *AR* is, as we shall see, that Tocqueville takes full account of variations within France as well as of differences among France, England, and Germany. His analyses of America are usually more coarse-grained, with many references to "the Americans" and little mention of class or regional differences (the South–North distinction is an exception).[12] He was simply more knowledgeable about France and Europe, so that he could rely more on facts and less on speculation.

TOCQUEVILLE AND HEGEL VERSUS MONTAIGNE AND PASCAL

In the first volume of *DA*, important discussions of belief formation occur in the chapter on the freedom of the press and in the chapter on the omnipotence of the majority. The former considers stages in belief

---

[12] He does say that "When I use the term 'Anglo-Americans,' I am speaking only of the vast majority of them. Outside the majority there are always a few isolated individuals" (p. 431 n. 60). But this is a far cry from admitting group differences.

formation, and the latter the role of conformism in belief formation. I now consider them in turn.

In the chapter on the freedom of the press, Tocqueville focuses not so much on the *content* of beliefs in democratic societies as on the *mode* in which they are held and the frequency with which they *change*. Implicitly, he also proposes a useful distinction between the depth and strength of beliefs. Unfortunately, the subsection on which I shall focus (*DA*, pp. 212–14) is incoherent. Tocqueville begins by making a strong statement that is contradicted by the immediately following paragraphs.

Because of freedom of the press, he first asserts, people in democratic societies are dogmatically attached to their opinions:

When an idea, whether just or unreasonable, takes possession of the American mind, nothing is more difficult than to get rid of it. The same thing has been observed in England, the European country which for a century now has exhibited the greatest freedom of thought and the most invincible prejudices. (*DA*, pp. 212–13)

The rest of the subsection is then devoted to a highly interesting analysis of why this is *not* always the case. Dogmatic adherence to beliefs, it turns out, is not an invariant feature of democratic societies, although it does characterize them in their early stages.

Tocqueville stages the scene for the discussion by citing "a great man [who] once said that *ignorance lies at both ends of knowledge*" (*DA*, p. 213). Although he does not identify the great man, it is no doubt either Montaigne or Pascal (writing under Montaigne's influence).[13] The Montaigne-Pascal theory of the development of belief may be contrasted with what we might call the Hegel-Tocqueville theory. Like the former,

---

[13] "It may be plausibly asserted that there is an infant-school ignorance which precedes knowledge and another doctoral ignorance which comes after it" (Montaigne 1991, p. 349); "Knowledge has two extremes which meet; one is the pure natural ignorance of every man at birth, the other is the extreme reached by great minds who run through the whole range of human knowledge only to find that they know nothing and come back to the same ignorance from which they set out, but it is a wise ignorance which knows itself. Those who stand half-way have put their natural ignorance behind them without attaining the other; they have some smattering of adequate knowledge and upset everything. They upset the world and get everything wrong" (Pascal, *Pensées* # 327, ed. Brunschwicg).

the latter theory stipulates three stages in the development of belief: naïve dogmatic belief, doubt and skepticism, and mature reflective belief.[14]

Tocqueville expresses his disagreement with the "great man" by claiming that "It might have been truer to say that deep convictions are found only at the two ends, and that in the middle lies doubt. Indeed, one can distinguish among three distinct and often successive states of human intelligence" (*ibid.*). The first stage is the "habit of believing firmly but uncritically." When freedom of the press finds people in this condition, it initially causes them to change "their uncritical beliefs from one day to the next. From one end of the intellectual horizon to the other, man therefore continues to see only one point at a time, but that point changes constantly" (*ibid.*). In this stage beliefs, we might say, are strong but not deep.

Repetition of this oscillation induces learning. "Soon . . . , the whole range of new ideas is explored. With experience comes doubt and universal mistrust" (*ibid.*). In this second stage, beliefs are neither strong nor deep. Paradoxically, this mistrust makes beliefs more stable, not less:

> It has been observed that in centuries of religious fervor men sometimes changed faiths, while in centuries of doubt each man clings stubbornly to his own beliefs. The same thing happens in politics under freedom of the press. Since all social theories are criticized and combated one after another, anyone who once adheres to one of them holds on to it not so much because he is sure that it is good as because he is not sure that anything else is better. In such centuries, people are not ready to die for their opinions, but they do not change them, and one finds both fewer martyrs and fewer apostates. (*DA*, p. 214)

In the third stage, which will never be attained by "more than a very small number of men," we observe a "reflective, self-assured conviction that grows out of knowledge and emerges from the agitation of doubt itself" (*ibid.*). It may not be a true Hegelian synthesis, however. Tocqueville asserts that he is not "sure however that reflective, self-assured convictions of this kind ever exalt men to the same degree of ardor and devotion that dogmatic beliefs inspire" (*DA*, p. 213 n. 2). Hence beliefs may be deep, but not necessarily very strong.

---

[14] In Hegelian language, these would be thesis, antithesis, and synthesis.

This three-stage model is certainly a plausible pattern of belief development. It may or may not contradict the Montaigne-Pascal model, depending on whether the two are supposed to apply to the same kinds of belief. And even if they are, one model may be applicable in some situations and one in others. The value of Tocqueville's analysis, here as elsewhere, lies in the uncovering of mechanisms rather than in the formulation of laws.

CONFORMISM

Tocqueville's analysis of conformism is one of his most striking achievements.[15] It is also, as is often the case in *DA*, severely ambiguous. In the subsection "On the power that the majority in America exercises over thought," it is not entirely clear whether he is dealing with inner conformism of thought or with outer conformism of behavior. He writes that "Tyranny in democratic republics . . . ignores the body and goes straight for the soul" (*DA*, p. 294). In a later section he elaborates on this idea:

As men come to resemble each other more, each individual feels weaker and weaker vis-à-vis all the others. Not seeing anything that lifts him far above the rest and sets him apart, he loses confidence in himself when they combat him. Not only does he doubt his strength, but he begins to doubt his rectitude and comes very close to admitting that he is wrong when most people say he is. The majority has no need to force him; it convinces him. (*DA*, pp. 757–58)

As we have seen, the mechanism that induces this inner conformism may be either cognitive or motivational. In the passages I cited earlier, there is no reference to *an action by the majority on the individual*, merely to an internalization by the individual of the majority opinion. Yet Tocqueville also refers to a mechanism that causes conformist behavior through active sanctioning of deviants. In an eloquent continuation of a passage cited above, Tocqueville spells out the

[15] Although it applies to preference formation as well as to belief formation, I limit myself to the latter. On preference formation, see for instance *DA*, p. 293: "A king's only power is material . . . ; it affects actions but has no way of influencing wills. In the majority, however, is vested a force that is moral as well as material, which shapes wills as much as actions and inhibits not only deeds but also the desire to do them."

mechanism of ostracism, including, importantly, the ostracism of non-ostracizers:

The master no longer says: You will think as I do or die. He says: You are free not to think as I do. You may keep your life, your property, and everything else. But from this day forth you shall be a stranger among us. You will retain your civic privileges, but they will be of no use to you. For if you seek the votes of your fellow citizens, they will withhold them, and if you seek only their esteem, they will feign to refuse even that. You will remain among men, but you will forfeit your rights to humanity. When you approach your fellow creatures, they will shun you as one who is impure. And even those who believe in your innocence will abandon you, lest they, too, be shunned in turn. (*DA*, p. 294)

We may note the revealing reference to *feigned* refusal of esteem. It suggests that the conformism it induces is no less feigned, outer rather than inner. This idea is developed at some length in the later chapter from which I just cited:

When an opinion takes hold in a democratic nation and establishes itself in a majority of minds, it becomes self-sustaining and can perpetuate itself without effort, because nobody will attack it. Those who initially rejected it as false end up accepting it as general, and those who continue to oppose it in the depths of their heart do not show it. They take great pains to avoid dangerous and futile struggle.... Time, events, or individual effort by solitary minds can in some cases ultimately undermine or gradually destroy a belief without giving any external signs that this is happening. No one combats the doomed belief openly. No forces gather to make war on it. Its proponents quietly abandon it one by one, until only a minority still clings to it. In this situation, its reign persists. Since its enemies continue to hold their peace or to communicate their thoughts only in secret, it is a long time before they can be sure that a great revolution has taken place, and, being in doubt, they make no move. They watch and keep silent. The majority no longer believes, but it appears still to believe, and this hollow ghost of public opinion is enough to chill the blood of would-be innovators and reduce them to respectful silence. (*DA*, p. 758)

The silence of the false believers, induced by fear of ostracism, is also cited as a factor explaining the appearance of irreligion in prerevolutionary France:

What with the loquacity of the opponents of Christianity and the silence of those who were still believers, there ensued a state of affairs that has often since been seen in France, not only as regards religion but in all other matters.

Those who retained their ancient faith became afraid of being alone in their allegiance, and, dreading isolation more than error, professed to share the opinions of the mass. So what was still the sentiment of only a part of the nation appeared as the opinion of all, and hence seemed irresistible to the very individuals who had given it this false appearance. (*AR*, p. 155)

The idea of "the hollow ghost of public opinion" has an interesting ancestor and a remarkable posterity. The second volume of *DA*, in which it was first proposed, was published in 1840. Hans Christian Andersen's tale "The Emperor's New Clothes," which rests on the same basic idea, was published in 1835. Unlike Tocqueville, Andersen also proposed a mechanism for the *unraveling* of conformism: it suffices for a single child to say that the emperor has no clothes on.[16] Recent ideas similar to and perhaps inspired by Tocqueville's argument include "pluralistic ignorance" and "the spiral of silence."[17] Next to "the Tocqueville paradox" (Ch. 9) it is probably the piece of analysis in his writings that has had the greatest influence on social science or, more weakly, has been most frequently cited as an important precursor of later work.[18]

DA also contains an additional conformity-generating mechanism and, moreover, one argument that undermines the importance of ostracism in inducing conformism. In several places, he notes that if men living in democracies have similar ideas it is because their circumstances are so alike. Similar causes produce similar effects. In the chapter in which he proposes the idea of ghost opinions, he also makes the following observation:

Men equal in rights, education and fortune – men of like condition, in short – necessarily have needs, habits and tastes that are not very dissimilar. Since they see things from the same angle, their minds are naturally inclined towards

---

[16] Kuran (1995) is a study of unraveling inspired by Schelling (1978). Experiments in which subjects are induced to make manifestly wrong judgments in order to conform with the judgment of others (confederates of the experimenter) also show that conformism unravels when a single confederate expresses the correct opinion (for these experiments, see Aronson 2003 or any other textbook of social psychology).

[17] For an overview, see Taylor (1982).

[18] A more complex mechanism for generating pluralistic ignorance is described in the section on the causes of the power of religion in America. Tocqueville argues (*DA*, pp. 345–46) that if those who do not believe hide their incredulity, it is not because of fear of ostracism but because they recognize the social usefulness of religion.

analogous ideas, and while each of them may diverge from his contemporaries and form beliefs of his own, all end up unwittingly and unintentionally sharing a certain number of opinions in common. (*DA*, p. 754)

Elsewhere he adds:

When equality is complete and long-standing, men having roughly the same ideas and doing roughly the same things do not need to agree with or copy one another in order to act and speak in the same way. You constantly see a host of minor variations in their manners but no major differences. They are never perfectly alike, because they do not share the same model; they are never highly dissimilar, because they do share the same condition. (*DA*, p. 712)

These passages suggest a very different and more innocent picture of conformism. It does not arise by the relentless pressure of individuals on one another, but by the fact that all live under the same external conditions.[19] Tocqueville argues, in fact, that conformism through fear of ostracism is *unlikely* in a society that, like America, is characterized by high social mobility that weakens the operation of norms of etiquette and codes of honor: "Men who live in democracies are too mobile to allow some group of them to establish and enforce a code of etiquette. Each individual therefore behaves more or less as he pleases, and manners are always to some extent incoherent because they are shaped by each individual's feelings and ideas rather than conforming to an ideal model held up in advance for everyone to imitate" (*DA*, pp. 711–12). Tocqueville applies the same argument to the work of artisans. In aristocratic societies, "the aim of the arts is to do the best possible work," because the artisans all know each other and have a "reputation to keep" (*DA*, p. 530). By contrast, "when each profession is open to all comers, and large numbers of practitioners are constantly entering and leaving ..., the social bond is destroyed, and each worker... seeks only to earn as much as he can" (*DA*, pp. 530–31). Similarly, "In democratic states ... where all citizens are indistinguishable members of the same crowd and in a state of constant agitation, public opinion has no hold. Its object is forever disappearing and slipping away. Hence honor in

---

[19] The draft manuscripts contain a long passage (*O II*, pp. 1146–48) in which Tocqueville clearly and explicitly distinguishes between a *common model* and *common conditions* as causes of similarity in behavior. In aristocracies, the former is more important; in democracies, the latter.

such states will always be less imperious and less oppressive, for honor acts only with the public in view" (*DA*, p. 736).

"In democratic states public opinion has no hold" – a far cry from the claims in the first volume denouncing the tyranny of public opinion in democracies. There is no way, I believe, in which these analyses can be reconciled. At the same time, if we cut each of them down to size, we can learn from both. In modern societies, some communities are sufficiently coherent and stable to generate pressure to conform, while others turn over so fast that norms fail to develop or to have much impact.[20]

BELIEFS AND INTERESTS

The desire to conform is not the only mechanism involved in motivated belief formation. Our beliefs can also be shaped by *our interests*, in one of two ways. One important variety is wishful thinking: the wish is the father of the thought. I have an interest in promotion that causes me to believe, against the evidence, that I will be promoted. Or, to take an example closer to Tocqueville's concerns, I may believe I can have my cake and eat it too. A frequent theme in *DA* is, in fact, that people often – but wrongly – think they can have the best of both worlds. Three examples follow:

When it comes to the press ... there really is no middle ground between servitude and license. In order to reap the priceless goods that derive from the freedom of the press, one must learn to accept the inevitable evils that it breeds. To seek the former without the latter is to succumb to the sort of illusion that sick nations indulge when, tired of fighting and exhausted by their exertions, they seek ways to oblige hostile opinions and contrary principles to coexist within the same territory. (*DA*, pp. 208–9)

Americans want the Union, but reduced to a shadow: they want it strong in certain cases and weak in all others. They pretend that in time of war it can gather all the nation's forces and all the country's resources in its hands, yet in time of peace that it can cease, as it were, to exist – as if this alternation of debility and vigor existed in nature. (*DA*, p. 454)

[20] We might ask, nevertheless, why modern societies develop norms that regulate *interactions among strangers*, such as the norm against walking up to a person at the front of a bus queue and asking to buy that person's place (Shiller, Boycko, and Korobov 1991, p. 393). Tocqueville would have answered, I think, that in democracies there is a general aversion to the public display of wealth differences (see *DA*, p. 204).

Democratic mores are so mild that even partisans of aristocracy find them attractive, and after savoring them for a time they are not tempted to revert to the chilly and respectful formalities of the aristocratic family. They would willingly preserve the domestic habits of democracy if only they could reject its social state and laws. But these things go together, and it is impossible to enjoy the one without enduring the other. (*DA*, p. 690)[21]

In addition to denouncing these motivated mistakes, Tocqueville also offered brilliant analyses of *unmotivated* causal fallacies. Because of their importance I reserve them for separate treatment later (Ch. 6). There I also discuss an idea that is closely related to the three passages just quoted, and which we may think of as the impossibility or *instability of halfway houses.*

A second variety of interest-based belief formation arises when we adopt a belief because *the fact that we hold it* will serve our interest. Asserting a falsehood may be more effective – because it is less easy to detect – when the speaker believes in it. In the *Recollections*, Tocqueville claims that he is incapable of deceiving himself in this manner, unlike "most party politicians." These, he says,

are often accused of acting without conviction; but my experience goes to show that this is much less frequent than is supposed. It is just that they have a faculty, which is precious and indeed sometimes necessary in politics, of creating ephemeral convictions in accordance with the feelings and interests of the moment; and in this way they can with a tolerably good conscience do things that are far from honest. Unluckily I have never been able to illuminate my mind with such peculiar and contrived lights, or to persuade myself so easily that my advantage and the general weal conformed. (*R*, p. 84)[22]

---

[21] It is also a central theme in the literature on modernization that governments in backward countries often strive for limited reforms, which will – or so they believe – give them the best of both worlds. Thus Chinese and Russian policy makers around the turn of the century wanted Western technology without Western values; capitalism without individual rights; modern education without freedom of the press, etc. (Levenson 1968, vol. 1, pp. 61 ff.; Knei-Paz 1977, pp. 100 ff.). Had they read Tocqueville, they might have been less sanguine about these prospects.

[22] Along similar lines, he comments on the conduct of Dufaure in the constitutional committee in 1848 that "Neither the swing of public opinion nor his own passions and interests would ever have persuaded him to adopt a cause he thought bad; but such motives were enough to make him wish to find it good, and often that was enough" (*R*, pp. 173–74).

IDEOLOGICAL BELIEFS

Tocqueville also considered at some length ideological belief formation. He believed in particular that the social fact of equality was
reflected in the intellectual constructions of the Americans: "Equality
suggests a number of ideas that would not otherwise occur to the
human mind and modifies most of the ideas it already holds" (*DA*,
p. 514). Among these ideas is that of "man's infinite perfectibility." On
this particular topic, as on many others, Tocqueville offers a mix
of arbitrary speculation and acute observation. He first writes that
"Every man . . . becomes a witness to constant change. Some changes
make his position worse, and he understands only too well that no
nation or individual, no matter how enlightened, is ever infallible.
Others improve his lot, and he concludes that man in general is
endowed with an infinite capacity to perfect himself " (*DA*, p. 515).
He might equally well have inferred that the constant flux induces
a tendency to believe in cyclical theories of the eternal return. Tocqueville here relies on what I called the first law of pseudo-science,
"Everything is a little bit like everything else." [23] Other examples will
be offered shortly.

He also, shrewdly, points to a more practical implication of the
incessant change and improvement: "I once met an American sailor,
and I asked him why his country's ships are not built to last. Without
hesitation he answered that the art of navigation was making such
rapid progress that the finest ship would soon be useless if its existence
were prolonged for more than a few years" (*ibid.*). This explanation is
matched by a similar argument to account for the short leases of land
in democratic societies: "In centuries of equality . . . it is easy to
imagine that nothing stays put. The mind is possessed by the idea of
instability. Given this attitude, both landlord and tenant feel a kind
of instinctive horror for long-term obligations. They are afraid that
the contract that is profitable today may some day prove limiting"
(*DA*, p. 681).[24]

---

[23] The number and complexity of causal chains in *DA* is such that one sometimes has the
impression that Tocqueville was also under the sway of what might be called the
second law of pseudo-science: "Everything is causally related to everything else."

[24] As both these passages show, Tocqueville sometimes identifies *equality* and *change*,
a central topic in Ch. 7 below.

Tocqueville asserts that "equality of conditions fosters a sort of instinctive incredulity about the supernatural" (p. 490). If an egalitarian society should nevertheless adopt a religion, it is more likely to be Catholicism than Protestantism: "People today are by nature not particularly inclined to believe, but if they accept religion at all, they soon discover in themselves a hidden instinct that propels them unwittingly toward Catholicism. Any number of the doctrines and customs of the Roman Church astonish them, but they harbor a secret admiration for the way it is governed, and its great unity attracts them" (p. 510). The relationship also works in the other direction: "Catholicism may dispose the faithful to obedience, but it does not prepare them for inequality" (p. 333). "Only the priest stands above the faithful: below him, everyone is equal" (*ibid.*).

The general principle is this: "Allow the human spirit to follow its bent and it will impose a uniform rule on both political society and the divine city. It will seek, if I may put it this way, to *harmonize* earth with Heaven" (*DA*, p. 332). Presumably, the causal relation is from earth to heaven, rather than the other way around. As an illustration, "Christianity itself has in some ways been affected by [the] influence of the social and political state on religious beliefs" (*DA*, p. 505). For instance, to the fragmentation of society after the fall of the Roman Empire there corresponded a fragmentation of religion: "If Divinity could not be divided, it could nevertheless be multiplied, and its agents could be magnified beyond all measure. For most Christians, homage to angels and saints became an almost idolatrous cult" (*DA*, p. 506). Later on, he observes that the opposite tendency is at work in democracies: "Even when equality does not undermine religions, it simplifies them. It distracts attention from secondary agents and focuses it primarily on the sovereign master" (*DA*, p. 555). That statement, however, stands in a puzzling relation to the proposition that equality favors Catholicism, which is precisely the religion that multiplies secondary beings.

In my opinion, these efforts to demonstrate an intrinsic connection between social structure and religious dogma are arbitrary and unconvincing. There will always be some similarities or resemblances between a complex social structure and a complex system of religious dogma, but to cite them as evidence for the claim that the specific form of religion is due to an impulse to harmonize heaven and earth is entirely speculative. There are so many different ways of harmonizing heaven and earth and, in choosing a religion, so many more important reasons than the desire for harmony, that it is more plausible to think that the harmony comes after the event, to consolidate a choice that has already been made or imposed on other grounds. One could equally well say that Catholicism, with its hierarchy of angels and saints, is especially well suited to an aristocratic society that is based on hierarchy, and that democracy predisposes people toward Protestantism, which, by doing away with all intermediaries between men and God, places them on an equal footing. In this respect Tocqueville resembles Marx, whose arguments about a natural affinity between capitalism and Protestantism are entirely arbitrary and, in fact, incoherent.[25] Tocqueville's sophomoric analyses of the *content* of religions form a strange contrast to his insightful comments on the psychological and social *effects* of religion.

[25] Elster (1985), Ch. 8.

3

Self-Interest and Individualism

Tocqueville stands firmly in the tradition of the French moralists. He cites Montaigne, Pascal, and La Bruyère. Although he does not cite La Rochefoucauld, many of his observations are in the spirit of the *Maximes*.[1] He must have read, although he does not cite it, a famous maxim by La Bruyère: "Nothing is easier for passion than to overcome reason; its greatest triumph is to conquer interest."[2] In Chapter 4 we shall see several examples of the triumph of passion over interest. First, however, we must determine how he conceived of interest.

Tocqueville's terminology on this point is somewhat unstable. My interpretation will therefore, more than elsewhere in this book, take the form of a "rational reconstruction." I shall propose a conceptual framework that seems consistent with the texts while being occasionally more explicit and elaborate than his own statements.

---

[1] Compare Maxime 107, "One kind of flirtation is to boast we never flirt," with Tocqueville's comment on George Sand, "I confess that with more adornment she would have struck me as still more simple" (*R*, p. 135); or compare Maxime 199, "The desire to appear clever often prevents our being so," with the observation that "nothing makes for success more than not desiring it too ardently" (*R*, p. 88). Tocqueville's definition of egoism, cited below, is also close to La Rochefoucauld's idea of amour-propre: "Self-love is the love *of* self, and of all things *for* self." (Maxime supprimée # 1). It also seems possible that his reproach of Machiavelli for being, as it were, insufficiently Machiavellian (*L*, p. 362) may have been inspired by La Rochefoucauld's Maxime 124.

[2] *Characters* IV.77.

Tocqueville uses several recurring terms. First, there is "egoism," "a vice as old as the world" (*DA*, p. 585), which is "to societies what rust is to metal" (*DA*, p. 316). Next, there is "interest" without any qualification, usually in the sense of material interest. Third, there is the key idea of "enlightened interest" (literally: "interest properly understood"). It may be synonymous with "true interest" (*DA*, pp. 7, 10, 104 n. 51). In addition, there is the rather different idea of "individualism,"[3] distinguished as follows from egoism:

> Individualism is a recent expression arising out of a new idea. Our fathers knew only the word *egoism*. Egoism is a passionate and exaggerated love of self that impels man to relate everything solely to himself and to prefer himself to everything else. Individualism is a reflective and tranquil sentiment that disposes each citizen to cut himself off from the mass of his fellow men and withdraw into the circle of family and friends, so that, having created a little society for his own use, he gladly leaves the larger society to take care of itself. (*DA*, p. 585)

Much of the time, I believe, Tocqueville uses "egoism" in a sense that differs from this Augustinian definition, which probably owes much to La Rochefoucauld. It can mean "material self-interest," as when he writes about "the inhabitants of some countries" that "they value their time too much to spend it on the interests of the community, and they would rather confine themselves within the narrow limits of egoism, precisely defined by four ditches lined with hedges" (*DA*, p. 279).[4] That may also be the sense in which he uses the word when writing that individualism "in the end will be subsumed in egoism" (*DA*, p. 585). Sometimes egoism seems to mean "unenlightened self-interest," as when he remarks that during the transition to democracy, "the poor man . . . accepts the doctrine of interest as the guide for his actions without understanding the science of that doctrine and his egoism is as unenlightened now as his selfless devotion was before" (*DA*, p. 11). The reference to egoism as a "blind instinct" (*DA*, p. 585) suggests the idea

---

[3] Not to be confused with "individuality." In *DA*, p. 780 n. 1, Tocqueville asserts that whereas "the spirit of individuality is very tenacious" in aristocratic societies, it is "almost destroyed" in democracies.

[4] Tocqueville also refers to "immaterial interests," which turn out not to be interests at all, but rather "love of equality and independence" (*DA*, p. 200). The phrase would have been more appropriate if used about the interest in the afterlife.

of "short-term self-interest." Without claiming exegetical accuracy, this is how I shall understand the term. We may note, for future reference, that egoism thus defined may cause problems on *two counts*: by the focus on the self and by the focus on the present. As La Bruyère wrote, a source of error in politics is "to think only of oneself and of the present."[5] Since egoism has *two antonyms*, altruism and foresight, it might seem that overcoming egoism would require both of these attitudes. Actually, as we shall see, one of them may be sufficient.

ENLIGHTENED SELF-INTEREST

Because of the shortsightedness of egoism, it prevents the citizens from forming *wise beliefs*, by which I mean beliefs that will make them take actions that make their life as a whole go well. The reason is that egoistic citizens will be poorly motivated to gather information about the long-term consequences of their choices. Since they care little about the future, they have no reason, for instance, to look into the long-term health consequences of their present behavior. And even if they *are* aware of, for instance, the dangers of smoking, the risk will not deter them. (In language to be explained below, their short time horizon may be due either to a cognitive or to a motivational deficit). Nevertheless, their beliefs and actions may be perfectly *rational*. As we saw in Chapter 2, a rational citizen may well decide to make up his mind on the basis of thin information, if the cost of collecting more is prohibitive. Similarly, he may rationally neglect to gather information about long-term consequences if he cares little about the future. Concern for the future is *not* a demand of rationality, as I understand it.[6]

"Enlightened self-interest," by contrast, *is* defined in part by concern for the future. To rebut a possible objection to his claim that if the poor have sole responsibility for making the laws they will always tax the rich heavily, Tocqueville asserts:

It is idle to object that if the people had a proper understanding of their own interest, they would spare the fortunes of the rich because they must soon feel

---

[5] *Characters* XII.87.
[6] For a defense of this claim, which some may find counterintuitive, see Ch. 11 of Elster (2007a).

the effects of any financial difficulties they create. Is it not also in the interest of kings to make their subjects happy and of nobles to know when to open their ranks? If long-run interests had always trumped the passions and needs of the moment, there would never have been tyrannical sovereigns or exclusive aristocracies. (*DA*, p. 240)[7]

Tocqueville also describes self-interest properly understood as the capacity for self-control and the ability to delay gratification. Endowed with this attitude, "a man, seeking to attain the happiness of this world, resists instincts at every turn and coldly calculates all the actions of his life, and . . . instead of blindly yielding to the ardor of his first desires, he has learned the art of combating them and has become accustomed to easily sacrificing the pleasure of the moment to the permanent interests of his entire life" (*DA*, p. 615).

In several passages that I cited in Chapter 1, Tocqueville asserts that democracies in general discourage long-term thinking. In another passage he refers to "the secret force by which equality causes the passion for material pleasures and the exclusive love of the present to predominate in the human heart" (*DA*, p. 742). This would seem to leave little scope for enlightened self-interest. Yet Tocqueville also claims that he does not "believe that egoism is a worse problem in Europe than in America. The only difference is that there it is enlightened and here it is not" (*DA*, p. 612). I do not see how this contradiction can be explained away by even the most charitable principles of interpretation.

COORDINATION AND COOPERATION

When we look more closely at the function that self-interest properly understood is supposed to serve in a democracy, we see that it is mainly to *ensure coordination and cooperation*. Tocqueville can be read, with a little bit of charity and exegetical leeway, in the context of a century-long effort to understand why largely self-interested individuals can be motivated to cooperate with each other. Modern contributions to this debate include game theory and evolutionary biology. Earlier pioneers include Montaigne, Descartes, and Hume, all of whom are cited below.

[7] Along the same lines, see also the passage in *DA*, pp. 441–42, cited in Ch. 4.

Tocqueville himself cites Montaigne and may have been inspired by Descartes. To my knowledge, he was not acquainted with the relevant works by Hume.

Let me first cite Hume, who stated with unsurpassable clarity the issues of coordination and cooperation. On coordination, he wrote, "Two men, who pull the oars of a boat, do it by an agreement or convention, tho' they have never given promises to each other."[8] It is in the interest of each that they coordinate their moves, just as it is in the interest of all drivers that they drive on the same side of the road. In Hume's example, the coordination is achieved spontaneously. Coordinating on left-hand or right-hand driving can prove more difficult. In Canada, different provinces used different rules until the 1920s.

On cooperation, Hume proposed the following parable:

Your corn is ripe to-day; mine will be so tomorrow. It is profitable for us both, that I should labour with you to-day, and that you should aid me to-morrow. I have no kindness for you, and know you have as little for me. I will not, therefore, take any pains upon your account; and should I labour with you upon my own account, in expectation of a return, I know I should be disappointed, and that I should in vain depend upon your gratitude. Here then I leave you to labour alone: You treat me in the same manner. The seasons change; and both of us lose our harvests for want of mutual confidence and security.[9]

To my knowledge, this was the first clear statement of the Prisoner's Dilemma, albeit in a slightly different form than the standard one, which involves simultaneous rather than successive decisions. In the standard example, each of two (self-interested) prisoners, who have been involved in the same crime but are now in separate cells, is told that if he informs on the other but the latter does not inform on him, he will go free and the other will go to prison for ten years; if neither informs on the other, both will go to prison for one year; and if both inform on each other, both will go to prison for five years. Under these circumstances, informing is individually rational whatever the other does, although both would be better off if neither informed.

The Prisoner's Dilemma is often used to explain the weakness of public institutions. Each citizen has an interest in public goods, which can only be

---

[8] Hume (1978), p. 490.
[9] *Ibid.*, p. 521.

funded by taxes, but also has an interest in avoiding paying taxes himself.[10]
In a passage that clearly relies on the logic of the Dilemma, Tocqueville uses
it to explain the *strength* of state institutions:

Democratic centuries are times of trial, innovation, and adventure. There are
always a host of men engaged in difficult or novel enterprises which they pursue
independently, unencumbered by their fellow men. These people accept the
general principle that the public authorities should not intervene in private
affairs, but each of them wishes, as an exception to this rule, help in the affair
that is of special concern to him and tries to interest the government in acting in
that area while continuing to ask that its action in other areas be restricted.
Because so many men take this particular view of so many different objectives
at the same time, the sphere of the central power imperceptibly expands in
every direction, even though each of them wishes to restrict it. (*DA*, p. 794 n.)

Important as it is (see Ch. 8), for present purposes this passage points
us in the wrong direction. The puzzle Tocqueville is grappling with in
much of *DA* is why citizens of democracies are willing to look beyond
their narrow personal horizon, not why they might be excessively willing
to do so.

Unlike Hume, Tocqueville does not explicitly distinguish between
coordination and cooperation. I focus, therefore, on passages that
directly address the latter issue. Morality, he argues, is a sufficient
condition for cooperation. He denies, however, that it is a necessary
one. He situates himself within a long French tradition according to
which enlightened self-interest is capable of *mimicking morality*:
"Most of [the Anglo-Americans] believe that the man who properly
understands his own self-interest has all the guidance he needs to act
justly and honestly" (*DA*, p. 432). This theme, struck in passing in
Volume 1, has a central place in Volume 2 of *DA*. Claiming that the
Americans "do their utmost to prove that it is in every man's interest to
behave honorably" (*DA*, p. 611), he cites Montaigne to the same effect:
"Should I not follow a straight path for its straightness, yet would I do it
because experience has taught me that in the end it is the happiest and
most profitable" (*ibid.*).

---

[10] "The attitude of the bourgeois to the institutions of his regime is like that of the Jew to
the law; he evades them whenever it is possible to do so in each individual case, but he
wants everybody else to observe them" (Marx 1845–46, p. 80).

Montaigne does not explain *why* this should be so. Exactly what is the invisible hand that causes morality and enlightened self-interest to converge on the same behavior? The first to my knowledge to suggest an answer was Descartes, in his correspondence with Princess Elisabeth of Bohemia.[11] It is possible, although I cannot prove it, that Tocqueville knew these letters and was influenced by them.

In one letter, Descartes merely affirms the existence of an invisible hand:

[It] is difficult to determine exactly how far reason orders us to interest ourselves in the public; yet that is not something in which one must be very exact; it suffices to satisfy one's conscience, and in doing that, one can grant very much to one's inclination. For God has so established the order of things, and has joined men together in so connected a society, that even if everyone related only to himself and had not charity for others, a man would nevertheless ordinarily not fail to employ himself on the behalf of others in everything that would be in his powers, provided he uses prudence.[12]

Challenged by Elisabeth to explain his argument more fully, Descartes replied as follows:

The reason that makes me believe that those who do nothing save for their own utility, ought also, if they wish to be prudent, work, as do others, for the good of others, and try to please everyone as much as they can, is that one ordinarily sees it occur that those who are deemed obliging and prompt to please also receive a quantity of good deeds from others, even from people who have never been obliged to them; and these things they would not receive did people believe them of another humor; and the pains they take to please other people are not so great as the conveniences that the friendship of those who know them provides. For others expect of us only the deeds we can render without inconvenience to ourselves, nor do we expect more of them; but it often happens that deeds that cost others little profit us very much, and can even save our life. It is true that occasionally one wastes his toil in doing good and that, on the other hand, occasionally one gains in doing evil; but that cannot change the rule of prudence that relates only to things that happen most often. As for me, the maxim I have followed in all the conduct of my life has been to follow only the grand path, and to believe that the principal subtlety [*finesse*] is never to make use of subtlety.[13]

---

[11] See discussion in Elster (2004).
[12] To Elisabeth October 10, 1645, in Descartes (1978), p. 164.
[13] To Elisabeth January 1646, *ibid.*, pp. 176–77 (translation modified).

A crucial premise of this argument is that the individual in question is capable of being motivated by the long-term consequences of present choices. By making a small sacrifice in the present, the individual builds a reputation for being helpful that will benefit him later when he, in turn, needs help. This "Descartes effect"[14] goes beyond simple bilateral tit-for-tat (you scratch my back, I'll scratch yours), since those who have a good reputation receive help "even from people who have never been obliged to them."

To explain mutual help among Americans, Tocqueville proposes an argument that is very close to the Cartesian one:

In Europe we see men who share the same profession voluntarily helping one another every day. All are exposed to the same ills. That is enough reason for them to seek mutual protection from those ills, no matter how hardened or selfish they may be in other respects. Thus, when one of them is in danger and others can save him by means of a small, temporary sacrifice or a sudden burst of energy, they do not fail to make the attempt. . . . There exists a sort of tacit and involuntary agreement among these men, under the terms of which each one owes the others temporary support and may in turn claim the same for himself. Extend to an entire people what I have just said about a single class and you will understand my thought. Among the citizens of a democracy there does in fact exist a compact [*convention*] analogous to the one I have just described. . . . In democracies, where great boons are seldom granted, small favors are done constantly. (*DA*, p. 668)[15]

In modern terminology, this "tacit and voluntary agreement" or "convention" of mutual help is an *equilibrium*. Given that others offer their help when needed, it is in the interest of the individual to do so as well. Going back to Hume's farmer example, the two farmers may be induced to help each other if their time horizon goes beyond the current harvest. If the farmer whose corn will be ripe in August knows that he will need the help of his neighbor next August, he will have an incentive to help him in September – *at least if he cares sufficiently about the future.* Knowing this, his neighbor will in fact

[14] Kolm (1984).
[15] One reason for suspecting the influence of Descartes is the idea that sacrifices will be *small*. This does not prevent Tocqueville from also asserting that in democracies, "citizens could . . . be summoned to make great sacrifices by appealing to their reason and experience" (*DA*, p. 10) and that "I have often seen Americans make large and genuine sacrifices to the public good" (*DA*, p. 593).

provide the help. In interactions over time, the willingness to delay gratification serves to mimic morality.

This argument may explain some forms of cooperation, for example, between the two farmers. It may even apply to the professional associations that Tocqueville mentions, if the members are able to keep a close watch on one another. The New York community of diamond merchants is a famous example.[16] When extended to society as a whole, the argument is more fragile. Each citizen would have to be implausibly well informed about whether others are meeting their obligations. The argument cannot explain, for instance, why people would pay their taxes. In the Introduction to *DA*, Tocqueville refers to a hypothetical state of society that is clearly intended to anticipate the analyses of America: "The people, instructed as to their true interests, would recognize that in order to enjoy the benefits of society one has to accept its burdens" (*DA*, p. 10). But even though the people will *vote* for high taxes if they understand that they are necessary for the provision of public goods, self-interest will not motivate them individually to *pay* taxes if they can avoid it. The idea that "I will comply with the tax code if and only if I can be sure that others comply" requires an unrealistically high level of information about the tax obligations of others and the extent to which they are meeting them. Compliance with the tax code requires a modicum of *civic duty* that has little place in Tocqueville's analysis. Although he asserts, in the same reference to a hypothetical society, that "all people would think of themselves as the authors of the law, which they would consequently love and readily obey" (*DA*, p. 9), the actual analyses of American society make little use of this idea.

Interaction over time can thus be an important mechanism for reconciling private interest and cooperation. A special case is that of *interaction under uncertainty*. Suppose that a governing majority has the opportunity to take a measure that will benefit it here and now, such as opening the archives of its predecessor. It may nevertheless decide to pull its punches since the precedent set by these measures may hurt it should it become a minority later on: "A Minister who wants to be protected in the future would see to it that former Ministers are likewise protected."[17] In the United States, the reason why Congress

---

[16] Rachman (2006).
[17] Cooray (1979), p. 73.

refrains from using its constitutional power to limit the jurisdiction of the Supreme Court may be that "once one political faction uses certain means that threaten judicial independence, other factions will be more willing to use those devices in the future."[18]

Tocqueville uses a similar argument, except that he focuses on the interest of the minority to comply with the majority:

[In] the United States each individual has in a sense a personal interest in seeing to it that everyone obeys the law. For a person who is not in the majority today may find himself in it tomorrow, and the respect that he professes for the will of the legislature now he may later have occasion to demand for himself. (*DA* p. 276)

[Because] the United States was settled by equals, no natural and permanent conflict among their interests yet exists. Social states do exist in which members of the minority cannot hope to win over the majority. . . . In the United States, political questions of such an absolute and general kind cannot arise, and all parties are prepared to recognize the rights of the majority, because all hope some day to exercise those rights. (*DA*, p. 285)

These claims must be understood on the background of Tocqueville's argument that in America politics, no less than private fortunes are in incessant flux (Ch. 8). The Americans know that the future may see alternations in power no less than the waxing and waning of private fortunes. Under these conditions, self-interest induces moderation. We may ask, however, why he applies the argument to the minority only. Would not uncertainty concerning the future also cause the majority to limit its tyranny over the minority, as in the two examples I cited? Perhaps the fact that "the majority lives in perpetual self-adoration" (*DA*, p. 295) makes it hard for its members to imagine they might come to be a minority.[19]

INDIVIDUALISM

Tocqueville's idea of *individualism* is not easy to grasp. Its core meaning is the tendency to withdraw from public life and to retreat into the private sphere of business, family, and friends. Even the idea of family

---

[18] Wilson (1992), p. 693.
[19] I owe this point to an anonymous reader of the manuscript.

has a restricted meaning in democracies. Unlike those who lived in aristocratic centuries, democratic citizens care neither about their ancestors nor about their progeny (*DA*, pp. 585–86), only about the immediate members of their families. Whereas "classes in an aristocratic society are highly differentiated and immobile [and] each becomes for its member a sort of homeland within a homeland" (*DA*, p. 586), the unstable nature of classes in democracies (Ch. 7) prevents these bonds from forming.

In a secondary meaning, individualism seems little different from unenlightened egoism. In the chapter on "How individualism is more pronounced at the end of a democratic revolution than at any other time," he begins by asserting that "Man's isolation from other men and the egoism that results from it become especially striking" in the aftermath of a democratic revolution (*DA*, p. 588): "[O]blivious of the fact that they may some day need to call on their fellow men for assistance, [they] make no bones about showing that they think only of themselves" (*ibid.*).

In either sense of the term, individualism is a vice. To each variety corresponds a distinct remedy. We have seen how individualism in the sense of egoism is overcome by the ability to defer gratification when one is interacting with others. To overcome individualism in the core sense, Americans "combat [it] with free institutions" (*DA*, p. 590). Born of equality, individualism is neutralized by liberty: "As soon as common affairs are dealt with in common, each man sees that he is not as independent of his fellow men as he initially imagined and that, in order to obtain their support, he must often lend them his cooperation" (*ibid.*). More telling than this vague phrase is an observation that I paraphrased at the end of Chapter 1 by saying that American politics gave rise to a cult of disinterestedness. What matters is not *esse*, but *percipi* – being *seen* as disinterested rather than being willing to work for the common good even when unobserved.

When Tocqueville returns to the idea of individualism in *AR*, it is clear that its core meaning is indeed what I said it is. The passage is worth citing at some length:

Our forefathers lacked the word *individualism*, which we have forged for our own use, because in their day there was no individual who did not belong to a group and who could regard himself as absolutely isolated. But each of the myriad small groups that made up French society had no thought for any group other than itself. There was, if I may put it this way, a sort of collective individualism, which prepared people for the true individualism that we have come to know. . . . Had anyone been able to plumb their inner depths, moreover, he would have discovered that these same people, being quite similar to one another, regarded the flimsy barriers that divided them as contrary to both the public interest and common sense and, in theory at any rate, already worshiped unity. Each clung to his own condition because others distinguished themselves by theirs, yet all were prepared to merge into a single mass provided no one stood out in any way or was elevated above the common level. (*AR*, p. 134)

This passage embodies a type of cooperation problem that we have not encountered so far. Recall that in the Prisoner's Dilemma, there is a tension between what is rational from the point of view of the individual and what is good for the collectivity. Each citizen would like everybody to pay taxes, except for him. Here, by contrast, each would prefer to sacrifice his parochialism on the condition that others do so too. In the Prisoner's Dilemma, the obstacle to cooperation is egoism; here it is lack of information about what others really want. The situation is one of pluralistic ignorance (Ch. 2) or, as economists would say, of an Assurance Game with incomplete information. As we shall see in Chapter 9, Tocqueville argued that this situation was a part of the general elite fragmentation that, when it was not engineered by the successive kings, at least worked to their benefit.

4

Passions

In the previous chapter I cited the classical trio of motives: interest, passion, and reason. It is fair to say that Tocqueville had little faith in reason or "virtue" as the original spring of behavior. At the individual level, it may be found in exceptional individuals such as Turgot (*AR*, p. 188) or George Washington (*O II*, p. 976), but at the social level, it may at best be approximated or mimicked by enlightened self-interest. It is not so much that he thought that what Madison called "the mild voice of reason" was easily overruled by the other two motives; rather, he seems to have believed that in most people it was not present at all (see, for instance, *L*, p. 384). As I noted, the simple idea of civic duty is absent from his work.

PASSION OVERRIDING INTEREST

Be this as it may, Tocqueville certainly believed that *passion* was capable of overriding interest. In Chapter 3 I cited a passage in which he asserts that long-term interest does not always trump the "passions and needs of the moment" (*DA*, p. 240), suggesting that enlightened self-interest can be undermined by passion as well as by short-term

interest.[1] Another important instance arises from ignoring the role of
religion. We saw in Chapter 1 that by virtue of the compensation effect,
citizens of democratic societies need religion. By virtue of a different
mechanism (Ch. 5), democratic *societies* also benefit from the stabilizing effects of religion (both effects are asserted in *DA*, p. 633).[2] Hence,
Tocqueville deplores the views of some otherwise well-intentioned
persons

who would sincerely like to prepare men to be free. When people such as these
attack religious beliefs, they obey their passions rather than their interests.
Despotism can do without faith, but liberty cannot. Religion is much more
necessary in the republic they advocate than in the monarchy they attack, and
most necessary of all in a democratic republic. How can society fail to perish if,
as political bonds are loosened, moral bonds are not tightened? (*DA*, p. 340)

In another passage he suggests that *envy* (*DA*, pp. 440, 442) among
the different American states might cause the breakup of the Union.[3] The
paradox is that although "southerners should feel most attached to the
Union, for it is they who would suffer most if left to themselves, [y]et
only they are threatening to break up the confederation" (*DA*, p. 440).

It would be a mistake to think . . . that states that lose power also lose population or wither away. There is no halt to their prosperity. . . . To them,
however, it seems that they are growing poorer because they do not grow richer

---

[1] Here and elsewhere (*DA*, pp. 68, 304, 633, 639) it is unclear whether Tocqueville refers
to *short-term* interests or *short-lived* interests. When he uses one of the French terms for
the latter expression ("intérêt passager" or "intérêt du moment"), it is most plausibly
understood in the sense of short-lived interests. Although these may be little more than
whims, they can also arise out of the passions, a key feature of which is precisely that
they tend to induce temporary preference change (see below). Anger and love, for
instance, tend to have "a short half-life." By contrast, being governed by short-term
interest can be a permanent feature of an individual: today I care only about today and
tomorrow, tomorrow I will care only about tomorrow and the day after tomorrow. For
a subtle discussion of these issues, see White (1987), pp. 254–55.
[2] Unlike some of the other founders of sociology, Tocqueville does not *explain* religion by
the social benefits it provides. His explanations rely throughout on the psychological
benefits religion provides for the *individual*, the social benefits being non-explanatory.
[3] He also makes the insightful comment that "It is difficult to imagine a durable union
between two peoples, one poor and weak, the other rich and strong, even if the strength
and wealth of the one are known not to be the cause of the weakness and poverty of the
other" (*DA*, p. 440). The breakup of Czechoslovakia illustrates the instability of feder-
ations with two members of unequal size (Elster 1995).

as rapidly as their neighbors, and they think they are losing power because they suddenly find themselves in contact with a power greater than their own. Thus their feelings and passions suffer more than their interests. Is that not enough, however, to place the confederation in peril? Had nations and kings looked only to their own true advantage since the beginning of the world, man would hardly know what war is. (*DA*, pp. 441–42)

In the *Recollections*, Tocqueville constantly appeals to the *vanity* of the main actors to explain their behavior (Ch. 9). In an amusing passage he tells us how, as minister of foreign affairs in the 2nd Republic, he was able to make leading politicians ignore their interest by flattering their vanity: he "found that negotiating with men's vanity gives one the best bargain, for one often receives the most substantial advantages in return for very little of substance" (*R*, p. 233). In his conversations with various politicians who "thought they had a special right to direct our foreign policy," he found that "it was more to their taste that I should ask for their advice without taking it than that I should take it without asking for it" (*ibid.*). Elsewhere he makes a general comment along the same lines, which anticipates his remarks on the self-destructive behavior of the elites in the ancien régime:

In France a government is always wrong to base its support on the exclusive interests and selfish passions of a single class. Such a policy could succeed only in a nation where self-interest counts for more and vanity for less than with us; with us, when a government so constituted becomes unpopular, the members of the very class for whose sake it becomes unpopular will prefer the pleasure of joining with everybody else in abusing it to the enjoyment of the privileges it preserves for them. (*R*, p. 41)

ENVY

A more important example – on a common reading the key to Tocqueville as a political theorist – concerns the tension between the passion for equality and the interest in liberty that characterizes democratic citizens. The two central passages both need to be cited:

There is . . . a manly and legitimate passion for equality that spurs all men to wish to be strong and esteemed. This passion tends to elevate the lesser to the rank of the greater. But one also finds in the human heart a depraved taste for equality, which impels the weak to want to bring the strong down to their level, and which reduces men to preferring equality in servitude to inequality in freedom. Not that people whose social state is democratic naturally despise liberty; on the contrary, they have an instinctive taste for it. But liberty is not the principal and constant object of their desire. What they love with a love that is eternal is equality. They lunge toward liberty with an abrupt impulse or sudden effort and, if they fail to achieve their goal, resign themselves to their defeat. But nothing could satisfy them without equality, and, rather than lose it, they would perish. (*DA*, p. 60)

Democratic peoples love equality in all ages, but there are times when their passion for it turns to frenzy. This happens when a long-threatened social hierarchy finally destroys itself in one last intestine struggle and the barriers that once separated citizens are finally knocked down. At such times men swoop down upon equality as upon conquered spoils and cling to it as a precious good that someone would snatch from their grasp. The passion for equality then inundates the human heart and fills it entirely. No use telling people that such blind surrender to an exclusive passion jeopardizes their most cherished interests: they are deaf. No use pointing out to them that liberty slips through their fingers while their attention is focused elsewhere: they are blind, or, rather, in all the world they see only one good worth coveting. (*DA*, pp. 583–84)

Although Tocqueville does not use the term "envy" in these passages, it is clearly what he has in mind.[4] The appeals to envy as an explicatory motivation are numerous and central in both *DA* and *AR*. I shall cite many of them later in this chapter, and then again in Chapter 9. First, however, I want to propose an interpretation of the two passages in terms of a distinction between "white envy" and "black envy." Writing (X, Y) for a situation in which person I has amount X of some good such as money and person II has amount Y, person I is subject to white envy if he prefers (3, 3) to (3, 7) and to black envy if he prefers (2, 2) to (3, 7). In black envy, the agent is willing to cut off his nose to spite his face, taking a loss to impose an even larger loss on another.[5] In white envy passion does not act to the detriment of interest. In black envy it

---

[4] When Tocqueville uses the terms "jealousy" and "jealous," as he does frequently, it is a judgment call whether they are to be read as synonyms of "envy" and "envious."

[5] In Tocqueville's 1836 essay on the ancien régime, he asserts the existence of black envy under the monarchy. The third estate assisted the king, *against their own interest*, in ruining the system of privileges: "It happened that they freely gave up their own rights, when they chanced to have any, in order to bring the nobles down with them in a common destruction" (*O III*, p. 30).

	A	B	C	D	E	F
INCOME	3, 7	3, 7	3, 3	2, 2	3, 3	2, 2
FREEDOM	4, 4	5, 5	0, 0	4, 4	4, 4	0, 0

FIGURE 4.1

does, especially if we assume (as I do below) that liberty itself is an interest.

The various cases may be illustrated by Figure 4.1 above, where the first number in each box refers to the level of income or freedom in one class of citizens and the second to the level in another. We shall compare the preferences of the members of the first class with regard to the various pairs of states defined by these numbers. Although incomes can be unequal, the liberties of the two classes are constrained to be equal (see Ch. 7 for a discussion of unequal liberties in the ancien régime).

Tocqueville repeatedly asserts that citizens in democratic societies favor liberty. This would be reflected in a preference for state B over state A. Assuming the same income distributions, the state that has more liberty is better. In the first of the two cited passages, Tocqueville refers initially to white envy, "which impels the weak to want to bring the strong down to their level." This would induce a preference for state E over state A. He then goes on to make the stronger statement about a preference for "equality in servitude to inequality in freedom." This amounts to a preference for state C over state A and perhaps even for state F over state A. Either of these would be forms of black envy, as would a preference for D over A. Since democratic citizens value liberty, giving it up with no gain in income, as in a move from A to C, would be a form of black envy. Moving from A to F would require the willingness to suffer a loss of *both* liberty and income for the sake of equality.

I believe we can safely assert that according to Tocqueville, members of the first group would (i) prefer B over A and (ii) prefer E over A. As suggested, he also seems to assert that they would either (iii) prefer C over A or (iv) prefer F over A. Are there any textual grounds for

thinking that he also believed they would (v) prefer D over A? Clearly, if
he held that (iv) is true, then he must have held that (v) is true, since the
citizens would obviously (vi) prefer D to F, but we do not know whether
he held (iv) or only the weaker statement (iii). For direct evidence that
he thought they might prefer D over A, we may revisit an example from
the previous chapter. Might the poor be so motivated by black envy as
to tax the rich heavily, even if by doing so they would kill the goose that
lays the golden eggs? As we saw in the previous chapter, Tocqueville
was willing to entertain this possibility. The poor may be willing to hurt
themselves because of their short time horizon. In doing so they would,
to be sure, go against their objective or enlightened self-interest, but not
necessarily against their interest *as they perceive it*. They might either
not understand that confiscatory taxes will hurt them in the long run (a
cognitive deficit) or they might not care enough about the long run to be
influenced by it (a motivational deficit). We observe a more radical
triumph of passion over subjective or perceived interest when a person
rejects an unfair proposal about how to share a sum of money with the
consequence that neither he nor the proposer gets anything.[6] Tocqueville's analysis of envy among the American states has perhaps a bit of
that flavor.

It is common, perhaps because of Tocqueville's work, to think of envy
as a passion that is more intense and frequent in democracies than under
other regimes: "We must not blind ourselves to the fact that democratic
institutions develop the sentiments of envy in the human heart to a very
high degree" (*DA*, p. 226). He refers to "the democratic sentiment
of envy" (*DA*, p. 359) and even to "the democratic disease of envy"
(*R*, p. 63). There may be something to these claims, although it is hard
to see how one could establish them. Anthropologists and historians
find envy in all sorts of societies.[7] Moreover, because of the stigma
that usually attaches to overt expressions of envy, the emotion tends
to go underground. Be that as it may, Tocqueville himself repeatedly
cites envy in *AR* to characterize relations between individuals and between classes in predemocratic France. To bring out the parallelism,

---

[6] See Camerer (2003), Ch. 2 for discussion of such "Ultimatum Games." In experiments, it turns out that resentment is a more likely explanation than envy for such
rejections.
[7] See, for instance, Foster (1972) and Walcot (1978).

we may compare two strikingly similar passages in which Tocqueville explains how rich individuals hide their wealth to avoid provoking the envy of their fellow citizens. An opulent American of the 1830s and an affluent French peasant of the eighteenth century are both compared to medieval Jews hiding their wealth:[8]

Do you see this opulent citizen? Does he not resemble a Jew of the Middle Ages, afraid lest anyone suspect his riches? His dress is simple, his demeanor modest. Within the four walls of his home, luxury is adored. Into this sanctuary he allows only a few select guests, whom he insolently calls his equals. (*DA*, p. 204)[9]

To escape this violent and arbitrary taxation, the French peasant, in the middle of the eighteenth century, acted like the Jew in the Middle Ages. He put on a show of being miserable even if by chance he was not. His affluence frightened him, for good reason. I find tangible proof of this in a document, which I take in this instance not from Vienne but from a hundred leagues away. The Agricultural Society of Maine announced in its 1761 report that it had conceived the idea of awarding prizes and incentives in the form of livestock. "The idea has been dropped," the report continued, "because of the risks to which the winners were exposed owing to the base jealousy of others, who could subsequently take advantage of the arbitrary way in which taxes were assessed in order to avenge themselves on the winners." (*AR*, p. 159)

In Chapter 9 we shall look more closely at the role of envy in Tocqueville's analyses of the preconditions for the French Revolution. Here I shall only cite a few references in *AR*. Amazingly, he says that

---

[8] The following passage confirms the accuracy of Tocqueville's description: "Encapsulated in Christian society, Jewish people worried about links that coreligionists had to the luxury trade. Occasionally, Christian regulations governed their dress; more often this was accomplished by sumptuary laws of their own communities. These laws advocated restraint, but less from religious conviction than to *avoid arousing envy* in Christians. Like the pochteca of the Aztec state, Jews were 'condemned to go about meanly clad in sad-coloured raiment.' Parents of children dressed in red or blue risked insult and extortion. Ownership of jewels, silks, and mixed colors was acceptable, but the ostentatious display of them was not, and the long black cloak was prescribed as the best concealment for finery" (Schneider 1978, p. 433; my italics).

[9] We may contrast his attitude with the conspicuous consumption that Veblen described almost a century later. A person who is mainly concerned with impressing others would not care about expensive items that others cannot observe. Wealthy Chinese women apparently love to display their furs but buy cheap lingerie, a fact that explains the failure of Victoria's Secret when it tried to establish itself in China. (I owe this observation to Lauren McFall.)

because of the "inexplicable and detestable" privileges of the aristocracy, "democratic [*sic*] envy flared up in the French heart so intensely
that it still burns there today" (*AR*, p. 225).[10] Elsewhere, he makes it
clear that the main target of envy in the ancien régime was status and
privilege rather than, as in democracies, inequality of wealth.[11] Within
the bourgeoisie, tax exemptions "filled with envy all who did not share
in them" (*AR*, p. 131). Across classes, "the system of ennoblements, far
from diminishing the commoner's hatred of the nobleman, increased it
beyond all measure. It was a hatred embittered by all the envy that the
new noble inspired in his erstwhile equals" (*AR*, p. 128). But as in the
text just cited (*AR*, p. 127), he also refers to economic envy within
classes, adding that "in this system of collective taxation, each taxpayer
had a direct and permanent interest in spying on his neighbors and
informing the tax collector of any increase in their wealth. All were
trained to outdo each other in slander and hatred" (*AR*, p. 159).

In *DA* Tocqueville has extensive discussions of the causes and effects
of envy. I have already mentioned some of the effects, and others will be
discussed shortly. First, however, let me try to sort out his complex
statements about the causes of envy in democratic societies.

In line with Tocqueville's general methodology (see Ch. 6), we first
need to distinguish between envy as the effect of equality and envy as
the effect of equalization. In the Introduction to *DA* he asserts that
"The breakup of fortunes has diminished the distance that once separated the poor from the rich. In coming together, however, they seem to
have discovered new reasons to hate one another. Gripped by terror or
envy, each rejects the other's claim to power" (*DA*, p. 11). As shown by
the context, this passage refers to the state of transition to democracy
rather than to democracy itself. Elsewhere he uses similar language:
"When, in the wake of a prolonged struggle between the various classes
of which the old society was composed, conditions become equal, envy,
hatred and scorn of one's neighbor . . . invade the human heart, as it

---

[10] For another reference to "the envious hatred of democracies" in the ancien régime, see
O III, p. 392.
[11] One might ask why the reaction of those who lacked the privileges did not take the
form of hatred of the king (who granted them) rather than envy of those who possessed them. In a letter Tocqueville simply notes that "what most prevented the French
from being worthy and capable of freedom was that they always detested the neighbor
more than the master" (*L*, p. 1098; same observation on p. 1107).

were, and for a time holds sway there. This, *independent of equality,* acts as a powerful influence that tends to divide men and make them mistrust one another's judgment" (*DA*, p. 487; my italics).

We may note for future reference that in both these passages, and in many others, Tocqueville confusingly lumps together envy and hatred as if they were one and the same emotion. Not only are they obviously different, but they also occupy, as we shall see in Chapter 9, distinct places in Tocqueville's analysis of the French Revolution. The reader simply has to decide when "hatred" means hatred and when it doesn't. The reference to fear in the first passage is more straightforward. Because envy characteristically triggers the desire to destroy the envied object, its possessor has good reason to fear.

A further confusing fact is Tocqueville's reference to *privilege* as the object of democratic envy. In the old regime, there were innumerable formal privileges (*AR*, II.9 and *passim*), tax exemption being the most important.[12] In democracies, legal privileges are almost nonexistent. Exemption from military service, in particular, is unthinkable in a democracy: "Since military service is compulsory, the burden is equally and indiscriminately shared by all citizens. This is also a necessary consequence of the condition of democratic peoples and of their ideas. Government in a democratic society can do almost anything it wants provided that it addresses itself to all the people at once. What leads to resistance is unequal sharing of the burden and not the burden itself" (*DA*, p. 768).[13]

---

[12] Surprisingly, Tocqueville never refers directly to the widespread bourgeois resentment caused by exclusion from high military office, only to the peasant resentment caused by the fact that the bourgeois were largely exempt from serving in the militia (*AR*, p. 161). The passage from *O III*, p. 1110 cited in Ch. 7 may be an indirect reference.

[13] In the first volume, though, we read that "In America, conscription is unknown. Men are induced to enlist for money. Compulsory recruitment is so contrary to the ideas and so foreign to the habits of the people of the United States that I doubt whether anyone would ever dare introduce it into law. What is called conscription in France is surely the heaviest of our taxes, but without conscription how could we sustain a major continental war?" (*DA*, p. 255). In light of this statement, the passage cited from *DA*, p. 768 may be one of those in which "democracy" should be read as meaning "France." It is then somewhat ironical that in the *Recollections*, Tocqueville comments critically on a proposal to "oblige everybody to do their military service in person [thus banning paid replacements], a measure that would have ruined all liberal education" (*R*, p. 181). Although the first draft of the 1848 constitution included a ban on replacement, it was reintroduced in the final draft that was shaped by the June insurrection of the Paris workers. It was abolished in 1873. In the United States, paid replacements were common during the Civil War.

The sole privilege that may arise is the right to vote, as long as it is not extended to everybody. Tocqueville argued that (male) universal suffrage would ultimately prevail (see Ch. 6), but until that happened, limitation of the suffrage remained a bastion of privilege, perhaps the only one, in democracy. Even in this case he might have said that restrictions on suffrage are not privileges in the sense of the ancien régime, as the latter were ascribed rather than achieved. Anyone may in principle acquire property or learn to read, if these are required for the right to vote. French revolutionaries, for instance, used this argument after 1789 to defend the restriction of the right to vote to taxpayers.[14]

With regard to the causes of envy, we need to distinguish two questions: How is envy determined by the overall level of equality in society? How is it shaped by the distance that separates the envious person from the envied person? Tocqueville's answer to the first question is clear: the greater the overall equality, the more intensely felt is the envy. This argument applies both to "advantage" and to "privilege":

When inequality is the common law of a society, the greatest inequalities do not call attention to themselves. When everything is more or less on a par, the slightest inequality becomes an eyesore. That is why the desire for equality becomes ever more insatiable as the degree of equality increases. (*DA*, p. 627)

[W]hen there is little difference in conditions, the slightest advantages are important. Since each person is surrounded by a million others who possess quite similar or analogous advantages, pride becomes exigent and jealous; it fastens on trifles and defends them stubbornly. (*DA*, p. 720)

The hatred that men bear toward privilege increases as privileges become rarer and less substantial, so that democratic passions seem to burn hottest precisely when they are most starved for fuel. . . . When all conditions are unequal, no inequality is great enough to be offensive, whereas the slightest dissimilarity seems shocking in the midst of general uniformity. The more complete the uniformity, the more unbearable the sight of inequality. . . . This hatred . . . which animates democratic peoples against the most insignificant privileges, powerfully encourages the gradual concentration of all political rights in the hands of the sole representative of the state. The sovereign, being of necessity and incontestably above all citizens, arouses no envy in any of them. (*DA*, p. 795)

---

[14] *Le Moniteur Universel*, May 29, 1791. Tocqueville makes a similar observation about England, in which "the aristocracy of birth is supplanted by the aristocracy of money. . . . Some people still enjoy considerable privileges, but the possibility of acquiring such privileges is open to all" (*DA*, p. 660).

These passages also point to an answer to the second question. Rather than asserting that envy is caused *even* by small differences, they suggest that it is *especially* likely to be triggered by "trifles." A big difference, such as that between the sovereign and the citizen, "arouses no envy."[15] These claims amount to the theory of "neighborhood envy." Stated simply, the idea is that we envy only those immediately above us in the relevant hierarchy, but not those who stand far above. In a draft manuscript, Tocqueville asserts that "by a strange peculiarity of our nature, the passion for equality which ought to increase with the inequality of conditions is on the contrary heightened when conditions are getting equal" (*O II*, p. 938). Only starlets envy stars and only princes envy kings. In a more complex and probably more adequate version, the theory says that our envy of those richer than us first increases and then decreases with the difference between our situation and theirs.[16]

The comments by Tocqueville I just cited suggest the simple version of neighborhood envy. A very general statement is the following: "A singular principle of relative justice lies deep within the human heart. Men are far more struck by inequalities within the same class than by inequalities between different classes" (*DA*, p. 410). Elsewhere, however, he seems to say that envy increases with the distance that separates the envious individual from the one he envies. He asserts, for instance, that "the low-level official is on almost the same level as the people, while the high official stands above (*domine*) them. Hence the former can still excite their interest, but the latter begins to arouse their envy" (*DA*, p. 243). In his explanation of why "great revolutions will become rare" in the democratic age, he writes that "[i]n any great democratic people there will always be some citizens who are very poor and others who are very rich. . . . Between these two extremes of democratic society stand a vast multitude of men

---

[15] Similarly, in the ancien régime "the nobles were not jealous of the King, but of those among themselves who rose above the others" (*O II*, p. 1170). Asserting, moreover, that "As long as the bourgeois were different from the nobles, they were not jealous of the nobles, but among themselves," Tocqueville concludes that "the hatred of inequality in proportion as inequality is less is therefore a truth of all time and applicable to all men" (*ibid.*). Although the claim that the bourgeois were not jealous of the nobles is inconsistent with what he writes elsewhere, the theory of neighborhood envy suggests that the nobles most likely to provoke their envy were the newly ennobled ones (Nicolas 2008, pp. 304–6).

[16] Elster (1999), p. 170.

who are almost alike and who, while not exactly rich or poor, own enough property to want order but not enough to arouse envy" (*DA*, p. 748). While perhaps consistent with the complex theory of neighborhood envy, these passages do not really allow us to say that Tocqueville held that view.

Among the effects of democratic envy, I have already cited the tendency to *envy-avoidance*: the rich hide their wealth. Recall also Tocqueville's conjecture that the union might break up because of envy among the states. The fact that military service in democracies is universal rather than selective may also be rooted in the envy that selection would trigger. A further effect is the tendency toward *mediocrity* in democratic politicians. On this point, Tocqueville offers a three-pronged explanation: "distinguished men . . . shun careers in politics, in which it is so very difficult to remain entirely true to oneself or to advance without self-abasement" (*DA*, p. 227); the people lack "the capacity to choose men of merit" (*DA*, p. 226); and even if they had the capacity, they would lack "the desire and the taste to do so" (*ibid.*). The last mechanism is explicitly related to "the sentiment of envy." In times of danger, however, "Genius no longer shuns the light, and the people, struck by the perils they face, forget for a time their envious passions. Under such circumstances it is not rare to see famous names emerge from the ballot box" (*DA*, p. 228).[17] In line with his claim about envy toward high officials, Tocqueville argues, finally, that this sentiment explains the fact that "salaries seem almost to decrease as an official's power increases" (*DA*, p. 244).

Tocqueville also has striking insights into mechanisms of *envy-alleviation*. Suppose that instead of hiding their wealth the rich try to prevent envy by sharing it. Tocqueville notes that this measure is more likely to fuel envy than to counter it, since "the very magnitude of benefactions, which highlights the difference of conditions, secretly irritates those who profit from them" (*DA*, p. 592). In America, the rich use the more effective strategy of *envy-preemption* by mingling with the people: "What is asked of them is not the sacrifice of their money; it is the sacrifice of their pride" (*DA*, p. 593). By contrast, mingling with the people would never have occurred to the

---

[17] One might ask whether the talented, like the rich, might not hide their assets in order to be elected. Reportedly, Bill Clinton tended to avoid mentioning that he graduated from Yale Law School. (I owe this observation to Tom Langer.)

well-intentioned reformers in prerevolutionary France: "to the striking expressions of interest that the people inspired in them they occasionally added public expressions of contempt. The people had already become the object of their sympathy without yet ceasing to be an object of their disdain. The provincial assembly of Haute Guyenne, while warmly pleading the cause of the peasants, called them *coarse and ignorant creatures, troublemakers, and uncouth, undisciplined characters*. Turgot, who did so much for the people, expressed himself in largely similar terms" (*AR*, pp. 208–9).

These are all effects on *behavior*. Tocqueville argues that envy can also affect *beliefs*, by a kind of self-poisoning of the mind:

> In a democracy, ordinary citizens see a man step forth from their ranks and within a few years achieve wealth and power. This spectacle fills them with astonishment and envy. They try to understand how a man who only yesterday was their equal today enjoys the right to rule over them. To attribute his rise to talent and virtue is inconvenient, because it requires them to admit to themselves that they are less virtuous and clever than he. They therefore ascribe primary responsibility to some number of his vices, and often they are right to do so. This results in I know not what odious mingling of the ideas of baseness and power, unworthiness and success, utility and dishonor. (*DA*, p. 253)[18]

ENVY AND HATRED

Envy is a *comparison-based* emotion. It does not presuppose any interaction between the envious individual and the one he envies: the mere knowledge of the latter's superior position is often sufficient. As we shall see in Chapter 9, this idea is a central premise in Tocqueville's analysis of the ancien régime. Moreover, the actions of the envied person owe nothing to the presence of the envier, of whose existence he may even be unaware. Other emotions are *interaction-based*. An example is *envy-provocation*, based on the enjoyment of other people's envy of oneself. Whereas display of superior wealth may create envy, the perception that the purpose of the display is to provoke envy will instead induce the interaction-based emotion of hatred. Although Tocqueville does not to my knowledge discuss envy-enjoyment and envy-provocation in his work on the ancien régime, these were very

---

[18] Anti-Semitism may have similar roots (Netanyahu 1995, p. 989).

common in that society. In official ceremonies, the nobles enjoyed wearing finery that was out of bounds for the third estate. Moreover, the nobility delighted in showing their *contempt* for the third estate. When expressed spontaneously, for instance by turning away, contempt induces shame. When expressed deliberately, for the purpose of inducing shame, it is as likely to cause anger or hatred. In a decaying aristocracy, "Indifference and contempt betray themselves on one side, jealousy and hatred on the other" (*DA*, p. 680). Conjecturally, some of the apparent confusions of envy and hatred in *AR* may be due to the fact that these emotions were actually intermingled for the reasons just stated.[19] However, the similar confusions in *DA* cannot be explained in this manner. Nor do the references to "envy and hatred" in the relation between the peasantry and the nobles (see below) lend themselves to explanation in this way, since the nobles took no pleasure in humiliating the peasants. On the contrary, "the lord who lived on his estate usually displayed a certain familiar bonhomie toward his peasants" (*AR*, p. 129).

In *AR*, *hatred* is the most important interaction-based emotion. Whereas envy arises mainly in the relation between the bourgeoisie and the nobility, hatred characterizes the relation between the peasantry and the nobles. Tocqueville shows vividly how this emotion arose from the daily frustrations and humiliations suffered by the French peasant in his encounters with his noble neighbors:

Now here come the same neighbors to drag him from his field and force him to work elsewhere without pay. When he tries to defend what he has planted from their game, they prevent him. They wait for him at the river crossing to collect a toll. He meets them again at the market, where they sell him the right to market his own produce, and when he returns home and wants to consume what remains of his wheat – wheat that he has grown with his own hands – he cannot until he has sent it to be milled in their mill and baked in their oven. . . . Whichever way he turns, he finds these inconvenient neighbors barring his path, interfering in his pleasures, impeding his work, and eating his produce. . . . Consider this man's condition, needs, character, and passions and calculate, if you can, the reserves of hatred and envy that his heart has amassed. (*AR*, p. 79)

[19] A different mechanism by which envy may lead to hatred is suggested by the passage from *DA*, p. 253 cited above. As I say in the previous footnote, hatred of Jews may originally have been due to envy of Jews. But I do not think Tocqueville had anything like that mechanism in mind.

Although, as he notes (*AR*, p. 77), feudal burdens were actually heavier on most of the European continent, they were felt more acutely in France because the French peasant was no longer a serf: he "had become a landowner and . . . had been completely emancipated from the control of his lord" (*AR*, p. 78). The frustrations encountered by a free man are subjectively worse than the objectively greater suffering of an unfree man. The phenomenon of status inconsistency (Ch. 7) may provide a key.

HOW PASSION CAUSES TEMPORARY PREFERENCE CHANGE

In his studies of the two revolutions – 1789 and 1848 – Tocqueville also made important contributions to our understanding of the impact of emotion on *preferences*. Unlike the mechanisms canvassed in Chapter 1, emotions induce *temporary* and hence reversible preference changes, which does not exclude that actions taken under their sway may be irreversible. Commenting on the measures adopted on the night of August 4, 1789, when the National Assembly in a collective frenzy abolished all feudal privileges, he asserts that they were "the combined result, in doses that are impossible to determine, of fear and enthusiasm" (*O III*, p. 593). Although these emotions did, predictably, abate,[20] the measures were not to be undone. As one deputy wrote in his journal (citing another), "the people had been penetrated by the measures one had promised them; they will not let themselves be de-penetrated."[21]

External events can trigger *several* emotions simultaneously, urging different actions. The sight of a friend's success may cause envy and sympathy at one and the same time. The net effect on action – do I disparage or praise him in front of third parties? – is often hard to predict. Or consider what we might call "the counterterrorist dilemma." Repressive measures intended to deter terrorist behavior by causing fear can also encourage it by causing hatred. In his analyses of the royal reactions to dissent before and during the revolution, Tocqueville repeatedly emphasizes this ambiguity: "The half-measure of

---

[20] As may be seen by comparing the entries in Duquesnoy (1894) for August 5 and August 10, 1789.

[21] Duquesnoy (1894), p. 349; see also Elster (2007b).

constraint imposed on the enemies of the Church at that time did not
diminish their power but rather increased it. . . . Authors were persecuted just enough to make them complain but not enough to
make them tremble. They were hobbled in a way that provoked
resistance without incurring the heavy yoke that might subdue it"
(*AR*, pp. 181–82). As we shall see in Chapter 9, this is a fundamental
theme in Tocqueville's analysis of the French Revolution.

In many such cases, *both* emotions, fear and hatred, are triggered
simultaneously in the same person. (Admittedly, the texts cited from
Tocqueville, here and in Ch. 9, do not say so.) One may be willing to
fight a tyrant in spite of one's fear, because the hatred triggered by the
same tyrannical measures is stronger. In other cases, we can imagine
that events may trigger *either* of two opposite reactions in different
individuals.[22] Tocqueville states the mechanism as follows:

It has been observed that a man facing urgent danger rarely remains as he
was: he will either rise well above his habitual level or sink well below it.
The same thing happens to peoples. Extreme peril does not always impel
a nation to rise to meet it; it is sometimes fatal. It can arouse passions without
offering guidance and cloud a nation's intelligence rather than enlighten
it. The Jews went on slaughtering one another amid the smoking ruins of
the Temple. In nations as well as individuals, however, it is more common to
see the very imminence of danger act as midwife to extraordinary virtues.
(*DA*, p. 228)

In the *Recollections*, Tocqueville offers more specific comments on
the "more common" case. In his analysis, the key factor explaining the
successful resistance to the insurrection of the Paris workers in June
1848 was not simply the danger in which the bourgeoisie found itself,
but the *level* of danger. In spite of a negative historical precedent, a divided leadership and limited military force,

we did triumph over this formidable insurrection; furthermore, it was exactly
the element that made it so terrible that saved us, and there has never been

---

[22] In Ch. I of Elster (1999), I characterize these two patterns as "type B" and "type A"
mechanisms. For an example of the latter, consider two different reactions to the Saint
Bartholomew massacre in 1572. Protestants in the North of France largely reacted by
converting to Catholicism, whereas those in the South and the West were stimulated to
fight (Jouanna 1998, p. 204).

a better application of the famous phrase: "We should have perished, had we not been so near to perishing." If the rebellion had been less radical and seemed less fierce, probably most of the bourgeoisie would have stayed at home; France would not have rushed to our aid; perhaps even the National Assembly would have yielded. . . . But the insurrection was of such a nature that any dealings with it were at once out of the question, leaving no alternative from the start but victory or destruction. (*R*, p. 144)

Schematically, if we represent the level of mobilization y as a function $y = f(x)$ of the level of danger x, and assume that the danger will be overcome if and only if $y > x$, then we can imagine that $f(2) < 2$, $f(4) > 4$, and $f(6) < 6$. Tocqueville does not make the third claim, but it seems obvious that there will come a point when the danger is too large to be resisted.

SOCIAL NORMS

I conclude this chapter with some comments on the role of *social norms* as motivations of action. The reason I discuss these in a chapter dealing with the passions is that I believe, and believe that Tocqueville believed, that social norms are maintained by the emotions of contempt and shame. At least, I believe this to be true of the second and more analytical of the two chapters in *DA* that deal with social norms, the chapter on "honor." The first, the chapter on "manners," is curiously lacking in incisiveness. In particular, Tocqueville never hints at the idea that manners – rules of etiquette – are sustained by the disapproval or, more specifically, the *contempt* meted out to those who breach them. By contrast, the discussion of honor relies explicitly on this idea.

He defines honor as "a particular rule based on a particular state that a people or class uses to assign blame or praise" (*DA*, p. 726) or "a distinctive set of opinions regarding what is to be praised or blamed" (*DA*, p. 730). As thus defined, the idea applies to many phenomena beyond those that belong to honor as usually defined. It applies, for instance, to the norm against free-riding in joint enterprises (Ch. 7) or to the norm against looting in revolutionary action (see below). In fact, as we shall see shortly, the way Tocqueville uses the term, it is virtually synonymous with our idea of a social norm. First, however, let us see how Tocqueville applies the idea to honor in the narrow sense, that is, "the aristocratic honor that arose in feudal society" (*DA*, p. 726). He notes that "in some cases feudal honor prescribed vengeance and stigmatized pardon for insults" (*DA*, p. 727). Although he does not say so, and although it is not the whole story, the stigma in such cases is prior to the prescription. Vengeance is mandatory *because* the man who does not take revenge for some conventionally defined insult will be ostracized and suffer a "civil death," compared to which the risk of being killed in a duel or a feud is often to be preferred. The same holds for the norm that a vassal must keep faith with his lord: "Public opinion condemned treachery by a vassal with extraordinary severity" (*DA*, pp. 728–29).

To explain norms, some scholars appeal to their effects. Social norms provide goods that cannot be produced by the market system.[23] The argument not only overlooks the existence of harmful norms, such as norms of footbinding and female genital mutilation, but also fails to produce a mechanism by which the need for a norm might cause it to emerge. Tocqueville also engages in this kind of functional explanation when he argues that the code of honor can be explained by the nature and the needs of the nobility: "In order to maintain [its] distinctive position, from which it derived its strength, it not only needed political privileges but also required virtues and vices tailored to its own use" (*DA*, pp. 726–27). He also offers functional explanations of the norm of courage in ancient Rome (*DA*, pp. 729–30) and of what one might call "norms of commerce" in America: "All the peaceful virtues that tend to regulate social activities and encourage trade should therefore enjoy special honor among Americans, and neglecting those virtues ought to incur the public's contempt" (*DA*, p. 730). In a passage already cited, he asserts that "Americans, who

---

[23] "It is a mistake to limit collective action to state action. . . . I want to [call] attention to a less visible form of social action: norms of social behavior, including ethical and moral codes. I suggest as one possible interpretation that they are reactions of society to compensate for market failure. . . . Non-market action might take the form of a mutual agreement. But the arrangement of these agreements and especially their continued extension to new individuals entering the social fabric can be costly. As an alternative, society may proceed by internalization of these norms to the achievement of the desired agreement on an unconscious level. There is a whole set of customs and norms which might be similarly interpreted as agreements to improve the efficiency of the economic system (in the broad sense of satisfaction of individual values) by providing commodities to which the price system is inapplicable" (Arrow 1971, p. 22).

make a kind of virtue of commercial recklessness, cannot in any case stigmatize the reckless" (*DA*, p. 731).[24] Whereas aristocracies stigmatize work, democracies stigmatize idleness (*DA*, p. 733).[25]

Yet, as I have also noted, Tocqueville then goes on to say that under equality of conditions (by which he here means high social mobility), "public opinion has no hold" (*DA*, p. 736). For this reason, honor in the broad sense of social norms is more likely to arise under conditions of permanent inequality, and then to take the form of honor in the narrow sense of codes of vengeance and loyalty.

Tocqueville has a striking comment on the social norms governing the behavior of revolutionary crowds. Commenting on the revolution in February 1848, he explains that he "never expected the rich to be looted. . . . [W]e have passed through such long years of insurrections that a particular kind of morality of disorder and a special code for days of riot have evolved. These exceptional laws tolerate murder and allow devastation, but theft is strictly forbidden" (*R*, p. 72).[26] The permission to destroy material goods but not to steal them is striking. Writing a few years later, Tocqueville claimed that this norm had in fact been present from the very beginning. In the correspondence between the deputies from Anjou and their constituencies, on which he relied heavily (and perhaps too much), he notes the following statement from July 13,

---

[24] This kind of reasoning remains very common. As an example, take the following statement from a standard work on France under Vichy. In a discussion of the prewar pro-natalist policies, the author asserts that "the urgent need to increase births meant [*sic*] that French culture maintained considerable tolerance towards illegitimacy" (Jackson 2003, p. 33). Similarly, one sometimes encounters the assertion that in periods of high male unemployment, social norms emerge to stigmatize women who work. The objection to such claims is not so much that they are false as that in the absence of mechanisms showing how the "social need" for these norms brings them about, we have no reason to believe them to be true.

[25] In a draft (*O II*, p. 1154) Tocqueville explicitly asserts that the norm against idleness has been created by "the needs" (presumably of society).

[26] He adds that even in such cases, there will always be some "rascals" who steal "when nobody is looking." My suggestion here is that the code is consistent with *everyone* stealing when nobody is looking. Social norms are triggered only when one is observed by others. Referring to another code of honor, Montaigne (1991, pp. 789–890) wrote that "When I was a boy noblemen rejected a reputation for fencing as being an insult; they learned to fence in secret as some cunning craft which derogated from true inborn virtue." This being said, it is more likely that Tocqueville is making a distinction between moral norms, which compel compliance even when nobody is looking, and social norms, which do not.

1789: "In the tumult the prisoners of common crimes escaped; the people opposed their release, declaring that criminals were not worthy to mix with the makers of liberty. . . . If an armed man committed something vile, he was immediately taken to prison by his comrades." He comments that "This is particularly French" (*ER*, p. 95).[27]

As we shall see in Chapter 7, Tocqueville also argued that in the ancien régime, what one might call "estate consciousness" (similar to class consciousness) was maintained by social norms. Although members of the nobility or of a profession might be tempted to defect from the implicit contract that bound them, peer pressure kept them in line. By contrast, Tocqueville claimed that the evanescent nature of classes in America prevented the emergence of class consciousness.

---

[27] For similar observations, see Duquesnoy (1894), p. 271, and Lefebvre (1988), pp. 141–42.

5

Desires, Opportunities, Capacities

INTRODUCTION

In the chapters so far I have considered the mental antecedents of action, notably beliefs and desires. In one standard model of action, people do what they believe will best realize their desires. If, moreover, these beliefs are rational, we have the *rational-choice model of action*.

In *DA* Tocqueville offers us a different toolbox for understanding individual choice.[1] While not necessarily inconsistent with the rational-choice model, it represents a rather different approach. The main elements are the desires, opportunities, and capacities of people in democratic societies.[2] For desires to lead to action, the opportunity to act and the capacity to act must both be present.[3] Moreover, these three elements are not independent of one another, since the "social state of democracy" or some other independent variable may foster or block any one of them. In the language of contemporary social science, their presence or absence is "endogenous" to democracy.

For a brief illustration, consider an example from the last chapter. In democratic societies, the people do not have the opportunity to choose

---

[1] For reasons I do not understand, he seems to have discarded this scheme in *AR*, with an important exception noted toward the end of the chapter.
[2] To see the relation between the two models, note that the beliefs of an agent include beliefs about the opportunities for action (often referred to as "the choice set"). The capacities to which Tocqueville refers are mostly capacities to form rational beliefs.
[3] On this point, see also White (1987), pp. 135–36.

eminent persons as their representatives, for no such individuals will stand for office (Ch. 8). Even if they did, the people would not have the intellectual capacity to recognize their merits. And even if they had, they would have no desire to choose them, because of their envy of anyone meritorious. These facts are not accidental, since each of them springs from the nature of democratic society itself.

This three-way interaction among desires, opportunities, and capacities is rare. Usually Tocqueville cites either desire-opportunity interactions or desire-capacity interactions.[4] I focus on the former, which are by far the most important, but first some brief comments on the latter.

DESIRES AND CAPACITIES

In addition to the example just cited, concerning the lack of discernment of and lack of preference for *merit*, the most important instance involves attitudes toward the *future*. As we saw in Chapter 1, Tocqueville argued that people in democratic societies are naturally myopic, in the sense of being unable to delay gratification. (As we saw in Chapter 3, he also argued the very opposite.) We may think of this as a *motivational deficit*. At the same time, he argued for the existence of a *cognitive deficit*: "what democracy often lacks is this clear perception of the future, based on enlightenment and experience" (*DA*, p. 256). This argument applies with particular force to the benefits to be derived from liberty and the dangers that equality might bring:

Political liberty, if carried to excess, can endanger the tranquility, property, and lives of private individuals, and no one is so blind or frivolous as to be unaware of this. By contrast, it is *only the attentive and clear-sighted who perceive the perils* with which equality threatens us, and they usually avoid pointing them out. They know that the miseries they fear are remote and are pleased to think that they will afflict only future generations, *for which the present generation evinces little concern*. The ills that liberty sometimes brings on are immediate. They are visible to everyone, and to one degree or another everyone feels them. The ills that extreme equality can produce reveal themselves only a little at

---

[4] I have also found one instance of an *opportunity-capacity* interaction, in Tocqueville's explanation of the American intolerance of extramarital affairs: "In a country where the woman always freely exercises her choice [of marriage partner], and where her upbringing has put her in a position to choose well, public opinion is inexorable in regard to her faults" (*DA*, p. 700). An American woman has the opportunity to choose her husband and the capacity to choose well.

a time. . . . The goods that liberty yields reveal themselves only in the long run, and it is always easy to mistake their cause. The advantages of equality are felt immediately and can be seen daily to flow from their source. (*DA*, p. 583)

The first of the two phrases that I have italicized refers to a cognitive deficit in all citizens except for the "attentive and clear-sighted". The second refers to a motivational deficit in (it would seem) all citizens. Even though the temporally distant effects of their present choices appear on the mental screen of members of the intellectual elite, they are not motivated to lend them any weight in their decisions. As for members of the majority, they lack foresight as well as prudence: the two deficits converge. This passage obviously presents a more complex picture of the equality-liberty relation than the one that I presented in Chapter 4. In the passages I cited there (*DA*, pp. 60, 584), the preference for equality over liberty seems to be entirely due to motivation. Further complications will be introduced in the next chapter.

DESIRES AND OPPORTUNITIES

I now turn to the desire-opportunity interaction. Standard theories of rational choice usually assume that desires and opportunities are given independently of each other. While certainly appropriate in many cases, we may think of two reasons why this assumption may be inadequate.

First, we cannot assume that all logically possible combinations of desires and opportunities could actually be realized. Sociology may tell us that desires and opportunities covary, so that certain logically possible combinations are unlikely or unstable. If we view action as an outcome of desires and opportunities, the covariation of the latter two implies that we can also expect certain limits on what actions will be observed. In other words, desires and opportunities act as intermediate variables between a common cause (often but not always the social state of democracy) and a dependent variable.

Second, there may be a direct influence of opportunities on desires[5] or vice versa. The influence might be mediated by intentional choice or

---

[5] An example often used to illustrate the irrationality of desire-opportunity interactions is the following. A customer enters a restaurant and asks what is on the menu. Having been told that they serve beef and chicken, he orders beef. The waiter comes back, however, to tell him that today they also offer fish, whereupon he changes his order to one of chicken.

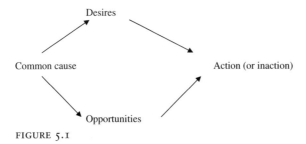

FIGURE 5.1

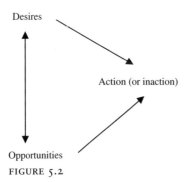

FIGURE 5.2

be due to a purely causal mechanism operating "behind the back" of the individual. Schematically, these two cases are represented in Figure 5.1 and Figure 5.2.

In considering the "common cause" situations, I shall distinguish among four cases, depending on whether the common cause increases or decreases the desire to take a certain action and on whether it increases or decreases the opportunity to take the same action. I first consider the two "convergent" cases in which the effects on desires and opportunities go in the same direction, and next the two "divergent cases."

POSITIVE IMPACT ON DESIRES, POSITIVE IMPACT
ON OPPORTUNITIES

This constellation can arise as an effect of *equalization*:

When [equality of conditions] first established itself in France, it immediately unleashed ambitions that were virtually without limit. . . . Not only is there no limit to desire, but the power to satisfy desire seems virtually unlimited. Amid the general and unexpected recasting of customs and laws . . . citizens rise and fall with unprecedented speed, and power passes so quickly from one hand to another that no one need despair of eventually grabbing some for himself. (*DA*, p. 738)

As we shall see shortly, the effects of *equality* differ in important respects.

Another instance of this pattern occurs in the context of a discussion of military advancement in wartime:

Those officers who have grown old in body and soul during peacetime are weeded out, retire, or die. Hastening to fill their place is a host of young men already hardened by war, and whose desires war has magnified and inflamed. These men want to achieve greatness at all cost, and they never stop wanting it. . . . Equality allows everyone to be ambitious, and death affords plenty of opportunity for all their ambitions. (*DA*, p. 775)

Here *war* is the common cause that both kindles the ambitions of military men and creates the opportunity to satisfy them.

A similar argument applies to the raising of large armies:

When it was possible to enlist troops of a type superior to all others, such as the Swiss infantry or French cavalry of the sixteenth century, people felt no need to raise very large armies, but this ceases to be true when one soldier is as good as another. *The same cause that gives rise to this new need also provides the means to satisfy it.* For as I have said, when all men are alike, all are weak. Social power is naturally much stronger among democratic peoples than it is elsewhere. Thus when these peoples feel the desire to call their entire male population to arms, they also have the ability to do so. (*DA*, pp. 780–81; my italics)

NEGATIVE IMPACT ON DESIRES, NEGATIVE IMPACT ON OPPORTUNITIES

These are not instances of causal (over)determination, as they would be if the effect of the common cause were to extinguish the desire *completely* and to eliminate *all* opportunities. The effect is merely to make it less likely that the action in question will be observed.

There are numerous arguments of this type, often recognizable by Tocqueville's use of the phrase "not only." (Below I cite several passages in which this phrase is used to make this point.) A famous example is his claim that "the law of inheritance [requiring equal partition] not only makes it difficult for families to keep their estates intact, it deprives them of the desire even to attempt to do so" (*DA*, p. 56). A few pages later he refers to the poor conditions for the "labors of the mind" in America: "the will to devote oneself to such works is lacking, and so is the ability" (*DA*, p. 59). This sounds like an argument about converging lack of desires and of capacities, but it is actually a condensed statement of two divergent desire-opportunity patterns: "In America, most of the rich started out poor. Almost all men of leisure were occupied in youth. Hence in the time of life when a person might have a taste for study, he has no time for it, and when he has acquired time to devote to it, he no longer has the taste" (*ibid.*).

A more consequential example concerns the impact of slavery on slave owners. In the first place, slavery creates few opportunities for profit, compared to free labor: "The free worker receives wages; the slave receives an upbringing, food, care, and clothing. The money that the master spends on the upkeep of the slave is meted out for specific purposes a little at a time; it is barely noticed. The wage paid to the worker is distributed in a lump sum and seems to enrich only the person to whom it is paid. In reality, however, the slave costs more than the free man, and his labor is less productive" (*DA*, p. 400). But "the influence of slavery extends still further. It penetrates the master's very soul and imparts a particular direction to his ideas and tastes" (*ibid.*). Because work is associated with slavery, the southern whites are "contemptuous not only of labor but of all enterprises that succeed by virtue of labor" (*DA*, p. 401). They lack both the opportunities and the desire to get rich: "slavery not only prevents the White from making a fortune but diverts his will to other ends" (*ibid.*). If Tocqueville is right, the classic debate over the economic stagnation of slave societies is spurious. There is no need to ask whether lack of investment desires or lack of investment opportunities provides the correct explanation: both sides could be right.[6]

---

[6] Hegel and more recently Eugene Genovese argued that the psychology of the slave owner channeled his desires toward conspicuous consumption and, by implication, away from investment. Marx asserted that the psychology of slaves, which makes them treat tools and instruments badly, destroyed any investment opportunities for the slave owner. Both could be right. See Elster (1985), pp. 275 ff.

In Chapter 4 I cited Tocqueville's discussion of a possible breakup of the union due to the envy of the more slowly developing southern states. This idea invites the question whether the other states would not then take measures to prevent the dissolution. In an earlier part of the same chapter in *DA*, Tocqueville addresses the issue more abstractly, claiming that it "appears certain that if one portion of the Union seriously wished to separate from the other, it could not be prevented from doing so; indeed, no one would even try to prevent it" (*DA*, p. 427).

Tocqueville offers another double-barreled argument to show the weakness of the American president. Although the constitution confers vast powers on him, "he has no occasion to use them" (*DA*, p. 142) because of the lack of important foreign policy issues. At the same time, "by introducing the principle of reelection [the lawgivers] conferred great power on the president and stripped him of the will to make use of it" (*DA*, p. 155). Although "power" in the second passage refers to domestic issues and not foreign policy, the mechanism stated there applies to foreign policy as well. If an important foreign policy issue came up, the need to maneuver for reelection could deprive the president of the will to take energetic action.

A final instance of this pattern occurs in Tocqueville's discussion of the fate of an occupied country under a democratic regime. Because individual citizens in a democracy are powerless and isolated, "no one can either defend himself or serve as a rallying point for others" (*DA*, p. 781). Moreover, they do not really have an interest in defending their country: "each citizen has only a small share of political power and in many cases no share at all. Furthermore, everyone is independent and has property to lose. People therefore fear conquest far less and war far more than they would in an aristocratic nation" (*DA*, p. 782). Hence, he concludes, "not only will the population then be unable to carry on the war, but there is reason to fear it will not even wish to make the attempt" (*ibid.*).

POSITIVE IMPACT ON DESIRES, NEGATIVE IMPACT ON OPPORTUNITIES

I have already cited an example to the effect that Americans never have the time to study at the age when they desire to do so. Much more important is the following text, which summarizes a central idea in DA: "The same equality that allows each citizen to entertain vast hopes makes all citizens individually weak. It limits their strength in every respect, even as it allows their desires to expand. . . . The constant tension that exists between the instincts to which equality gives rise and the means it provides for their satisfaction torments and tires the soul" (*DA*, p. 627). In the language of sociology, *anomie* is a permanent and inevitable feature of democratic societies. This is not in line, however, with more recent views, which rather tend to see anomie as an effect of change and social disruption.[7]

Disconcertingly, Tocqueville also asserts the latter idea. His argument is that when opportunities become more restricted, desires also become more modest, but that the adjustment is subject to a time lag:

Passions prompted by revolution do not disappear when the revolution ends. . . . Vast desires remain, while the means of satisfying them diminish daily. The taste for great fortunes persists, even though great fortunes themselves become rare. . . . Little by little, however, the last traces of conflict fade from view. . . . Desires proportion themselves to means. Needs, ideas, and sentiments follow from one another. Leveling is complete: democractic society finally has found its footing. (*DA*, p. 739)

Is it possible for Tocqueville to escape the charge of contradicting himself on this point? Can it both be true that in democracies "desires proportion themselves to means" *and* that there is a "constant tension that exists between the instincts to which equality gives rise and the means it provides for their satisfaction" (*DA*, p. 627), so that in "democracies one . . . finds large numbers of people whose fortunes are on the rise but whose desires nevertheless outpace them" (*DA*, p. 531)?

The contradiction unravels when we see that there are two different time scales involved. As Tocqueville notes, "One must be careful to distinguish the kind of permanent agitation that exists in a peaceful, established democracy from the tumultuous revolutionary movements that almost always accompany the birth and development of a democratic society" (*DA*, p. 523). Or again, whereas "great revolutions are

---

[7] Even if I had the competence to do so, this would not be the place to discuss the complex idea of anomie that originated with Durkheim. Let me simply state that the idea I discuss here is closer to Durkheim's analyses in *Suicide* than to *The Division of Labor in Society*.

no more common in democratic nations than in other countries," the former have in common "a constant turnover of people" (*une sorte de roulement incessant des hommes les uns sur les autres*) (*DA*, p. 524). This distinction between *change of regime* and *change within regime* dispels the appearance of contradiction.[8] Although each form of change is characterized by an interplay of desires and opportunities, they differ in their fine grain.

The European transition from the ancien régime to democracy was a one-shot world historical process. In the beginning, as Tocqueville observes, huge opportunities opened up, to match the new desires that were created. As he certainly knew, many of Napoleon's generals were between twenty-five and thirty years old. After the Restoration, when things settled down in a more peaceful pattern and it was no longer realistic to entertain huge ambitions, many still continued to do so because of the time lag. Julien Sorel, the hero of Stendhal's *Le rouge et le noir* (1830), idolized Napoleon. In one scene of the novel he watches a bird of prey circling in the sky, and asks himself, "It was the destiny of Napoleon, would it one day be his own?"

After another generation had passed, the scope of ambitions finally adjusted to the opportunities for satisfying them. Although Tocqueville asserts that in this "permanent and normal state" of democracy "leveling is complete" (*DA*, p. 739), that statement is quite misleading. It rests on an ambiguity that I shall consider more closely in Chapter 7, between equality in the sense of equal fortunes at a given point in time and equality in the sense of a rapid turnover of fortunes. As I shall argue, the second idea is in some ways the more powerful explanatory variable in *DA*. It implies that *change is a permanent feature in democracies* – not the world historical change that was illustrated by the French Revolution, but incessant social (and geographical) mobility.

As Tocqueville acutely notes, downward as well as upward social mobility may cause desires to outstrip opportunities: "In democratic nations there are always many citizens whose patrimonies are divided and whittled away. In better times they acquired certain needs that stay with them after the ability to satisfy them no longer exists.... In

---

[8] As we shall see in Ch. 7, however, Tocqueville suggests that in the realm of politics, rapid within-regime change may induce between-regime change.

democracies one also finds large numbers of people whose fortunes are on the rise but whose desires nevertheless outpace them" (*DA*, p. 531).[9]

The first of these mechanisms is the time lag that we also noted in the large-scale change of regime. The second is one often used to characterize Tocqueville's explanation of the French Revolution in *AR*. In that context, it is usually called "the revolution of rising expectations": When conditions improve, desires will improve even faster, causing discontent rather than satisfaction. As a result, the citizens turn to collective revolutionary action to close the cap between aspirations and reality. As we shall see in Chapter 9, this was *not* the theory Tocqueville proposed in *AR*.[10] To my knowledge, the idea that rising opportunities cause desires to expand even faster occurs only in the passage just cited. In *DA* we find, nevertheless, two arguments that explain revolutionary or rebellious behavior by the discrepancy between desires and opportunities. The first relates to democratic armies, the second to slavery.

Tocqueville argued that in democratic armies, neither the regular officers nor the rank and file soldiers are particularly bellicose. By contrast, the precarious existence of the noncommissioned officer creates a "desperate ambition" for advancement (*DA*, p. 771): "The non-commissioned officer therefore wants war; he wants it always and no matter what the cost, and if war is denied him, he will desire revolutions, which suspend the authority of rules and give him hope that, abetted by confusion and political passions, he may drive out his officer and take his place" (*ibid.*). This remark points to a connection between desires and opportunities that differs from the ones we have seen so far: rather than desires and opportunities having a common cause, opportunities may be *shaped* by desires (more accurately: by the actions these desires inspire). I shall return to this idea later in the chapter.

Once we accept this new connection, a further implication follows. If an authority wants to reduce the likelihood of rebellion of an

---

[9] In the language of reference group theory, the second effect may be due to *anticipatory socialization*, the internalization of the desires of the group to which one aspires to belong. By analogy, the first effect might be called "retrospective socialization."

[10] See notably note 25 to Ch. 9 with accompanying text.

oppressed group, it may be more efficient to shape the desires of members of that group than to limit their opportunities. Tocqueville makes this point in a remarkable discussion of slavery: "In Antiquity, people sought to prevent the slave from breaking his chains; nowadays they seek to sap his desire to do so" (*DA*, p. 417). The crucial strategy for stifling the desire was to ban manumission:

> The Americans of the South understood that emancipation is always dangerous if the freed slave cannot some day assimilate with the master. To give a man freedom yet leave him in ignominious misery – what does this accomplish other than to provide some slave rebellion with a future leader? It was noticed long ago, moreover, that the presence of the freed Negro was vaguely disquieting to the souls of the unfree, in whom it aroused the first glimmering of an idea of their rights. In most cases, therefore, Americans in the South stripped masters of the prerogative to free their slaves. (*DA*, pp. 417–18)

The argument goes as follows. Individual slave owners might want to emancipate their slaves. The slave states forbid them from doing so, however, because of the consequences that might ensue. First, in the newly emancipated slaves, the gap between the desire for material well-being suggested to them by their freedom and the lack of opportunities for satisfying that desire would lead to discontent. Secondly, in the unemancipated slaves, the presence of free blacks would create a desire for freedom that, once again, would not be matched by opportunities. One day potential leaders and potential followers would join in a slave rebellion. Instead of using force against the slaves to limit their opportunities for rebellion, the American slave-holding states used the law against the slave owners to limit the desire of the slaves to rebel.

After this digression on the impact of desires on opportunities, let me conclude on the question of anomie. I believe that the passages I cited allow us to assert that high social mobility does in fact induce a low-grade anomie as a permanent feature of democracies in equilibrium, to be contrasted with the acute anomie illustrated by Julien Sorel. In the latter, "overweening and frustrated ambitions secretly consume the hearts that harbor them" (*DA*, p. 739). In the former, the effect is mainly that citizens "settle for less than complete satisfaction" (*DA*, p. 532). In this case, at least, a close reading of Tocqueville's text enables us to go beyond the appearance of contradiction.

NEGATIVE IMPACT ON DESIRES, POSITIVE IMPACT ON OPPORTUNITIES

This pattern is exemplified by the statement that Americans have no taste for studying when they finally acquire the means to do so. A similar argument occurs in a strange paragraph in which it is not clear whether Tocqueville is referring to America, to France, to democracies in general, or even (as suggested by the following paragraph) to China:

Hatred of privilege and the difficulty of selection . . . create a situation in which all men, regardless of stature, are forced to follow the same course and are indiscriminately subjected to a host of trivial preliminary exercises, in which they squander their youth and see their imagination stifled, so that they despair of ever being able to enjoy fully the goods they are offered. And by the time they finally reach the point where they are able to do extraordinary things, they have lost the taste for them. (*DA*, p. 741)

Another argument of the same general form has a central place in Tocqueville's explanation of the stability of democratic societies: "even as the law allows the American people to do anything and everything, there are some things that religion prevents them from imagining or forbids them to attempt" (*DA*, p. 338). As noted in Chapter 1, one mechanism by which this effect comes about is the tendency of religion to make citizens think in terms of the distant future rather than giving in to sudden impulses. To see that the opportunity for imprudent, violent, or licentious behavior and the lack of any desire to behave in such ways have a common cause, it suffices to observe that for Tocqueville, religion is itself a product of democracy. In a passage already quoted, he says that if man "has no faith, he must serve, and if he is free, he must believe" (*DA*, p. 503). The ills or dangers of democracy are cured or neutralized by democracy itself.

In another instance of this argument, Tocqueville relies on *interest* rather than on religion to neutralize the dangers that liberty, in the abstract, might generate. In the chapter on "Why great revolutions will become rare," the key variable is the fact that in democracies, everybody has some property and hence something to lose (*DA*, p. 749).[11] Hence, in the succinct statement from the draft manuscript, "if people

---

[11] See also the quote from Bismarck in note 19 to Ch. 9.

who live in democratic centuries have greater facility and liberty to make changes, they have less interest in change" (*O II*, p. 1159). Whereas in the religion-based argument the cure for the ills generated by political democracy was itself a product of that regime, the interest-based argument relies on "the social state of democracy" to counteract the ills of political democracy.

INTERACTION BETWEEN DESIRES AND OPPORTUNITIES

I now turn to various forms of direct interaction between desires and opportunities. Implicitly, I have already alluded to one such mechanism: the adjustment of desires to opportunities, in recent literature sometimes called "adaptive preference formation."[12] Tocqueville has an explicit reference to this mechanism in one of his comments on American women: "Their desires seem to contract with their fortunes as readily as they expand" (*DA*, p. 696). In a discussion of officers in democratic armies, he asserts that whereas "those who have the greatest ambition and the most resources leave the army," the rest adjust "their tastes and desires to the mediocrity of their lot" (*DA*, p. 774). Several of the passages on slavery that I have cited (*DA*, pp. 366–67, 417–18) assert how the slave adjusts to his condition and even develops a "depraved taste" for it. As we shall see in Chapter 9, Tocqueville also argued that what one might call the "release from adaptive preferences" was one of the most important causes of the French Revolution.

In all these cases but one, this adjustment of desires to opportunities takes place unconsciously, "behind the back of" the individual, offering another example of the self-poisoning of the mind to which I referred in Chapter 4. The exception concerns American women, who are said to embrace their situation consciously and with Stoic calm. In some of his most extraordinary statements, Tocqueville asserts that "it is through the use of independence that [the young American woman] develops the courage to endure the sacrifice of that independence without a struggle or a murmur when the time [to marry] comes" (*DA*, p. 695). Or again, "it seemed to me that in a way [the most virtuous among American women] prided themselves on the voluntary sacrifice of their will and demonstrated their greatness by freely accepting the yoke

[12] Veyne (1976) has the first sustained analysis of this phenomenon.

rather than seeking to avoid it" (*DA*, p. 706). He makes similar and equally extravagant claims about voluntary servitude in the ancien régime: "There was a time under the old monarchy when Frenchmen felt a kind of joy at surrendering utterly to the arbitrary rule of their monarch" (*DA*, p. 269).[13] Or again, "It is not unknown for a people to take pleasure and pride of a sort in sacrificing their will to that of the prince, thereby marking a kind of independence in the very act of obedience" (*DA*, p. 296).[14]

In the last two paragraphs I have discussed conscious and unconscious causal mechanisms through which opportunities may affect desires. Earlier I mentioned that, conversely, desires may affect opportunities, if, for instance, noncommissioned officers or slaves succeed in the attempt to expand their choice set through violence. We might, then, draw a distinction between two reactions to the discrepancy between desires and opportunities: *resignation* (caused by contraction of the desires) and *rebellion* (aimed at expanding the opportunities). We may speculate, moreover, that in both cases the reactions can *overshoot*. In resignation, there may be overadaptation to the choice set ("sour grapes").[15] Tocqueville observes that "The French needs a little license in everything, even in servitude. He likes to go beyond his original commands; when in servitude, he exceeds in that too" (*ER*, p. 159). In rebellion, Tocqueville argues, "the same energy that impels a man to rebel in a violent way against a common error almost always carries him beyond the bounds of reason" (*DA*, p. 701).

Even if some individuals may try to expand their choice set, we would not, perhaps, expect desires to aim at *reducing* the choice set. Yet there is by now a considerable body of writing on how rational

[13] This sentimental idea is also taken up in the work on the Revolution: "Their compliance with the orders [of the king], even the most arbitrary, was a matter less of compulsion than of love, and often they managed to preserve their freedom of spirit even in conditions of the most extreme dependence" (*AR*, p. 153).

[14] To complete the picture, it may be worth citing a passage in which Tocqueville condemns rather than praises the independent abdication of independence. Referring to political associations in Europe, he writes that their members "respond to orders as soldiers in the field. They profess the dogma of passive obedience, or perhaps it would be better to say that upon enlisting they offer up all they possess of judgment and free will in a moment of sacrifice" (*DA*, p. 222). Anyone who watched students in the 1960s passing from their normal state of skeptical questioning to a state of unconditional obedience to the (usually Maoist) party will recognize the phenomenon.

[15] This is a central idea in Veyne (1976).

individuals might want, for a large variety of reasons, to discard some of their options.[16] Like Ulysses binding himself to the mast, they might want to take precautions against yielding to passion. Tocqueville refers to this idea, but only to make fun of it:

Americans, whose laws authorize freedom and even license of speech in all matters, have nevertheless imposed a kind of censorship on dramatic authors. Plays can be performed only when town officials allow. This shows clearly that peoples are like individuals. They indulge their principal passions to the hilt and then take care lest they yield more than they should to tastes they do not possess. (*DA*, p. 567)

In his analyses of the Bank of the United States, for instance, Tocqueville praises "the benefits that the country derives from the Bank" (*DA*, p. 448). He is very far, however, from making the argument that has become a dogma or a mantra in the last few decades, namely, that the creation of an independent central bank could constitute an act of *collective self-binding* against momentary interests or passions.[17] On the contrary, he describes how the state banks, "impatient of the salutary control" exercised by the Bank, "arouse local passions and the country's blind democratic instincts against the central bank" (*DA*, p. 449). The actions of the Bank may be a "salutary control," but they are in no way a form of *self-control*.

---

[16] See, for instance, Schelling (1960); Elster (1984, 2000).
[17] Cukierman (1992).

6

Patterns of Social Causality

INTRODUCTION

In the Preface to his analysis of English capitalism, Marx told his German readers, "De te fabula narratur" – the story is told about you. And he added, "The country that is more developed industrially only shows, to the less developed, the image of its own future." *DA* is also a book about a foreign country that is held up to native readers as the image of their future. In the Introduction to the work, Tocqueville tells his readers that "There is no doubt in my mind that sooner or later we will come, as the Americans have come, to an almost complete equality of conditions" (*DA*, p. 14).

Tocqueville believed that his French readers would recoil before this prospect. *DA* as a whole may be read as an attempt to persuade them that their fears were ungrounded.[1] His rhetorical strategy can be represented as follows. "You, my French readers, claim that democracy is pernicious. To support that claim you point to this or that dangerous effect of democratic customs and institutions. For each of these alleged flaws of democracy, I will show you that it rests on one of the following causal fallacies. You misidentify the causes of the facts you cite; you fail to take a sufficiently long time perspective; you ignore how the flaws of democracy are remedied or offset by democracy itself; or you make

---

[1] I am deeply indebted to Stephen Holmes for urging this point on me some twenty-five years ago. It completely transformed my reading of *DA*.

a fallacious inference from the effects of a marginal practice to the effects that would arise were the practice to become generalized. Once you have seen through these errors, your objections will cease."

I may add that some of his readers might have raised – and almost certainly did raise – an objection that cannot be put to rest in the same way. It refers to the essential mediocrity of democracies, which provide comfort for the many but fail to nourish outstanding achievements in the arts or sciences. Tocqueville acknowledged this fact, and to the extent he remained an aristocrat, deplored it. To the extent he was able to take a more impartial perspective, he embraced it. In his concluding chapter, he writes that "It is natural to believe that what is most satisfying to the eye of man's creator and keeper is not the singular prosperity of a few but the greater well-being of all: what seems decadence to me is therefore progress in his eyes; what pains me pleases him. Equality is less lofty, perhaps, but more just" (*DA*, p. 833). In addition to being a methodological individualist, he was an ethical individualist. In his view, the value that should guide us is the good of individuals, not the good of Mankind.

TOCQUEVILLE'S IDEA OF A SOCIAL EQUILIBRIUM

The first of the four causal fallacies I listed involves a confusion between transitional effects and equilibrium effects. Usually this implies a confusion between the effects of equalization and the effects of equality, but we shall see that the distinction is more broadly applicable.

First, we need to characterize Tocqueville's idea of a social equilibrium. The French terms he uses, *assiette* and the corresponding verbal form *assis,* are not easy to translate, nor is the idea easy to understand. Another phrase used to express the same idea, "the natural state" of a society (e.g., *DA*, pp. 259, 754), is not very illuminating.

I believe the best entry into the subject is provided by a passage partly cited in Chapter 5, taken from the discussion of why there are so few great ambitions in the United States:

Desires proportion themselves to means. *Needs, ideas, and sentiments follow from one another.* Leveling is complete: democratic people society has finally found its footing [*est enfin assise*]. If we consider a democratic people that has achieved this permanent and normal state . . . we will easily come to the conclusion that if ambition becomes great while conditions are tending toward equality, it loses that character when equality becomes a fact. (*DA*, p. 739; my italics)

Tocqueville clearly intends to assert that America has found this "permanent and normal" state, in which there are no internal tensions that would presage a major social upheaval.[2] In another passage, however, he asserts that American society "has yet to achieve a settled and definitive form" (*une assiette tranquille et definitive*) (*DA*, p. 247). On my reading of this text, he is not claiming that the society is unstable, only that the dust has not yet quite settled. Admittedly, while plausible, this interpretation is not compelling. It is supported, however, by a number of texts, which taken together imply that Tocqueville viewed the various aspects of American life as *mutually reinforcing each other.* As we shall now see, the idea that "Needs, ideas, and sentiments follow from one another" can be generalized.

Needs, ideas, and sentiments belong to the category of *mores*, "habits of the heart" (*DA*, p. 331). These constitute one of the three main variables of the analyses in *DA*, the other two being the *laws* and "the *social state*" of society. The last usually but not invariably refers to equality in either its static or its dynamic form (see next chapter). Tocqueville makes a number of seemingly contradictory claims concerning the causal relations among these three variables. I shall argue that the contradiction can be resolved if we view him as grappling with the idea of *circular social causality* in which the three main variables do indeed "follow from one another."

In the title of one chapter, mores are explicitly said to be more important than the laws: "Laws do more to maintain a democratic republic in the United States than physical causes do, and mores do more than the laws" (*DA*, p. 352). Toward the end of the chapter he asserts that mores are supremely important (and not just more important than laws): "The importance of mores is a common truth, which study and experience have repeatedly confirmed. It is a truth central to

---

[2] In a draft manuscript Tocqueville draws a contrast between European society in which there is "confusion in the intellectual world, opinions are not in harmony with tastes nor interests with ideas," and America in which "everything *hangs together*" (*tout s'enchaîne*) (*O II*, p. 940; his italics). In another draft he notes that "Laws act on mores and mores on laws. Wherever these two things do not support each other mutually there is unrest, division, revolution" (*O II*, p. 960).

all my thinking, and in the end all my ideas come back to it" (*DA*, p. 356). Now, saying that A is more important than B could mean several things. It could mean that A offers an explanation of B, typically through being a cause of B, that A explains more phenomena or more important phenomena than B, or that A contributes more powerfully to the explanation of the phenomena jointly caused by A and B. Which-ever of these ways we choose to understand it, the idea that mores are more important than laws is incompatible with a number of other passages that I shall now cite.

Tocqueville writes: "More than once in the course of this book I have sought to explain the prodigious influence that the social state seems to me to exert on the laws and mores of men" (*DA*, p. 379). Or consider the opening sentence of the second volume: "The democratic social state of the Americans has naturally suggested certain laws and certain political mores" (*DA*, p. 479). But if laws and mores are both the effects of a common cause, one can hardly claim that mores are fundamental. One may still claim, perhaps, that they are more important than laws. That claim, however, is hard to reconcile with passages in which laws are said to shape the mores. Such is the case with the legal institution of slavery, which "explains the mores and social state of the South" (*DA*, p. 35). By giving priority to the laws over the social state of slavery, this passage also goes against the two passages cited at the beginning of this paragraph. Another assertion of this priority comes in the discussion of inheritance laws: "I am astonished that ancient and modern writers on public matters have not ascribed greater influence over human affairs to the laws governing inheritance. Such laws belong, of course, to the civil order, but they should be placed first among political institutions because of their incredible influence on a people's social state" (*DA*, pp. 53–54).

In these passages, then, we have seen Tocqueville asserting the prior-ity of mores over laws (*DA*, p. 352), the priority of the social state over laws and mores (*DA*, p. 379), the priority of laws over mores (*DA*, p. 35), and the priority of laws over the social state (*DA*, pp. 53–54). Although some of the passages assert a general priority and others simply the priority in special cases, the overall impression they leave is one of sheer muddle. However, we can dispel the confusion by a simple decoding principle, replacing two or more statements that stipulate causal chains working in opposite directions by a single statement about circular causality. In equilibrium, social conditions, legal institutions, and mores support one another mutually, just as do needs, ideas, and sentiments within the mores.

For another example of how apparently contradictory statements may be reconciled by the idea of circular causality, we may consider two of Tocqueville's comments on slavery. On the one hand, he asserts that the slave "finds his joy and his pride in a servile imitation of his oppressors" (*DA*, p. 367). Slavery, in other words, causes servility. On the other hand, we find him comparing the two oppressed races in America in the following terms: "The Negro would like to blend in with the European, and he cannot. The Indian might to some degree succeed in such an enterprise, but he disdains to attempt it. The servility of the Negro delivers him to slavery and the pride of the Indian condemns him to death" (*DA*, p. 369). Servility, in other words, causes slavery. Charitably interpreted, the two passages need not contradict each other. We can read them simply as saying that slavery generates mental attitudes in the slaves that tend to stabilize the institution.

A third apparent contradiction can be resolved in the same way. In Chapter 1 I cited Tocqueville as asserting both that "Americans almost always carry the habits of public life over into private life" (*DA*, p. 352) and that their "habits of private life carry over into public life" (*DA*, pp. 245–46). In a social equilibrium, private and public life would tend to mutually support one another. This is not to say that the spillover effect is invariably stabilizing. In another passage I cited in Chapter 1, Tocqueville writes that the nation "carried over into politics all the habits of literature" (*AR*, p. 177), adding that "what is merit in the writer may well be a vice in the statesman."

To complete the picture, I ought to add that Tocqueville in various places does suggest some tensions in American democracy that might cause its demise or radical transformation. Some of these are intrinsic to *American* democracy rather than to democracy per se, notably the fragmentation of the union (see passages cited above) and the risk of civil war over the issue of slavery (*DA*, p. 752). The rise of a mild and tutelary despotism, sketched in Part IV of Volume 2 of *DA* and summarized in Chapter 8, probably applies more to France than to democracies in general. There is also the possible emergence of an aristocracy of industrialists that may constitute a danger more specific to democracies. In the succinct formulation of a draft manuscript, "democracy leads to trade and trade recreates aristocracy" (*O II*, p. 1129).[3] More generally, Tocqueville observes that what strikes participants and observers as stability may only be motion that is too slow to be perceptible (*DA*, pp. 199–200).

I think it is fair to say, however, that these are minor dissonances in what is otherwise a portrait of a remarkably stable society. In the somewhat disorganized chapter on "Causes that tend to maintain the democratic republic in the United States," we even find an anticipation of Frederick Jackson Turner's "frontier hypothesis," sometimes called "the safety-valve hypothesis":

I have it on good authority that in 1830 thirty-six members of Congress could trace their birth to the small state of Connecticut. . . . Yet the state of Connecticut itself sends only five representatives to Congress. The other thirty-one represent the new states of the West. If those thirty-one people had stayed in Connecticut, they would very likely have remained small farmers instead of becoming wealthy landowners, would have lived in obscurity without any possibility of a political career, and would have become not useful legislators but dangerous citizens. (*DA*, p. 325)

By contrast, Tocqueville asserts that French society from the revolution up to his own time was in constant disequilibrium. In the notes for the second volume of *AR* we read the following: "I have already heard it said in my lifetime on four occasions that this new society made by the Revolution has now finally found its natural and permanent form (*son assiette naturelle et permanente*). Four times events afterwards proved that people were wrong" (*ER*, p. 166). Taking into account regime transitions that occurred before his lifetime, he elsewhere counts five such occasions:

The Constitutional Monarchy had succeeded the Ancien Régime; the Republic followed the Monarchy; the Empire the Republic; after the Empire the Restoration; then there had come the July Monarchy. After each of these successive changes it was said that the French Revolution, having finished what was presumptuously called its work, was finished. . . . Under the Restoration, I, too,

---

[3] Somewhat surprisingly, Tocqueville goes on to assert that "this danger can be exorcized only by the discovery of means (associations or others) by which one could engage in trade without accumulating so much capital in the same hands" (*O II*, p. 1129). Tocqueville is not usually associated with the idea of workers' cooperatives.

unfortunately hoped for that, and I continued to hope after the Restoration government had fallen. (*R*, p. 66)

This passage follows directly upon one in which he asserts that "whatever might be the fate of our posterity, it was our lot to spend a wretched life between alternate swings to license and to oppression" (*R*, p. 65). This gloomy statement echoes a comment on Mexico "lurching from anarchy to military despotism and back again" (*DA*, p. 187). More generally:

For the past quarter of a century, people have been astonished to see the new nations of South America repeatedly convulsed by revolution, and they keep waiting for those countries to return to what they call their *natural state*. But who can say that, for the Spaniards of South America, revolution is not today the most natural state? (*DA*, p. 259)

As we saw in the last chapter and will see more fully in the next, Tocqueville believed that in democracies, change due to social mobility was endemic. In the three intriguing passages I just cited, he suggests that in some societies *violent* change may be endemic – that regime change may be, as it were, part of the regime itself. Although he thought stability might be achieved after his lifetime, recent writers have argued that the permanent effect of the French Revolution was to create a cyclical change between Bonapartism and Orleanism.[4] But as Chou En-lai is reported to have said when asked what he thought of the French Revolution, it may be "too early to tell."

TRANSITION EFFECTS AND EQUILIBRIUM EFFECTS

Be this as it may, Tocqueville warns the reader against confusing the effects of a transition from state A to state B and the effects of state B itself. In most of the examples to be given below, B is democracy, but in one it is absolutism. In most of the examples I shall cite, the effects of the transition are negative and those of the final state more positive. There are also, as we shall see, cases in which the transition is more fertile in achievements than the equilibrium state.

[4] Aron (1962), p. 292; Lévi-Strauss (1960), p. 94.

Tocqueville formulates the warning very explicitly toward the end of the work: "one must be careful not to confuse the fact of equality with the revolution that is responsible for introducing it into the social state and laws. Therein lies the reason for nearly all the phenomena that we find surprising" (*DA*, p. 814). He proposed a fuller development of this distinction in a review from 1848 of a book *On Democracy in Switzerland*:

M. Cherbuliez has called his book *On Democracy in Switzerland*, which might give the impression that the author thinks Switzerland can provide the basis for a book treating of the theory of democracy and that that country offers an opportunity to judge democratic institutions in themselves. That is the origin, in my view, of almost all the mistakes in the book. The title should have been *On the Democratic Revolution in Switzerland*. Switzerland has in fact for fifteen years been a country in the state of revolution. . . . One can well study there the particular phenomena which go with a state of revolution, but one cannot take it as the basis for a description of democracy in its *permanent and peaceful established state*. (*O I*, p. 637)[5]

Let me mention some examples of the use Tocqueville makes of this distinction. I have already cited the following: "If ambition becomes great while conditions are tending toward equality, it loses that character when equality becomes a fact" (*DA*, p. 739). In the three-stage model of belief formation that I discussed in Chapter 2, he asserts the pernicious effect of the *introduction* of freedom of the press: "Woe unto those generations that abruptly introduce freedom of the press for the first time!" (*DA*, p. 213). By contrast, in an established democracy freedom of the press "is the only cure for most of the ills that equality can produce" (*DA*, p. 824).[6] Moreover, whereas democracy generates mutual indifference, the transition causes mutual hatred: "Democracy tends to make men unwilling to approach their fellows, but democratic revolutions encourage them to shun one another and perpetuate in the midst of equality hatreds originating in inequality" (*DA*, p. 589). Elsewhere he writes that "If equality of conditions encourages good morals,

---

[5] The translation is taken from pp. 737–38 of the Lawrence translation of *DA*, which includes this review as an appendix. The French original of the phrase I have italicized is "son assiette permanente et tranquille."
[6] In a different argument, he appeals to the net effect idea: "the ills [newspapers] cause is . . . far less than the ill they heal" (*DA*, p. 600).

the social travail that makes conditions equal is very damaging to morality" (*DA*, p. 703). And whereas democracy produces conformism, the transition generates diversity: "The more closely I consider the effects of equality on the mind, the more I am persuaded that the intellectual anarchy we see all around us is not, as many people assume, the natural state of democratic peoples. In my view it should be looked upon rather as an accidental consequence of their youth, and it manifests itself only in this era of transition" (*DA*, p. 754).

As I noted in Chapter 5, Tocqueville argued that religion was endogenous to democracy. In a brief aside on the state of affairs in Europe at his time, he asks himself: "Why does this picture not apply to us?" In his answer he first cites the existence of "lukewarm allies and ardent adversaries" of religion, and adds that there are "a small number of believers [who], having seen that the first use their own countrymen made of independence was to attack religion . . . , fear their contemporaries and recoil in terror from the liberty those contemporaries seek" (*DA*, pp. 346–47). These defenders of religion, therefore, confuse the effects of democratization with the effects of democracy: to defend religion, they think that they must attack democracy.

In some analyses Tocqueville contrasts the effect of the transition from state A to state B with the equilibrium effects of A, as well as with the effects of B. Typically, he claims, the transitional stage will be worse than either equilibrium state. In the Introduction to *DA* a major theme is how, in the transition to democracy, "we have abandoned what was good in our former state without acquiring what useful things our present state might have to offer" (*DA*, p. 11).

A more specific development of this idea occurs in a section on "The public spirit in the United States" in which he distinguishes between the "unreflective" patriotism of the ancien régime and the "more rational form of patriotism," which is "born of enlightenment" rather than of passion (*DA*, p. 269). In the transition from the one to the other, however, "there may come a time when ancient customs are transformed, mores decay, faiths are shaken, memories lose their prestige, but enlightenment has yet to complete its work. . . . Lacking both the instinctive patriotism of monarchy and the considered patriotism of a republic, [men] find themselves stuck somewhere between the two, surrounded by confusion and misery" (*DA*, p. 270).

We find another three-stage comparison in the chapter on "How democracy modifies the relations between servant and master":

In aristocratic nations, domestic service is commonly an estate that does not debase the soul of those who submit to it, because they neither know nor imagine any other, and the extraordinary inequality they observe between themselves and the master strikes them as a necessary and inevitable consequence of some hidden law of Providence. Under democracy, there is nothing degrading about the estate of domestic service because it is freely chosen and temporarily adopted and because it is not stigmatized by public opinion and creates no permanent inequality between servant and master. During the transition from one social condition to another, however, there is almost always a moment of hesitation between the aristocratic notion of subjection and the democratic notion of obedience. . . . The master is malevolent and mild, the servant malevolent and intractable. (*DA*, p. 677)

In these passages, Tocqueville tells us that in the turbulence of transition we observe bad morals, intellectual anarchy, irreligion, swelling ambitions, mutual hostility, lack of patriotism, and insolence. In all respects, the end state of the transition is to be preferred. In the two last-cited cases, the state prior to the transition is also to be preferred. In one exceptional case, however, the transition to democracy allows for greater achievements than what democracy itself allows for: "Although the French made remarkable progress in the exact sciences at the exact moment they were finishing off what was left of feudal society, that sudden burst of creativity must be attributed not to democracy but to the unprecedented revolution that attended its growth" (*DA*, p. 524).

In the chapter on "The literary aspects of democratic centuries," he turns the master–servant argument on its head, arguing that in the arts, the transition from aristocracy to democracy yielded greater achievements than either of the two equilibrium states. In aristocracies, "style will seem almost as important as ideas and form almost as important as substance" and "writers will devote more effort to perfecting their works than to producing them" (*DA*, p. 540). In democracies, "Form will usually be neglected and occasionally scorned" and "authors will seek to astonish rather than to please" (*DA*, pp. 542–43). Yet in the transition from one state to the other, "there is almost always a moment when the literary genius of democracy encounters that of aristocracy and the two seem to want to reign in harmony over the human spirit.

Such periods are fleeting but very brilliant. They are fertile without exuberance and dynamic without confusion. French literature was like that in the eighteenth century" (*DA*, p. 543).[7]

Great art can also be produced in the transition to absolutism:

Almost all of the great works of the human mind were produced during centuries of liberty. It does not seem true that the spirit of literature and of the arts is recharged or that they attain high perfection when liberty is destroyed. Looking closely at what happens, we will see that certain absolute governments inherited certain forms, certain intellectual practices, and the liberty of imagination which free habits and free institutions had created before them. The despots then contributed the sole benefit of absolutism: a degree of tranquility was added to the continued usage of those intellectual treasures acquired from the previous government they had destroyed. It might, therefore, seem that certain absolute governments were spiritually fruitful ones. But this is a false semblance which quickly pales with the passing of time: soon the true face and the true tendency of these absolute governments appears. (*ER*, pp. 168–69).

SHORT-TERM EFFECTS AND LONG-TERM EFFECTS

A constant theme of *Democracy in America* is that the advantages of democracy emerge only in the long run, whereas at any given point in time its performance is inferior to aristocratic or monarchical governments. Later, Joseph Schumpeter made a similar distinction, in the context of comparing capitalist and communist regimes.[8] Much earlier, it had also been made by Leibniz.[9] Since both the short-term and the

---

[7] I cannot help thinking that Tocqueville's own preference (like my own) was for the seventeenth century (see, for example, *L*, p. 304).

[8] "A system – any system, economic or other – that at every given point of time fully utilizes its possibilities to the best advantage may yet in the long run be inferior to a system that does so at no given point of time, because the latter's failure to do so may be a condition for the level or speed of long-run performance" (Schumpeter 1961, p. 83). To illustrate, the patent system prevents existing knowledge from being fully utilized and thus entails waste at any moment in time, yet provides incentives for the creation of new knowledge and hence has good effects over longer stretches of time.

[9] "The infinite series of all things may be the best of all possible series, although what exists in the universe at each particular instant is not the best possible" (Leibniz 1875–90, vol. VI, p. 237).

long-term effects of regimes belong to their equilibrium features, the distinction must not be confused with the previous one.

The most explicit statement of this idea is perhaps the following: "I believe that democratic government must in the long run increase the real strength of society. But at a given time and in a given place it cannot assemble as formidable a force as an aristocratic government or an absolute monarchy" (*DA*, p. 256). An implication is that "In order for a democratic republic to survive easily in a European nation, all the other nations of Europe would have to establish democratic republics at the same time" (*ibid.*). Along similar lines, Tocqueville asserts that "administrative centralization can gather all of a nation's available forces at a specific time or place, but it impedes the reproduction of those forces. It ensures the nation's victory on a day of battle but over the long run diminishes its might" (*DA*, pp. 98–99). An implication is that "An aristocratic people that does not succeed in destroying a democratic nation in the first campaign of a conflict is always at great risk of being defeated by it" (*DA*, p. 776).

In a passage that I cited earlier when discussing the spillover effect, Tocqueville justifies democratic government by its long-term effects on economic growth: "Democracy will often abandon its projects before harvesting their fruits, or it will embark on dangerous adventures. In the long run, however, it achieves more than despotism. It does each thing less well, but it does more things" (*DA*, p. 280).

Another application of the distinction concerns the level of public expenditures in democracies:

Is the government of democracy economical? First we must know what we intend to compare it to. The question would be easy to answer if we wished to establish a parallel between a democratic republic and an absolute monarchy. We would find that public expenditures in the former are considerably higher than in the latter. But this is true of all free states, in contrast to states that are not free. There can be no doubt that despotism ruins men more by preventing them from producing than by depriving them of the fruits of production. It dries up the source of riches but often respects acquired wealth. Liberty, by contrast, begets far more wealth than it destroys, and in nations familiar with it, the people's resources always increase faster than taxes. (*DA*, pp. 238–39)

In these passages, Tocqueville compares short-term and long-term effects from the objective standpoint of an outside observer. As we have seen in several earlier chapters, we may also ask how citizens and politicians assess and compare the two effects from their subjective point of view. If they are unaware of the long-term benefits, or tend to give them little weight in their decisions, the system that works best in the long run may never be established.

In particular, the long-term benefits of liberty are less clear and less motivating than the short-term costs. In addition to the texts from *DA* that I cited in the previous chapter, the following eloquent passage is relevant:

> Nor do I think that a genuine love of liberty ever arises out of the sole prospect of material rewards, for that prospect is often barely perceptible. It is indeed true that in the long run liberty always brings comfort and well-being and often wealth to those who are able to preserve it. At times, however, it temporarily hinders the use of such goods. At other times despotism alone can ensure their fleeting enjoyment. Those who prize liberty only for the material benefits it offers have never kept it for long. . . . Whoever seeks in liberty anything other than liberty itself is born for servitude. (*AR*, p. 195)

It is worthwhile to digress a moment on the last remark, which amounts to a claim that the benefits of freedom are *essentially by-products* of the love of freedom for its own sake.[10] To exhort people to seek freedom because it leads to prosperity would be self-defeating. For the same reason, it would be self-defeating to publicly recommend the democratic form of government by the argument that, although inefficient as a decision-making system, it generates a valuable spillover to economic life. Nor would it be coherent to encourage jurors to work hard on reaching a correct judgment by the argument that "I do not know if juries are useful to civil litigants, but I do know that they are very useful to the people who judge them" (*DA*, p. 316).

A similar idea applies to religion: although "Christianity tells us that we must prefer others to ourselves to gain entry to heaven," it also tells us "that we must do good unto our fellow men for love of God" (*DA*, p. 614).[11]

---

[10] See Ch. 2 of Elster (1983a) for the idea of "states that are essentially by-products."

[11] To complicate matters, Tocqueville observes that religion yields a *second benefit* that, presumably, is also essentially a by-product. He notes that even false religions "impose a salutary discipline on the intellect" so that "if religion does not save men in the other world, it may yet contribute greatly to their happiness and grandeur in this one" (*DA*, p. 502). Yet nobody could *decide to believe* on these grounds.

If the Americans in fact do "work more ardently for the happiness of all ... only to be worthy of the blessings of the other world" (*ibid.*), the reason could be – in Tocqueville's terminology – that they "carry" the idea of instrumental rationality from the secular realm "over into" the spiritual one. Out of charity, Tocqueville nevertheless refuses to believe their claim to obey the precepts of religion out of self-interest. Be that as it may, the love of freedom and the love of God have in common that the benefits they produce – prosperity or salvation – are essentially by-products.[12]

In these cases, the point of view of the observer and that of the agent *necessarily* diverge. The causal structure, therefore, is not analogous to other trade-offs between short-term costs and long-term benefits. An observer and an economic agent may both agree that it makes instrumental sense for the agent to consume less today in order to invest and consume more tomorrow. A person may, to be sure, prefer an ascetic lifestyle for its own sake and receive the benefits from saving and investing as a windfall, but that preference is not a *condition* for profit making. By contrast, the noninstrumental love of freedom or of God *is* a condition for its instrumental value.

Suppose, however, that a political leader, having read *DA* and *AR*, wanted to create political freedom "behind the back" of the subjects for the sake of these instrumental benefits. Tocqueville doubts that the attempt would be successful: "A very civilized society finds it relatively difficult to tolerate experiments with local independence. It rebels at the sight of numerous errors and despairs of success before the final result of the experiment is achieved" (*DA*, p. 67). As recent French history also suggests, projects of centrally imposed decentralization never go very far. As has been said, "Liberty cannot be granted; it must be taken." In Tocqueville's words, "local independence is beyond the reach of human effort. It is seldom created but in a sense springs up of its own accord" (*DA*, p. 68). In the draft manuscripts the tone is even stronger: "Decentralization, like freedom, is thus something the leaders of the

---

[12] The same argument applies to Tocqueville's claim that "excessive love of well-being can impair it" (*DA*, p. 638). Perfecting the soul may perhaps as a by-product improve the agent's capacity to acquire material goods, but it would be paradoxical to claim that a person concerned only with the latter goal should engage in the former task for that purpose. (Tocqueville does not make that claim.) By contrast, the idea that "it is in the interest of the soul that the body prosper" (*O II*, p. 1127) can, without paradox, be harnessed to instrumental action.

people may promise, but which they never give. To achieve it and retain it nations can count only on their own efforts, and if they do not have a taste for it, the ill has no remedy" (*O II*, p. 965). Decentralization is a *state*, but it cannot be an *act* (*O II*, p. 1172).

PARTIAL EFFECTS AND NET EFFECTS

The general pattern of this argument is the following. Tocqueville first observes an effect of democracy that, if taken in isolation, would count against adopting that mode of government. He then goes on to observe that democracy also tends to have other effects that offset or neutralize the danger inherent in the first. When opponents of democracy focus on the partial, negative effects, Tocqueville hopes to persuade them by presenting the full set of consequences and arguing that the net effect is in fact positive.[13]

The argument has two subvarieties. In the first, the positive effect outweighs the negative one, but does not make it disappear. In the second, the positive effect provides an antidote to the negative one, so that its harmful consequences are no longer felt. A trivial but amusing example of the first is provided by Tocqueville's observation that "Because preventive measures are not taken in the United States, fires are more common there than in Europe, but generally they are extinguished more quickly, because neighbors are always quick to respond in case of danger" (*DA*, p. 853). A more substantial example arises in a comparison of municipal life in France and the United States:

I find most French *communes*, mired, despite their impeccable bookkeeping, in profound ignorance as to their true interests and in a state of apathy so invincible that the society seems to vegetate rather than thrive. Meanwhile, in the same American towns whose budgets are so unmethodical and so utterly lacking in uniformity, I find an enlightened, active, enterprising population; there I contemplate a society that is always at work.... I wonder, therefore, if it might not be possible to ascribe the prosperity of the American town and the disorderly state of its finances to the same cause, and, likewise, the distress of the

---

[13] Strictly speaking, the previous distinction between long-term and short-term effects is a special case of this one. Yet because of the crucial importance of the temporal dimension – both objective and subjective – in Tocqueville's work, it seemed appropriate to single it out as a separate category.

French *commune* and the perfection of its budget. In any case, I am suspicious of a good that I find mingled with so many ills and find it easy to console myself for an ill that is compensated by so many goods. (*DA*, p. 104 n. 51)[14]

In a very different kind of example, Tocqueville draws on the fact that the expected punishment for a political crime is a function both of the severity of punishment if convicted and of the probability of conviction: "One should be *careful not to be misled* by the apparent mildness of American legislation regarding political judgments.... Although political judges in the United States cannot pronounce sentences as severe as those pronounced by political judges in Europe, there is . . . a smaller chance that they will render an acquittal" (*DA*, pp. 123–24; my italics). By contrast, "in despotic states . . . the sovereign can instantly punish any faults that he perceives, but he cannot presume to perceive all the faults that he ought to punish" (*DA*, p. 235).

The second subvariety is illustrated by several of the desire-opportunity patterns we examined in the previous chapter, a paradigm being the observation that "even as the law allows the American people to do anything and everything, there are some things that religion prevents them from imagining or forbids them to attempt" (*DA*, p. 338). A more complex example can be taken from Tocqueville's analysis of political associations in the United States. The argument goes as follows. As we have seen, democracies tend to produce conformism and tyranny of the majority. Fortunately, political associations – also an endogenous product of democracies – provide "a necessary guarantee against the tyranny of the majority" (*DA*, p. 218). However, such associations can also be dangerously destabilizing: "Most Europeans still look upon association as a weapon of war, to be organized in haste and immediately tried out on some field of battle" (*DA*, p. 220). In the United States, however, the danger is contained, as the last step in this "triple negation," by the democratic practice of universal suffrage:

[O]f all the causes that help to moderate the violence of political associations in the United States, the most powerful, perhaps, is universal suffrage. In

[14] As I note in the Conclusion, Tocqueville later came to see the same combination of disorder and energy in the British political system.

countries where universal suffrage is allowed, the majority is never in doubt, because no party can reasonably portray itself as the representative of those who did not vote. . . . In Europe, there is virtually no association that does not claim to represent, or believe that it does represent, the will of the majority. This claim or belief adds prodigiously to the association's strength and serves marvelously to justify its actions, for what is more excusable than violence in the cause of righteousness oppressed? Thus in the immense complexity of human laws it is sometimes the case that extreme freedom corrects the abuses of freedom and extreme democracy guards against the dangers of democracy. (*DA*, pp. 221–22).

MARGINAL AND GLOBAL EFFECTS

The fourth fallacy Tocqueville denounces is closely related to the fallacy of composition: what may be true for *any* member of a set might be true for *all* the members simultaneously.[15] Although I have detected only one instance of this particular denunciation in *DA*, it is extremely interesting. It arises with respect to the democratic habit of people marrying for love rather than as a by-product of property consolidations. Tocqueville begins by noting that

[our] fathers had a peculiar opinion of marriage. Having observed that what few marriages of inclination were made in their time almost always ended badly, they resolutely concluded that it was very dangerous to consult one's own heart in such matters. Chance struck them as more clairvoyant than choice. (*DA*, p. 700)

He then proceeds to give three arguments against this inference. The first is a capacity-opportunity argument (Ch. 5), while the second and the third take the form of denouncing a fallacy of composition.

Tocqueville first observes that in this case as in many others, the ills of democracy can be cured by more democracy. If women in democracies were uneducated, love marriages would be disastrous – as they tend to be in effect when they occur in aristocracies. Since, however, the education of women is itself an endogenous effect of democracy, this

---

[15] Elster (1978), pp. 97 ff. A Keynesian example is the following. *Any* entrepreneur may be able to alleviate the effects of a recession by firing some workers or by reducing their wages. (*Pace* Henry Ford, the wages of his workers were not a major component in the demand for his cars.) Yet the negative impact on aggregate demand would make such behavior self-defeating if *all* entrepreneurs engaged in it.

danger does not arise. Whereas in aristocratic societies women are kept cloistered and not granted either "time to get to know (their husbands) or capacity to judge" (*DA*, p. 701) democracies offer them both the opportunity to learn and the capacity to judge. Even if marrying for love is disastrous in societies that allow women neither the capacity nor the opportunity to judge, we cannot infer that the same effect will be produced in democracies.

Second, Tocqueville shows that the inference rests on a further fallacy. Suppose that in an aristocratic society two young, well-educated, and well-acquainted people marry for love. By going against the current they will tend to encounter the hostility of their friends and relatives, a situation that "soon breaks their courage and embitters their hearts" (*ibid.*). In a society in which this practice was general, this effect would not arise.

Third, Tocqueville points to another mechanism that explains why we cannot generalize from exceptional cases to the general case. For a man to marry for love in societies in which this practice is uncommon, he must have "a certain violent and adventurous cast of mind, and men of this character, no matter what direction they take, rarely arrive at happiness and virtue" (*ibid.*). And one might add that a marriage of *two* people of this disposition is even less likely to be happy.

The last two arguments are quite remarkable. The first rests on a causal aftereffect: the fact of going against the current generates a causal process that has unhappiness as the outcome. The second, by contrast, rests on a selection effect: only those individuals who are destined to become unhappy in any case are likely to go against the current in the first place. The distinction is of fundamental importance for the interpretation of social processes.[16] Tocqueville, characteristically, does not make much of it. It is embedded in the flow of the discussion, and it is left to the reader to appreciate its explanatory potential.

---

[16] For the general distinction between aftereffects and selection effects, see Feller (1968), pp. 199 ff. For an application, consider the problem of unemployment. The longer the time an individual has already been without work, the smaller the chances that he will find work again. This fact can be explained by invoking an aftereffect: being out of work changes the individual (or the employer's perception of him) so as to make him less employable. One may also appeal to a selection effect: those who are naturally less employable tend for that reason both to be unemployed for longer periods and to have greater difficulties in finding work.

NO HALFWAY HOUSES

In Chapter 2 I noticed Tocqueville's objections to wishful thinking – the belief that one can have one's cake and eat it too. For instance, "when it comes to the press . . . there really is no middle ground between servitude and license" (*DA*, p. 208). He also denounces a number of other compromises or "halfway houses," without implying that anyone had actually thought them to be feasible. As he notes, "There are certain great social principles that a people either embraces in every aspect of its existence or roots out entirely" (*DA*, p. 686). A halfway house must be distinguished from a transitional state. The concept of transition refers to a temporal succession, that of a halfway house to location on a conceptual scale. Among the examples of halfway houses I have cited and the others I shall give, some are naturally seen as transitional stages between one stable situation and another. Others, such as the idea of having equality within the family but not in society, define situations that are not so much unstable as impossible.

The most important example is the impossibility of a limited extension of (male) suffrage: "Once a people begins to tamper with the property qualification, it is easy to foresee that sooner or later it will eliminate it entirely. Of the rules that govern societies, this is one of the most invariable" (*DA*, p. 64). The reason, arguably, is *envy of privilege*: "The ambition of those who remain below the qualification level is spurred in proportion to the number who stand above it" (*ibid.*). Nor is it possible to use fine-tuning in allowing some political associations while forbidding others: "When certain types of association are prohibited and others permitted, it is difficult to tell in advance to which category a particular association belongs. Being in doubt, people avoid associations in general" (*DA*, p. 606). Finally, "between the extreme inequality created by slavery and the complete equality to which independence naturally leads, there is no durable intermediate state" (*DA*, p. 418). I believe Tocqueville would have been surprised by the perpetuation into the present of the de facto inferiority of descendants of slaves.

In one case Tocqueville refrained, wisely, from putting his speculations about halfway houses into print. In several letters written during his travels in America, he conjectured (as he also does in *DA*, pp. 510–11) that in religious matters democracies will tend toward

Catholicism. In the correspondence he writes, moreover, that "I have always thought that in the matter of Christian religion, Protestantism is what constitutional monarchy is in politics, a form of compromise between opposite principles, a kind of resting point between two different states, a system, in one word, that could not bear the weight of its own consequences" (*L*, p. 244; see also *ibid.*, p. 190). While the observation about constitutional monarchy is right on target, the claim that Protestantism is intrinsically unstable is off by a wide margin.

In Chapter 9 I offer further examples of halfway-house arguments in Tocqueville's analysis of the ancien régime. Here, the constant theme is the inadequacy of moderate concessions and of moderate repression, both of which tend to exacerbate popular unrest rather than alleviate it. It is an intriguing question, to which I can offer no conclusive answer, whether Tocqueville deliberately drew on the same mental model that he had applied twenty years earlier. As in other cases, my inclination is to think that the recurrent patterns and mechanisms are indeed deployed in a very self-conscious manner.

7

Equality and Mobility

The themes of equality and inequality pervade Tocqueville's two major works.[1] Because of their importance and their complexity, it may be useful to offer a preview of the rest of the chapter.

In *AR*, the resentment and envy caused by inequality of rank, taxation, access to office, and military service have a central explanatory role. As I remarked in Chapter 4, these take the form of legal privileges rather than of differences in wealth or income. I do not think there is a single place in *AR* where Tocqueville cites *economic* inequalities as a cause of the revolution, except in the indirect sense that imprudent denunciations of such inequalities may have contributed to popular ferment (Ch. 9). The economic roots of the revolution are to be found in the burdens on the French peasantry and not in the difference between their situation and that of any other group.

The causal role of equality in *DA* is much more complex. The main dimensions of equality are income and property, although political equality in the form of universal suffrage also matters. While the idea of political equality is relatively unambiguous, that of economic equality is not. Often, it involves *static equality* in the sense of equal income or property at a given moment in time. At other times, equality means

---

[1] In this chapter I do not consider the effects of *equalization* that were examined in the previous chapter.

dynamic equality, in the sense of a high level of de facto social mobility. This idea, of course, implies static *in*equality. Hence, the statement that "When conditions are almost equal, men change places constantly" (*DA*, p. 673) is a non sequitur.[2]

Although absence of legal privilege is a necessary condition for dynamic mobility, it is not a sufficient one. The possibility of mobility is one thing, its actual presence another. Tocqueville was struck, as many observers have been, by the extremely rapid metabolism of American society compared to other societies – notably France – in which there were no *legal* obstacles to mobility. One might go further and say that dynamic equality goes beyond the equality of opportunity that is provided by the absence of legal *and material* obstacles. For Tocqueville, action springs from desires and opportunities. In a society governed by the norm "Don't stick your neck out," the desire for self-improvement and economic gain will be weak and de facto mobility rates be low, even in the absence of legal and material constraints. Even affirmative action will not create upward mobility if potential beneficiaries are reluctant to take advantage of it.

As we have seen, static equality often serves as an independent variable in the explanations proposed in *DA*. In many cases, equality produces its effects by making citizens *equal and weak* (e.g., *DA*, p. 781). Many of the desire-opportunity-capacity explanations that I discussed in Chapter 5 rely on equality as the "common cause." Equality is also said to "suggest" the idea of the perfectibility of man (*DA*, p. 514), an excessive taste for general theories (*DA*, p. 500), and "several penchants that are quite dangerous to liberty" (*DA*, p. 825), notably lack of respect for forms and contempt for individual rights. At the same time, "equality naturally gives men a taste for free institutions" (*DA*, p. 787). In some of the more extravagant chapters of the second volume, static equality is also said to favor certain sources of poetry over others, Catholicism over Protestantism, a bombastic style of expression, and so on. In many explanations, the dependent variables are bimodally

---

[2] The confusion has deep roots, as explained in a classic study by Gordon Wood (1972, p. 70): "The doctrine [of equality] possessed an inherent ambivalence: on the one hand it stressed equality of opportunity which implied social differences and distinctions; on the other hand it emphasized equality of condition which denies these same social differences and distinctions. These two meanings were intertwined in the Americans' use of equality and it is difficult to separate them."

distributed. Americans either produce big monuments or very trivial objects (*DA*, p. 536); their ideas are either extremely abstract or extremely concrete (*DA*, p. 561); their attitudes are either extremely materialistic or extremely spiritualistic (*DA*, p. 623). I shall mostly ignore these armchair speculations. In other arguments, it is the *absence* of (complete) static equality that serves to explain behavior. As we saw in Chapter 4, a number of Tocqueville's explanations hinge on the desire for static equality and the democratic sentiment or disease of envy.

Dynamic equality is in some ways an even more important explanatory variable. Beyond the effect it has on the individual who is upwardly or downwardly mobile, it undermines the stability of aggregate groups, such as classes. When individuals are highly mobile, the classes or occupational groups between which they move have a very *high turnover rate*, so high, in fact, that they may not even form classes or professions with all the attributes these usually have. In particular, class consciousness and class struggle remain undeveloped.

Social mobility and political equality are not unique to democracies. Tocqueville also paid some attention to upward (but not to downward) social mobility in his writings on the ancien régime. Moreover, at the local level we also find forms of collective self-government in prerevolutionary France, although by the eighteenth century these had mostly turned into make-believe forms of citizen participation.

INEQUALITY IN THE ANCIEN RÉGIME

As I argue in Chapter 9, Tocqueville's key idea in *AR* – what he might have called (but did not) his "idée mère" – was that the successive French kings undermined their own power by playing the various classes out against each other. As a result of these policies, the nobility and the clergy became obsessed with distinguishing themselves from the third estate; the third estate with what separated them from the peasantry; and the different occupations within the third estate with matters of relative rank.

In the chapter on "How, though in many respects so similar, the French were split up more than ever before in small groups that were indifferent and as foreigners to each other," Tocqueville claimed that tax exemptions were the most important divide-and-conquer strategy invented by the kings. Once they were established, no further efforts were needed:

Of all the ways of distinguishing men and marking class divisions, unequal taxation is the most pernicious and the most apt to add isolation to inequality, making both incurable. Consider its effects: when the bourgeois and the nobleman are no longer subject to the same tax, the annual assessment and collection of taxes will sharpen the class boundary between them. Year after year, each beneficiary of privilege will feel an immediate and urgent need to differentiate himself from the masses and once again set himself apart. Since nearly every matter of public interest either arises from a tax or culminates in one, once the two classes are not subject to equal taxation, they have virtually no reason to deliberate together and no occasion to experience common needs or sentiments. It is no longer necessary to keep them apart, since the opportunity and desire to act together have in a sense been eliminated. (*AR*, p. 127)

Tocqueville emphasizes that for the nobles, the tax exemption mattered mainly for the status, not for the income they derived from it. In a memorable formulation, he notes that "The inequality, though great, was, to be sure, more apparent than real, for the noble was often affected indirectly, through his tenants, by the tax from which he was himself exempt.[3] But in such matters, the inequality one sees hurts more than the inequality one feels" (*AR*, p. 126). In fact, the nobles and the clergy might be willing to take a financial loss to retain their privilege:

In [an assembly in Lower Normandy], the orders of the nobility and the clergy, after denouncing the evils of compulsory road work (*la corvée*), spontaneously offered to contribute 50,000 *livres* to the improvement of the provincial roads to make them practicable at no cost to the people. It might have cost these men of privilege less to replace the compulsory labor system with a general tax of which they would have paid a share, yet while they were ready to forgo the benefits of unequal taxation, they chose to maintain the appearance. (*AR*, p. 208)

In these passages, Tocqueville imputes to the privileged orders pretty much the exact opposite motivation of the one he attributed to democratic citizens (Ch. 4). Whereas the latter are willing to sacrifice

---

[3] What the tenants paid in taxes he had to deduct from their rent, since otherwise the burden would exceed their ability to pay. See also *O III*, pp. 540, 596, endorsing the claim by Abbé Sieyes that the abolition of the tithe without compensation simply amounted to a transfer of income from the parish priest to the seigneur.

their freedom and perhaps some material well-being for the sake of economic equality, the former renounce the financially less onerous scheme for the sake of keeping their formal privileges. The passion for rank and privilege is no less capable of overriding interest than is the passion for equality.

As always in the old régime, the desire for rank cascaded downward: "When we turn from the nobility to the bourgeoisie, we are confronted with a similar spectacle, as the bourgeois was almost as distant from the people as the noble was from the bourgeois" (*AR*, p. 128). Often, as we shall see, the town dwellers came from the countryside, yet town and country entertained a mutual hostility. The source, again, lay in tax exemptions:

> There were many justified complaints about the privileges of the nobility in matters of taxation, but what to say about those of the bourgeois? There were thousands of official posts that carried with them partial or total exemption from public charges.... These miserable prerogatives filled with envy all who did not share them and with the most egoistic pride those who possessed them. There is nothing as visible throughout the eighteenth century as the hostility of the urban middle class towards the peasantry living around the towns and the jealousy of the latter towards the towns. (*AR*, pp. 130–31)

Consider finally inequality of rank within the town itself. We may compare the democratic obsession with small differences to the obsession in the ancien régime with small privileges. In one town, a vital issue was whether the holy water should be given to the judges of the presidial court before being given to members of the town corporation (*AR*, p. 133). In the same town, Tocqueville found no fewer than thirty-six distinct groups busy with "purging themselves of any heterogeneous elements" (*AR*, p. 132). In another town, the guild of wigmakers decided to "express its justified pain at the award of priority to the bakers" (*AR*, p. 133) by withdrawing from public affairs.

The *effects* of this isolation between and within classes will concern us in Chapter 9. There we shall also see that Tocqueville's *explanation* of the phenomena is somewhat speculative. In fact, he sometimes verges on the brink of saying that the effects *provide* the explanation. As I noted in the Introduction, he does not often indulge in functional explanation, but this may be an instance.

EQUALITY AND STATUS CONSISTENCY

Earlier, I suggested that Tocqueville wanted to explain the extension of suffrage in terms of envy: the more citizens have been enfranchised, the more intense the resentment of those left behind. This is, as it were, a within-sphere mechanism. In addition, he suggests a between-sphere mechanism that might bring about the same outcome: "It is impossible to imagine that equality will not ultimately enter into the world of politics as it enters into everything else. It is impossible to conceive of men as eternally unequal in one respect but equal in all others. Eventually, therefore, they will be equal in everything" (*DA*, p. 60). Sociologists refer to this idea as the pressure for *status consistency*. Having low status on both of two dimensions may cause *less* discontent and *less* pressure for change than having high status on one and low on another. Alternatively, having high status on one dimension might compensate for having low status on another, but Tocqueville does not mention this possibility.[4]

In the notes for the second volume of *AR*, Tocqueville once more appeals to status inconsistency as a resentment-generating factor: "It is a commonplace to say that inequality of rights, while no greater as the Revolution approached, seemed more unbearable because the real equality of conditions was great. I add that inequality of rights was in certain respects much greater and of a far more shocking nature than at any previous time" (*O III*, p. 1110).[5] Tocqueville does not tell us,

---

[4] The two possibilities – inconsistency and compensation – are clearly spelled out in the following passage: "Equality among the full Spartan citizens was something consciously adopted, or so the ancient sources imply, in order to reduce envy among these citizens and thus prevent a Helot revolt. Athenian democracy had no such origin – but a consequence of the development of democracy at Athens was a restriction on the scope offered for feelings of envy because of an equality of voting rights. In one respect at least a citizen could feel himself to be as good as the next citizen, and this was in an area of the greatest importance, political life. But *perhaps democracy actually intensified rather than reduced the feeling of envy*: the very fact that all citizens were equal as voters in the assembly simply may have made some that much more aware of their inequality in birth or wealth or even good luck, and so Plutarch refers frequently to envy in his biographies of fifth-century Athenians. To put it another way, if one is 'entitled' to an equality of rights as a voter, this is a strong inducement to expect a comparable equality across the board. In fact if equality is to curb envy it must be a full equality which covers all of life, and the Spartan system did attempt to be comprehensive" (Walcot 1978, p. 64; my italics).

[5] The last remark may refer to the rigid rules for access to officer status introduced in 1781.

however, under which conditions the status inconsistency will lead to individual efforts (e.g., for rich commoners to seek ennoblement) and when it will trigger collective action (e.g., to demands for the abolishment of noble titles or even the physical extermination of the nobility).

Tocqueville observes that (what we now call) the desire for status consistency can be satisfied in two ways: "rights must be given either to each citizen or to none" (*DA*, p. 60). As he was writing about post-aristocratic societies, these two options correspond to universal suffrage and to despotism. In an aristocracy, however, extending the privileges of nobles to all citizens would be meaningless, since the extension would cause them to lose their mainly symbolic value. As the saying has it, when everybody is somebody, nobody is anybody. In democracies, Tocqueville argued, what matters is *not to have less* than others; in aristocratic regimes, it is *to have more than* others, whence the endless combats over rank and precedence.

Tocqueville was acutely aware of this difference between rights and liberties on the one hand and privileges on the other. Modern conceptions of rights imply that if anyone is free to do X or has the right to do X, then everyone has the right or freedom to do X. In the ancien régime, one could enjoy only "a kind of irregular and intermittent liberty, always limited by class distinctions, always bound up with the idea of exception and privilege, which allowed people to defy the law almost as much as it allowed them to stand up to arbitrary power and seldom went so far as to guarantee to all citizens the most natural and necessary rights" (*AR*, p. 153). Although "limited, twisted ... disorderly and unwholesome" (*AR*, pp. 153–54), it was nevertheless, as we shall see in Chapter 9, a second-best defense against the arbitrary despotism of the royal administration.

POLITICAL EQUALITY IN THE ANCIEN RÉGIME

As we shall see in the next chapter, Tocqueville had great admiration for the practice of local self-government in America. In *AR*, he points to similar practices, and especially to how they degenerated. In both town and village there existed initially the reality of collective self-government, which by the eighteenth century had lost all real substance.[6] A curious

---

[6] A modern analogy could be that of "consultative" worker participation in the management of firms.

difference is that on his account, the villagers but not the common people in the towns were taken in by the make-believe practices.

Tocqueville asserts that "until almost the end of the seventeenth century, towns still resembled small democratic republics, in which officials were freely elected by, and responsible to, all the people" (*AR*, p. 88). Yet with the increasing importance of sales of offices, the elections lost their significance:

The people, who are less easily fooled by the mere semblance of freedom than one might imagine, everywhere lost interest in town affairs and lived as strangers within their own town walls. From time to time officials would try to revive the municipal patriotism that had worked such wonders in the Middle Ages, but the people remained deaf to their appeals. Ordinary citizens seemed completely indifferent to the most important issues. In towns where officials felt they had to maintain the appearance of free elections, they tried to persuade the people to vote, but they stubbornly abstained. Nearly every ruler who set out to destroy liberty attempted initially to preserve its forms.... Nearly all failed, soon discovering that it is impossible to keep up such deceitful appearances for long when the reality is no longer there. (*AR*, pp. 90–91)[7]

A parallel development took place in the villages. Tocqueville explains his astonishment when he first read the records of an intendancy in order to understand the parish administration and found "several of the features which had struck me so much in the rural towns of North America" (*AR*, p. 93). Yet on closer inspection, the American and the French town "resemble each other ... only insofar as the living resemble the dead" (*ibid.*). Although "these municipal officials are usually still elected, or are supposed to be,... everywhere they have become instruments of the state rather than representatives of the community." Village assemblies were still called, in which everyone could express their opinion, but no decisions were made or votes taken: "When we recognize that these empty semblances of liberty went hand in hand with the absence of any real power, we can already see on a small scale how the most absolute rule can be combined with some of the most extreme forms of democracy, leaving the oppressed in the ridiculous position of seeming not to notice their own oppression" (*AR*, p. 95). The contrast

---

[7] For a similar comment on the inefficacy of make-believe elections, see the draft to *DA* in *O II*, p. 960.

with the town appears in Tocqueville's claim that "the peasants still cherished these last vestiges of the old parish government.... So much weight remains in even the hollowest of forms " (*AR*, p. 96).[8]

These observations may be read in the light of the statement, cited earlier, that a "civilized" government "finds it relatively difficult to tolerate experiments with local independence" (*DA*, p. 67). Because granting real independence allows for the possibility of costly errors, the government may prefer the semblance of independence, not realizing that make-believe autonomy will fail to have the invigorating effects of genuine self-government.

SOCIAL MOBILITY IN THE ANCIEN RÉGIME

Tocqueville often refers to the caste-like nature of the ancien régime, implying that there were few possibilities of upward social mobility.[9] His terminology, unfortunately, is not consistent. He is liable to use "caste," "class," and even "race" as if they were synonymous. Although a caste may be a class, not every class is a caste. By and large, nevertheless, his terminology is reasonably well captured by saying that he defines a caste by the fact that "no one may either exit or enter" (*DA*, p. 710) and that "birth was its distinguishing characteristic" (*AR*, p. 122).

Tocqueville clearly intended to say (with exceptions to be discussed shortly) that in prerevolutionary France, the nobility formed a caste in this sense. By contrast, the forced celibacy of the clergy prevented them from being a caste.[10] In *AR* Tocqueville never discusses ascension into the clergy as a form of upward mobility for the third estate, and so I shall not do so either.[11] He does discuss, however, the practice of

---

[8] The present tense reflects the fact that Tocqueville here is referring to the situation in his own time.

[9] I shall ignore, but only because Tocqueville does so, the possibility of *downward* social mobility. Under the ancien régime a nobleman might lose his title if he engaged in industry or in the retail trade. In the 1836 essay on the revolution, he refers to the ban as reflecting a harmful prejudice (*O III*, p. 12) and notes (see below) that it might lead to hypogamy, but he does not refer to any actual violations with subsequent loss of noble status.

[10] In the high clergy, the practice of favoring one's nephews and other relatives nevertheless imparted an element of caste.

[11] He does refer to this fact in *DA*, p. 4.

ennoblement as offering a chance of moving out of the third estate. Before I consider his observations on this matter, I want to comment on his analyses of upward social mobility – from the countryside to the towns – *within* the third estate.

In the chapter on which I have been drawing heavily, Tocqueville explains two mechanisms of intragenerational social mobility: "push" and "pull." The push mechanism involves the "almost infinite inso-lence" that the local seigneur would display toward his bourgeois neighbors (*AR*, p. 129). Even more important, according to Tocque-ville, is a pull mechanism that, once again, involves tax exemption:

The bourgeoisie gathered in the towns had a thousand ways of alleviating the burden of the *taille* [land tax] and often of evading it altogether, yet none of these means of evasion would have been available had they remained isolated on their estates. More important still, they thus avoided the obligation to collect the tax, which they feared even more than the obligation to pay it, and rightly so. . . . Rather than accept this charge, the wealthy commoner rented out his land and withdrew to the closest town. (*AR*, p. 129)

In a later chapter, he considers how *inter*generational mobility has the same effect: "Contemporary records all agree on the fact that in the countryside one almost never saw more than one generation of rich peasants. No sooner did an industrious farmer manage to acquire some wealth than he told his son to abandon his plow, sent him to town, and purchased a minor office for him" (*AR*, p. 156). The implication is that this a *one-way process*: upward mobility that is not followed by down-ward mobility in subsequent generations. In a superficially similar com-ment about the United States, we read that "wealth circulates there with incredible rapidity, and experience teaches that it is rare for two successive generations to garner its favors" (*DA*, p. 57). The idea of *circulation*, however, suggests a very different mechanism. In the United States, the pattern of rags to rags (or shirtsleeves to shirtsleeves) in three generations is part of the equilibrium state. In prerevolutionary France, the effect of upward social mobility was to drain the country-side, irreversibly, of its natural leaders: "the peasant was separated from those of his own class who might have been able to help and guide him" (*AR*, p. 157). Among the many mechanisms described in this chapter, entitled "How, despite the progress of civilization, the lot of the French peasant was sometimes worse in the eighteenth century than it had been in the thirteenth," this is perhaps the most fateful one. It left the peasants ignorant, miserable, backward, and uneducated (*AR*, p. 165).

Tocqueville discusses two channels of upward social mobility for the bourgeoisie: by marrying their daughters into the nobility and by ennoblement. Although he does not consider hypergamy in *AR*, he has an interesting comment on the topic in the 1836 essay on "The social and political state of France before and after 1789." Having cited the disastrous economic effect on the nobility of the ban on engaging in commerce and retail trade, he adds that in spite of the norm against hypogamy, "it was not rare for nobles to [marry the daughter of a rich commoner]. . . . These vulgar alliances, which enriched a few members of the nobility, had the effect of taking away from the body as a whole the power of opinion which was the only thing it had left" (*O III*, p. 13). In the language of contemporary social science, those who married downward acted as free riders.

In the 1836 essay, he also offers comments on the extent and the effect of ennoblement that differ from the discussion in *AR*. Tocqueville proposes what we might call a "safety-valve" theory of the prospect of upward mobility:

What moves the human heart is less the certainty of a small success than the possibility of a great fortune. Increase the size of the gain and you may without risk reduce the chance of obtaining it. In a country where it is not impossible that a poor man ends up governing the State, it is easier to keep the poor permanently out of government than in the countries where one does not offer him the hope of power; the idea of this imaginary greatness, to which he might one day be called, stands always between him and the sight of his real misery. It is a game of chance in which the enormity of the possible gain affects his soul in spite of the likelihood of loss. He loves aristocracy as a lottery. (*O III*, p. 17).

If taken literally, the text says that there would be virtually no *actual* ennoblements. Just as, say, one chance in ten million of winning ten million dollars in the state lottery may serve as "opium of the people" and distract it from its real misery and from rebelling against its condition, the infinitesimal chance of the cobbler's son ending up as the king's first minister might quell social unrest at its inception. The argument is ingenious, but not exactly plausible.

The more penetrating 1856 text focuses on the effects of actual rather than of potential ennoblement. Perversely, the effect was to increase discontent all around: in the third estate, among the old nobility (*noblesse d'épée*), and among the newly ennobled (*noblesse de robe*):

> The system of ennoblements, far from diminishing the commoner's hatred of the nobleman, increased it beyond all measure. It was a hatred embittered by all the envy that the new noble inspired in his erstwhile equals. That is why the grievance books of the Third Estate invariably show greater animosity toward the ennobled than toward the old nobility. . . . In no other period of French history was it so easy to acquire a title of nobility as in 1789, and yet the gap between bourgeois and noble had never been so great. Not only did nobles refuse to tolerate in their electoral assemblies anything that smacked of the bourgeoisie, but the bourgeois were equally firm in rejecting anything that resembled nobility. In some provinces, the newly ennobled were rejected by one group because they were not noble enough and by the other because they were already too noble. (*AR*, p. 128)[12]

To conclude on this point, all forms of upward mobility in the ancien régime – within or between estates – tended to deepen the crisis of the regime, to undermine its legitimacy, and to increase its vulnerability.

ARE THERE CLASSES IN AMERICA?

In a famous comment, Joseph Schumpeter said that "a class or a class-stratum is like a bus or a hotel – always full, but of different people."[13] This turnover criterion does indeed enable us to distinguish classes from castes. Does it also provide a sufficient condition for the existence of classes? Tocqueville denied that it does. He would have said that a hotel where people do not stay for more than one night, or a bus where nobody travels for more than one stop, is a poor metaphor for a class in the full sense of the term, whatever that sense may be.

The Marxist tradition distinguishes between "class in itself" and "class for itself." Although Marx himself did not use these terms, the distinction is clearly expressed in a famous statement on the French peasantry:

---

[12] Confusingly, the 1836 text says more or less the same thing (*O III*, p. 15), even using the same example (Lavoisier) as the 1856 text.

[13] Schumpeter (1955), p. 130.

In so far as millions of families live under economic conditions of existence that separate their mode of life, their interests and their culture from those of the other classes, and put them in hostile opposition to the latter, they form a class. In so far as there is merely a local interconnection among these small-holding peasants, and the identity of their interests begets no community, no national bond and no political organization among them, they do not form a class.[14]

Let me use the phrase "class consciousness" as a blanket term for the ideas of community, national bond, and political organization. It is not merely a matter of shared ideas and sentiments, but above all a capacity to overcome the free-rider problem in collective action.[15] Marx argues that the main obstacle to class consciousness of the French peasantry is to be found in their geographical isolation from one another. In a brief aside, he also refers to "the United States of North America, where, though classes exist, they have not yet become fixed, but continually change and interchange their elements in constant flux."[16] As a result, in that country the republic is only a "conservative form of life" and not "the political form of revolution of bourgeois society." I take him to be saying that in the United States the obstacle to class consciousness lies in the rapid turnover of membership in the various classes.[17] This, as we shall see, was exactly Tocqueville's view.[18]

Tocqueville states that "In America, few people are wealthy" (*DA*, p. 58) and that the country "in a sense has no rich people" (*DA*, p. 647). These and many similar statements are assertions of static equality. Yet on this topic more perhaps than on any other, Tocqueville was equally prone to seeing the glass as half full as viewing it as half empty, since he often characterizes America as combining static inequality with dynamic equality. In a passage I partly quoted earlier, he writes:

[14] Marx (1852), p. 187.
[15] Elster (1985), Ch. 6.
[16] Marx (1852), p. 111.
[17] See Elster (1978), pp. 134–50, for a general argument to the effect that communicational isolation and high turnover are the main obstacles to successful collective action.
[18] Did Marx take this idea from Tocqueville? We know that he had read *Democracy in America*, since he refers to it in his article on "The Jewish question." That reference, however, is to Tocqueville's claim about the importance of religion in the United States, not to classes. In light of the close similarity of the arguments, it nevertheless seems plausible that Marx took his idea of the uncrystallized nature of classes in America from Tocqueville.

Not that there are no wealthy people in the United States, just as there are everywhere. Indeed, I know of no other country where the love of money occupies as great a place in the hearts of men or where people are more deeply contemptuous of the theory of permanent equality of wealth. But wealth circulates there with incredible rapidity, and experience teaches that it is rare for two successive generations to garner its favors. (*DA*, p. 57)[19]

Elsewhere we read that "The law of inheritance . . . constantly pulls citizens back toward a common level from which they constantly escape" (*DA*, p. 519). Tocqueville also affirms that in democracies, "everyone works in order to live, or has worked, or was born to people who worked" (*DA*, p. 642), implying that the children of the third group would also work (from shirtsleeves to shirtsleeves in three generations). And finally, "Most of [the] wealthy people [that he met] had been poor" (*DA*, p. 619). These general statements of a high metabolic rate are in line with many of the specific facts that I have discussed in earlier chapters. These include notably:

- the frequency and tolerance of bankruptcies;
- the tendency toward shorter leases of land;
- the incessant technical progress (cited by a sailor to explain why ships were not built to last) that offers occasions for rapid accumulation and loss of wealth in what Schumpeter called "creative destruction";
- the fact that public opinion and social norms have little grip on the mind in a society whose members are "forever disappearing and slipping away";
- the risk-taking or even risk-loving character of the Americans.

The importance of dynamic equality is further enhanced by the claims, to be discussed in the next chapter, that Tocqueville makes about the high rate of metabolism in American *politics*.

I am tempted, in fact, to claim that in *DA*, dynamic equality is more important than static equality. Important for what? The answer is that

---

[19] Somewhat confusingly, we also read that since "the great fortunes that one finds in a democratic country are almost always commercial in origin, it takes several generations for the possessors of those fortunes to shed the habits of trade entirely" (*DA*, p. 646). Perhaps he was thinking of France, where risk-taking, downward social mobility, and bankruptcies were less common.

dynamic equality explains more phenomena, or at least more important ones, than does static equality. In the beginning of this chapter, I
provided a short and admittedly incomplete list of the phenomena
examined in *DA* that static equality (or the desire for it) is supposed
to explain. The most important set of these explananda are perhaps
those related to *envy and its behavioral manifestations*. One explan-
andum to which dynamic equality offers a key is the *absence of class-
consciousness and hence of class struggle* in the United States, due to
the fact that, as Marx wrote, classes there "continually change and
interchange their elements in constant flux."[20] Although geographical
mobility is no doubt a contributing factor to the weakening of classes,
Tocqueville puts more emphasis on (upward and downward) social
mobility.[21]

Before turning to class consciousness, we may note that Tocqueville
also invokes high turnover to explain other social phenomena. In Chapter 2 we considered how beliefs might arise from authority. Among the
possible sources that Tocqueville discusses and discards is the authority
of class: "Nor can the inhabitants of [a democratic] society derive their
beliefs from the opinions of the class to which they belong, because in
a sense there are no longer classes, and those that do still exist are so
variable in their composition (*sont composées d'éléments si mouvants*)
that the body can never exert any real power over its members" (*DA*,
p. 484). Elsewhere he cites turnover to explain the uniformity of language in democratic societies: "when men, no longer bound to their
place in society, see and communicate with one another constantly,
when castes are abolished and classes are replenished with new recruits
and become indistinguishable, all the words of the language get mixed
together" (*DA*, p. 551).

Earlier I cited how Tocqueville's 1836 essay refers to the free-rider
problem that arises from the temptation for nobles to marry their
daughters to commoners. Another free-rider temptation is that of
engaging in trade and commerce. I mentioned that this practice was

[20] Although it would be tempting to speculate on whether envy might also contribute to
the lack of class solidarity, I shall refrain from doing so.
[21] Although geographical mobility is obviously one source of social mobility, Tocqueville does not single it out as especially important. The references to the West are more
frequent in the first volume of *DA* than in the second, whereas the opposite is true of
references to the turnover of classes.

banned in the ancien régime, but matters were in fact more complex. An edict of 1701 allowed the French nobility to engage in wholesale commerce (not retail), but it took more than fifty years before they overcame the norms of their class and actually did so.[22] In Tocqueville's phrase, if a member of the aristocracy "should by chance wish to go into trade, the corporate will of the aristocracy as a whole will immediately stand in his way" (*DA*, p. 645). As Paul Veyne notes in a somewhat similar context, he would be deterred from violating the class norms by "the precise fear of vague sanctions and the vague fear of precise sanctions."[23] In other words, the aristocracy possessed class consciousness.

The bourgeoisie, too, were subject to social norms and peer pressure that protected them from free-rider temptations. These norms did not apply to the third estate as a whole, but to each of the many groups of which it was composed and whose stability of membership allowed for the development of class consciousness:

> The immunities of all sorts that so regrettably separated the bourgeoisie from the common people tended to make the former into a false aristocracy that often exhibited the pride and recalcitrance of the true one. Though divided among many small associations that readily forgot the general good, the bourgeoisie was constantly preoccupied with its interests and rights as a group. The members of this group had a common dignity and common privileges to defend. No one could seek refuge in the crowd or try to conceal unseemly bargains. The stage on which each man played his part was small but brightly lit, and he always faced the same audience, ever ready to applaud or hiss (*AR*, pp. 149–50)

By contrast, "in democracies, the rich never constitute a corporation with its own mores and discipline" (*DA*, p. 646). The lack of "discipline" implies that the class will not engage in collective action. As an example, recall the discussion in Chapter 3 of how each entrepreneur "tries to interest the government in acting in [the affair of special concern to him] while continuing to ask that its action in other areas be restricted" (*DA*, p. 794 n. 1). This free-rider behavior indicates lack of class consciousness in the entrepreneurial class.

---

[22] Mousnier (1974), vol. 1, pp. 154–55.
[23] Veyne (1976), p. 279.

Before we consider an important exception to this statement, let us consider the mechanism that sustains it. In the chapter on why great revolutions will become rare, Tocqueville asserts that neither the rich nor the poor constitute classes-for-themselves: "The rich . . . are scattered and impotent. . . . Just as there are no longer races of paupers, so, too, are there no longer races of the rich. The wealthy emerge from the crowd daily and time and again lapse back into it. Hence they do not constitute a separate class easy to define and despoil" (*DA*, p. 748). The emphasis here is not on inability of the rich to engage in collective action, but on how their fleeting existence protects their wealth, which, "no longer incorporated into the earth and represented by it, is intangible and almost invisible" (*ibid.*).

In another passage he asserts both the permanence of the "race of paupers" and the fact that the rich are "not solidly united among themselves" (*DA*, p. 651):

The poor have few ways of escaping their condition and becoming rich, but the rich are always becoming poor or quitting business with the profits they have amassed. Thus the elements of the poor class are almost fixed, but the elements of the rich class are not. To tell the truth, although there are rich people, the rich do not exist as a class, because rich people have no common spirit or objectives or traditions or hopes. Hence there are members but no body. (*Ibid.*)[24]

Industrialists obviously have a common interest in keeping wages as low as possible. In Adam Smith's words, "Masters are always and everywhere in a sort of tacit, but constant and uniform combination, not to raise the wages of labor above their actual rate. To violate this combination is everywhere a most unpopular action, and a sort of reproach to a master among his neighbors and equals. Masters, too, sometimes enter into particular combinations to sink the wages of labor even below this rate."[25] Although in the light of the statements I have cited it would seem that Tocqueville would have to claim America as an exception to this statement, he actually endorses it: "Since a person must already be very wealthy to launch a venture in one of the major industries . . . , the number who do so is quite small. Being few in number,

---

[24] Note the near-contradictory aspect of this passage – if some of the rich become poor, the poor are not a "fixed" class.

[25] Smith (1976), p. 84.

they can easily conspire to set whatever price for labor they choose" (*DA*, p. 683). Here, observation and common sense seem to have gotten the better of the abstract logic of turnover, according to which the rich would be too "scattered and impotent" to reach even a tacit agreement.

Tocqueville next launches a different argument, by claiming that even an individual master can force down the wages of the workers and that the latter will be unable to resist. It is basically a question of unequal bargaining power. In the language of modern bargaining theory, owners and workers have different "inside options" that determine how long they can hold out in a conflict:[26] "Suppose that by common accord the workers refuse to work: the master, who is a wealthy man, can easily wait without driving himself into bankruptcy until necessity brings them back to him, while they must work every day or die, for they have virtually no property other than their brawn" (*DA*, p. 683). Somewhat confusingly, however, he also claims that "nearly all workers have some secure resources [e.g., a plot of land] that allow them to withhold their services when others are unwilling to grant them what they consider a just reward for their labor" (*DA*, p. 682).[27]

The resources that enhance the bargaining power of the worker constitute a strictly individual advantage. In spite of the fact that Tocqueville thought (at least sometimes) that "the race of paupers" was becoming permanent, he nowhere in *DA* envisages collective action on the part of the workers. (Moreover, he could not, as Marx did with respect to the French peasantry, impute their lack of organization to physical separation.) Although the passages I cited in the preceding paragraph show that with regard to wage bargaining his understanding of a capitalist economy was superior to that of Marx, he did not realize the extent to which the workers are "trained, united, and organized by the very mechanism of the capitalist process of production."[28] The only references in his writings to working-class collective action are to *political* movements rather than to strikes for higher wages.[29] The

---

[26] For explanation and examples, see Elster (1989), Ch. 2.

[27] As shown by the draft manuscripts (*O II*, p. 1139), this second claim should probably be read as applying only to France.

[28] Marx (1867), p. 929.

[29] In a letter from 1835 (*L*, p. 329), he nevertheless recognizes that in England, "the rich begin to agree perfectly among themselves, but the poor also agree among themselves better than in any other country in the world."

relevant passages occur in the *Recollections*, where he explains the June insurrection of the Paris workers in terms of a "mixture of greedy desires and false theories" (*R*, p. 136), adding that "this terrible insurrection was not the work of a certain number of conspirators, but was the revolt of one whole section of the population against another" (*R*, p. 137).

A final illustration of the turnover argument can be taken from the chapter on the relations between servant and master in democracies: "When conditions are equal, men change places constantly. A class of valets still exists, as does a class of masters, but neither is composed of an unvarying group of individuals, much less of families, and there is no more perpetuity in command than in obedience. Since servants do not constitute a separate people, they have no customs, prejudices, or mores of their own" (*DA*, p. 673). The terminology is a bit confusing. By "people," Tocqueville is obviously referring to what he elsewhere calls "class," and by "class" to a more evanescent category. Also, the substantive criterion for class-hood (or "people-hood") is said to be a matter of shared "customs, prejudices, or mores," rather than of the capacity for collective action. He would, presumably, also have excluded the possibility of servants striking collectively for higher wages.

The main aim of this chapter has been to document Tocqueville's intense concern with and striking insights into *social dynamics*. In *AR*, the movements within and among the three estates are central explanatory variables for understanding the revolution. In *DA*, the incessant turnover in classes is vital for understanding the undeveloped nature of class formation and of class conflict. If asked, Tocqueville might have said it provides the key to the question "Why is there no socialism in the United States?"

8

Democratic Government

INTRODUCTION

In *DA*, "democracy" sometimes means equality and sometimes democratic government. The two are obviously related, both conceptually and causally. The conceptual link is clear: democratic government is based on equality of voting power. As in the utilitarian calculus, each (male) citizen counts for one and no one for more than one. The causal links are numerous and complex. As an illustration, recall how democratic envy, born of equality, may lead to the election of mediocre politicians.

Tocqueville was concerned both with explaining the workings of democratic government and with assessing it from a normative point of view. Although I have quoted (and will quote more) passages in which he asserts the inefficiency of democracy as a system of political decision making, this is not the only relevant normative dimension. In a passage I have cited earlier, he praises democracy for promoting "the greater well-being of all" rather than "the singular prosperity of a few," a statement that is perfectly compatible with the claim that democracy is an inefficient system.

In Figure 8.1, the distribution of welfare at point A represents an aristocratic society and that of point B a democratic one. The curve represents the technically feasible combinations of welfare of the two groups. Any point that is strictly below the curve is inefficient, since one could in theory make both groups better off by moving to some point

Welfare of the few

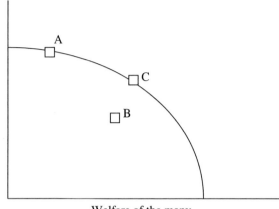

Welfare of the many

FIGURE 8.1

on the curve. (Economists refer to such a move as a Pareto-improvement.) While the efficient aristocratic society is very unfair, the inefficient democracy is superior on grounds of fairness. (Economists refer to this as an efficiency-equality trade-off.) The leaders of aristocracies are capable of making efficient decisions, but only to promote the welfare of their own caste. Democratic leaders are mediocre and inefficient, but they care about the common good rather than the interest of a few.

One may ask whether institutions exist that would sustain efficiency *and* fairness, as in point C of the diagram. If that point is, as assumed, feasible, what prevents one from realizing it? A Tocquevillian answer would be that C is technically feasible since there are no *objective* constraints that prevent the citizens of democratic societies from choosing excellent rather than mediocre politicians.[1] Yet the psychology of democracy makes it less likely that outstanding candidates will present themselves and, if they do, that the electorate will choose them. In aristocracies, no systematic mechanism of this kind prevents the most competent from exercising power. More strongly, "an aristocratic

---

[1] The standard economic illustration is that redistribution through taxes may cause deadweight losses by reducing the labor supply of the most heavily taxed. Although one might in theory overcome this problem by imposing lump-sum taxes rather than taxes that depend on earnings, that solution presupposes an unrealistic ability to assess the skills and labor–leisure trade-off of the citizens.

body is too numerous to be ensnared yet not numerous enough to yield readily to the intoxication of mindless passion" (*DA*, p. 263). "Democracy's resources are therefore more imperfect than those of aristocracy. ... But its goals are more utilitarian (*plus utile*)" (*DA*, p. 265).

THE METABOLISM OF DEMOCRATIC POLITICS

As we saw in the previous chapter, the "social state" of democracy is characterized by a very high rate of turnover in class membership. Tocqueville argued that the legal, political, and administrative arenas had a similarly high metabolic rate, partly by design and partly by accident, sometimes with negative effects and sometimes with positive.

The positive effect of a short tenure of office is that it makes it more difficult to corrupt the officials. Examples include the Electoral College and the jury:

> The Americans ... felt that if the legislature were charged with electing the chief executive, its members would become the target of corrupting maneuvers and pawns of intrigue long before the election, whereas special electors, like jurors, would remain unknown to the populace until the day they were called upon to act, and would come forward only long enough to make their decision known. (*DA*, p. 149)

A similar logic would dictate that the president not be reeligible, to shield him from intrigue and corruption. The reeligibility of the president is indeed one of the main criticisms that Tocqueville directs against the American political system (*DA*, pp. 153–55). Although Tocqueville was aware of the seeming paradox "of excluding a man from government just when he had proved that he was capable of governing well" (*DA*, p. 153), he thought the argument against reelection "more powerful."

In the first sentence of the section on "Administrative instability in the United States," Tocqueville asserts that "In America, men remain in power for but an instant before fading back into a population which itself changes from day to day, so that the record of society's actions there is often scantier than that of an ordinary family's action" (*DA*, p. 237). Hence, "It is very difficult for American administrators to learn from one another" (*DA*, p. 238). They have no collective memory.

A more specific cause with the same effect is the spoils system: "the fate of all federal employees hangs in the balance with each new election" (*DA*, p. 146). Hence, "In a democratic nation, each new generation is a new people" (*DA*, p. 542). The same high rate of turnover prevents the citizens of democracy from acting consistently with regard to the future: "Because the views of democracy change frequently, and the agents of democracy more frequently still, its undertakings are sometimes poorly managed or left unfinished" (*DA*, p. 242). The last passage presumably refers to legislators rather than to administrators, echoing an earlier statement that legislative power "constantly changes hands" (*DA*, p. 100). This claim needs to be distinguished from the idea that in democracies "the people proceed by momentary efforts and sudden impulses" (*DA*, p. 103). The legislative body is in fact *doubly unstable*, by virtue of the constant renewal of its members and because of its tendency to be swept away by passion.

Changes in personnel and change of laws or policies are closely interwoven in Tocqueville's argument, and it is not always clear whether he is referring to the one or the other. In one passage, the second is said to be an effect of the first: "When one election follows rapidly on the heels of another, their frequency keeps society in feverish activity and public affairs in a state of constant volatility.... The result of this is a singular mutability in legislation" (*DA*, p. 231). Citing what I called the "net effect" argument, he adds that "Many Americans regard the instability of their laws as a necessary consequence of a system whose general effects are useful" (*ibid.*). (He does not here say whether he agrees.) Expanding on this theme, he asserts that "Legislative instability is an evil inherent in democratic government" but especially so in America where "sovereign power is vested in the authority that makes the laws. It can quickly and irrevocably indulge its every desire, and each year it is supplied with new representatives" (*DA*, p. 286).

Later he tells us that he does *not* agree with the "many Americans." We may recall from the last chapter the idea that social mobility has a stabilizing effect by attenuating the class struggle. By contrast, he argues that *political* volatility could destabilize the regime:

I believe that the Americans, by changing their administrative procedures as often as they do, are compromising the future of republican government. If the people's projects are repeatedly thwarted by constant changes in the law, there is reason to fear that they will ultimately come to regard the republic as an inconvenient way of living in society. The harm done by instability in the secondary laws would then call the existence of [constitutional] laws into question and lead indirectly to a revolution. (*DA*, p. 460)[2]

A Tocquevillian question would be whether social mobility without political instability might not be one of those halfway houses that he decries as figments of wishful thinking. In that case the "many Americans" would be right.

The example of Athens in the fourth century B.C. shows, however, that turnover of individuals in office and instability of the laws need not go together. When Tocqueville writes that "in America men remain in power for but an instant before fading back into a population" (*DA*, p. 237), his words equally apply to the Athenian democracy, in which the citizens were "to rule and be ruled by turns."[3] The beneficial effects of democracy on economic life are presumably greater the more frequent the rotation in office and, hence, the more numerous the individuals who have held office or aspire to it. Although Tocqueville does not make that claim, it would seem to follow from his argument.

DEMOCRATIC GOVERNMENT AT THE LOCAL LEVEL

Tocqueville analyzes American politics at four levels: town, county, state, and the federal republic. Broadly speaking, the closer he is to the ground the more interesting are his analyses, not surprisingly given his view that "it is at the local level that the strength of a free people lies" (*DA*, p. 68). What he says about politics at the state and federal level mostly lacks the focus and sharpness of detail that characterize his analyses of local democracy, which enable us to observe his fertile and almost febrile mind at work in ways that few other parts of the book do.

---

[2] An example of the kind of thing he had in mind may be the birth of the Fifth French Republic, which owes its existence at least in part to the perceived volatility of the previous regimes.

[3] Aristotle, *Politics*, 1317b; see also Hansen (1991), pp. 313–14. For the relative stability of Athenian legislation, see *ibid.*, p. 176.

Rather than summarizing Tocqueville's analyses of local self-government, I prefer to look at one of them in some detail to display the moving parts of the argument.[4] In the section on administration in New England, he offers a comparative analysis of how officials can be held responsible for their actions or inactions. The reprehensible behaviors for which an official may be sanctioned fall in three categories: "He can do what the law commands him to do but without ardor or zeal. He can fail to do what the law commands him to do. Or, finally, he can do what the law forbids him to do" (*DA*, p. 86). The two last cases may be collapsed into the single category of *disobedience*, whereas I shall refer to the first as *negligence*.

With regard to negligence, one can check it either through administrative hierarchy, as in France, or through elections, as in America (*DA*, p. 87). With regard to disobedience, "society has as its disposal only two means of obliging officials to obey the law: It can entrust one of them with the discretionary power to direct the others and remove them in case of disobedience. Or it can charge the courts with imposing judicial penalties on violators" (*DA*, p. 82). When officials are elected rather than appointed, only the second means is available (*DA*, p. 83).[5] This solution is imperfect, however, since a court "can act, in legal terms, only when suit is filed" (*DA*, p. 87). In some cases, one may be able to count on this happening: "When an individual suffers immediate and palpable harm as a result of an administrative offense, it is indeed plausible to assume that personal interest is enough to assure that suit will be filed" (*DA*, p. 88). But this motive will not always be present:

It is easy to foresee ... that if it is a question of a legal prescription that, while useful to society, is not currently felt to be useful by any individual, each person will hesitate to come forward as the accuser. In this way, by a sort of tacit agreement, laws might well fall into disuse. Thus, forced by their system to adopt an extreme remedy, the Americans are obliged to motivate potential plaintiffs by authorizing them in certain cases to share in the proceeds of any fines. This is a dangerous procedure, which ensures the execution of the laws by degrading the morality of the people. (*DA*, pp. 88–89)

---

[4] In Ch. 9 I present a similar micro-level analysis of Tocqueville's discussion of the triggers of the 1848 revolution.

[5] For reasons that are not clear to me, Tocqueville does not explain why disobedience could not also be sanctioned by elections.

In this passage, Tocqueville points to a free-rider problem that may arise in any system that rests on private rather than public prosecutions. In the previous chapter, we noted some instances in which Tocqueville argued that free-rider problems are overcome by social norms. Norms cannot, however, be created at will and, as we saw in previous chapters, are in any case unlikely to shape behavior in the highly mobile American society. The more reliable procedure that Tocqueville notes in the cited passage operates by *selective incentives* that make it individually rational to act in the public interest.[6] The *side effects of this remedy* may, however, prove as bad as the disease, since the practice of denunciations is likely to favor venality and malice. There are interesting analogies between this case and that of classical Athens, in which all prosecutions were privately initiated. The Athenians also provided a *remedy against the side effects*, by imposing a severe fine on any informer (sycophant) who failed to get more than one-fifth of the votes in the court.[7]

This little argument is a model of its kind. From the basic premise of a decentralized or "flat" administration,[8] it leads the reader, step by step, to the conclusion of moral degradation. The chain of reasoning is held together by institutional facts (courts have to be seized), by assumptions about individual motivation (citizens will seize the court only out of self-interest), and by psychological facts (informing undermines trust).

CHECKS AND BALANCES

Tocqueville claimed that "Two principal dangers threaten the existence of democracies: The complete subjugation of the legislative power to the will of the electorate. The concentration in the legislative power of

---

[6] Puzzlingly, he also says that the reason why "in [no] other country crime so seldom goes unpunished" is that "everyone believes he has an interest in providing evidence of crime and in apprehending criminals" (*DA*, p. 108).

[7] Doganis (2007) has a full treatment.

[8] Although one might think that Tocqueville would explain the absence of administrative hierarchies in terms of the democratic obsession with equality, his account relies instead on a claim that "when all public offices are filled by election..., no true official hierarchy can exist" (*DA*, p. 83). The practice of choosing public officials by election is explained by the sovereignty of the people (*DA*, p. 64), which is of course closely related to political equality.

all the other powers of government" (*DA*, p. 175). By contraposition, democracy needs some distance between the electorate and the legislature, for example, by two-stage elections or by longer periods of parliamentary tenure, as well as some form of checks and balances. In his view, the federal government had provided these safeguards, but the states had not.

Consider first the several states. In an extravagant comparison with revolutionary France, Tocqueville claims that there are no checks and balances at the state level, because the state legislatures "tend to accumulate [the remnants of governmental power] in themselves, just as the Convention did" (*DA*, p. 100). Or again, "In America no state legislature has to contend with any power capable of resisting it" (*DA*, p. 99). Moreover, "In a number of states, the law made the judicial power subject to election by the majority" (*DA*, p. 284). This is to ignore, however, the power – recognized elsewhere (e.g., *DA*, p. 160) – of the (unelected) Supreme Court to strike down state legislation.

He first praises bicameralism in the state legislatures for its tendency to "slow the movement of political assemblies, and to create an appellate tribunal for revision of the laws" (*DA*, p. 95) and then claims that because the two houses are so similar, "the passions and wishes of the majority manifested themselves just as easily, and found an organ and an instrument just as rapidly, in one house as in the other" (*DA*, p. 173). The first (half-full) statement occurs in a discussion of the superiority of bicameral assemblies over unilateral ones, and the second (half-empty) statement in the section on the superiority of the federal constitution over the state constitutions. We shall shortly see another instance of how Tocqueville's assessments of institutions are shaped by the comparative context in ways that are liable to confuse the reader.

Tocqueville believed that the federal Senate was superior in its wisdom both to the state senates and to the House of Representatives. The reason is that federal senators are chosen by two-stage elections, a procedure that, while fully democratic, is "capable of partially correcting democracy's dangerous instincts" (*DA*, p. 229). The reason presumably is that although the voters lack, as we have seen, both the capacity and the motivation to choose outstanding individuals to represent them, they will nevertheless choose for their representatives persons who possess these two qualities.[9] Also, outstanding candidates may be more willing to stand for a chamber that constitutes "the elite of the nation" (*DA*, p. 229) than for one that is "made up of so many vulgar elements" (*ibid.*). In Tocqueville's opinion, this two-stage procedure is so vital that "It is easy to foresee a time in the future when the American republics will be forced to multiply two-stage elections in their electoral system or else come to grief on democracy's shoals" (*DA*, p. 230). As we know, however, indirect elections were not only not adopted in the states, but abolished at the federal level by the seventeenth Amendment. Indirect elections to the Senate may, in fact, have been an unstable halfway house between democracy and aristocracy.[10]

In his analysis of judicial review, Tocqueville's main concern is to explain to his readers why it could never work in France. In its role as a check on the state legislatures and on Congress, the Supreme Court can declare a law to be unconstitutional. The judge is thus "vested with immense political power" (*DA*, p. 113), a danger that is nevertheless neutralized by two factors. First, "the nation can always oblige magistrates to obey [the law] by amending [the] Constitution" (*DA*, p. 115). Second, "by leaving it up to private interest to instigate censure of the laws, and by tying the case brought against the law intimately to the case brought against an individual, one ensures that legislation will not be subject to frivolous attack" (*DA*, p. 116).

In France, the absence of a clause in the 1830 Charter governing its own amendment would remove the first neutralizing factor: "If courts in France could disobey the laws on the grounds that they found them unconstitutional, constituent power would really be in their hands, since they alone would have the right to interpret a constitution whose terms no one else could change" (*DA*, p. 114).[11] Hence, if someone is going to have the right to change the real constitution without formally

---

[9] There is a puzzle, however. Let us make a stylized division of society into bottom, middle, and top. Tocqueville's argument would seem to presuppose that the bottom would elect the middle but not the top, and that the middle would elect the top. But this is inconsistent with the idea of neighborhood envy.

[10] At least this may have been true of the United States. In some federal systems, members of the upper house are elected by state legislatures or appointed by state governments.

[11] As Dicey (1915), p. 63 n. 38, points out, Tocqueville was wrong on this point: "As a matter of fact one provision of the Charter, namely, art. 23, regulating the appointment of Peers, was changed [in 1831] by the ordinary process of legislation."

amending it, "it is ... better to grant [that power] to men who imperfectly represent the will of the people [e.g., the legislature] rather than to men who represent only themselves [e.g., the judges]" (*ibid.*).

In *DA* Tocqueville does not emphasize the extraordinary difficulty of amending the American constitution. As a consequence, he misses a point he was to make later. He writes that when the court declares a law to be unconstitutional, "either the people change the Constitution, or the legislature repeals the law" (*DA*, p. 115). But there is a third possibility: if the law has strong popular support and the constitution is very hard to amend, there might occur extra-constitutional legal change in the form of a revolution. In the *Recollections* he wrote that "I have long thought that, instead of trying to make our forms of government eternal, we should pay attention to making methodical change an easy matter. All things considered, I find that less dangerous than the opposite alternative. I thought one should treat the French people like those lunatics whom one is careful not to bind lest they become infuriated by the constraint" (*R*, p. 181). Here, the suggestion seems to be that the very fact of being tightly constrained – even by a law one approves – might cause rebellion.[12] Psychologists refer to this mechanism as *reactance*. More plausibly, rebellion might be triggered if it is very hard to change by legal means a law of which many people strongly disapprove.

The second neutralizing factor removes the danger of ex ante or abstract judicial review. At the time, this system did not exist anywhere. Yet Tocqueville may have had in mind the notoriously obstructionist practices of the French *parlements*, which did indeed have the power to review royal legislation before it was promulgated. De jure, the king might override their objections. De facto, they could retaliate by using their power to bring the legal system to a standstill. Perhaps Tocqueville thought that if judicial review were to be reintroduced in France, it would take this form. Spelling out the pernicious effects of abstract

---

[12] For an analogous idea, see Montaigne (1991, p. 698): "We thought we were tying our marriage-knots more tightly by removing all means of undoing them; but the tighter we pulled the knot of constraint the looser and slacker became the knot of our will and affection. In Rome, on the contrary, what made marriages honoured and secure for so long a period was freedom to break them at will. Men loved their wives more because they could lose them; and during a period when anyone was quite free to divorce, more than five hundred years went by before a single one did so."

review, Tocqueville writes that "Had the judge been allowed to attack laws in a theoretical and general fashion, had he been permitted to seize the initiative and censure the legislator ..., he would have invited all the passions that divide the country to join the fray" (*DA*, p. 115). It is perhaps worthwhile noting that today abstract review is practiced in most European countries, including France, without producing these consequences.

In his discussions of the relative powers of the president and Congress, Tocqueville again displays his half-full/half-empty rhetoric. When he wants to deemphasize the powers of the American president compared to those of the king of France, he writes that "even if [the president] withholds his consent, he cannot prevent a law from existing" (*DA*, p. 139) and that "he may nominate but cannot appoint federal officials" (*DA*, p. 140). Both statements are technically true, yet misleading. When he wants to emphasize the powers of the president compared to those of Congress, he writes more insightfully that "the lawgivers ... granted extensive prerogatives to the president and armed him with the veto so that he might resist the encroachments of the legislature" (*DA*, p. 155) and that "the Americans rightly judged that ... the chief executive.... ought to be left as free as possible to choose his own agents" (*DA*, p. 146).

With regard to the mode of election of the president and the extent of his powers, we observe an interesting development from *DA* to the *Recollections*. Writing in 1835, Tocqueville obviously had no idea that as member of the constitutional committee in parliament in 1848, he would be directly involved with the choice between direct and indirect election of the president. Instead, in *DA* he compares a monarch to a directly elected president with a view to determining the powers with which they may be entrusted: "in my opinion it is a contradiction to want the representative of the state to be both armed with vast power and elected. I know only one way of transforming a hereditary monarchy into an elective power: its sphere of action must first be limited, and its prerogatives gradually reduced" (*DA*, p. 144). Thirteen years later he devised another means to the same end: to have the president elected by the national assembly rather than by the people at large. Writing in March 1851, after the election of Louis Napoleon as president but before the coup d'état by which he took absolute power, Tocqueville comments that in a country with a strong tradition of administrative centralization, a direct election of the president would be disastrous:

> In such conditions who could be the president elected by the people, unless he were a pretender to the throne? The institution could serve the turn only of somebody wishing to transform presidential into royal power. I thought it clear then [in 1848], and today it is obvious, that if one wanted to have the president elected by the people, without danger to the Republic, the sphere of his prerogatives must be strictly curtailed. ... If, on the other hand, the president was to be left with his powers [that had been proposed by the constitutional committee], he should not be elected by the people. (R, p. 177)

If we address the issue in the abstract and ignore the fact that in 1848 the presidential contenders included a member of a former reigning dynasty, one could imagine the following arguments for Tocqueville's claims. The powers that the written constitution assigns to the president are multiplied by the legitimacy conferred on him by direct election.[13] Vast formal powers combined with direct election are too dangerous. Conversely, with indirect election he might safely be entrusted with large powers because he would not dare to use them.[14] Moreover (a closely related point), the assembly might deliberately choose a weak president who would not risk a confrontation.[15] None of these arguments, however, supports the idea that a powerful monarch is preferable to a powerful and directly elected president.

THE QUALITY OF DEMOCRATIC GOVERNMENT

I now return to some of the questions I raised in the Introduction to the present chapter. In earlier chapters I have argued that Tocqueville believed that the typical citizen of democracies suffers both from motivational and cognitive deficits. On the motivational side, I have notably cited envy and the inability to delay gratification. On the cognitive side, the most striking flaws are the inability to discern merit and the

---

[13] The power index for presidents proposed in Shugart and Carey (1992) is inadequate because it does not take the last factor into account.

[14] The non-use of the formal dissolution powers of the indirectly elected president in the Third French Republic is an example.

[15] To pursue the example from the previous note, Gambetta was never elected to the presidency in spite of – and probably because of – his dominant position.

inability to comprehend the long-term benefits of free institutions. As a result, democracies perform badly as decision-making mechanisms. They are redeemed only by their energizing effects on economic performance and by the fact that their potential dangers are largely neutralized by features or effects of democracy itself.

In Chapter 6 and Chapter 7 of Part II of Volume I of *DA*, Tocqueville nevertheless offers a more positive appreciation of political democracy. To frame his ideas, we may first note that the policy preferences that an individual expresses by his vote derive from his more fundamental value preferences and from his beliefs about the best way to realize the latter. Hence, if democracy is seen as a system for aggregating policy preferences through universal suffrage, it will also, albeit indirectly, aggregate fundamental preferences and causal beliefs.[16] To assess the quality of the system we may ask, therefore, whether it tends to produce wise aggregate beliefs and just aggregate values.

Tocqueville does not offer a firm positive answer to the question of belief aggregation. He claims that "the moral ascendancy of the majority rests in part on the idea that there is more enlightenment and wisdom in an assembly of many than in the mind of one, or that the number of legislators matters more than the manner of their selection" (*DA*, p. 284). In this chapter he neither endorses nor refutes this idea of the "wisdom of crowds."[17] His insistence elsewhere on the value of two-stage elections and on the superiority of the Senate over the more numerous House of Representatives suggests, however, that in his view the manner of selection *was* important and that the few *could* be wiser than the many. The wisdom of the many is part of the ideology of democracy, not of its reality.

By contrast, when he goes on to claim that "the moral ascendancy of the majority also rests on the principle that the interests of the many ought to be preferred to those of the few" (*DA*, p. 285), it is an idea that he unambiguously endorses. The underlying principle is more or less that of utilitarianism. I have cited his comment that compared to aristocracy, the goals of democracy are "more utilitarian" (*plus utile*). In

---

[16] Social choice theorists have drawn attention to the fact that direct aggregation of preferences combined with the direct aggregation of beliefs may yield a different policy choice from the one following from indirect aggregation (e.g., List 2006). For my purposes here, this anomaly can be ignored.

[17] For different views on this topic, see Page (2006) and Caplan (2007).

general, "the aim of legislation in a democracy is more useful (*utile*) to
humanity than that of legislation in an aristocracy" (*DA*, p. 265). As an
objection to the aristocratic mode of government, he cites the fact that
"society is often sacrificed to the individual and the prosperity of the
majority to the grandeur of a few" (*DA*, p. 823). The class interest of
aristocratic leaders will encourage them "to work together to achieve
a result that is not necessarily the happiness of the greater number"
(*DA*, p. 267). Hence, although Tocqueville never explicitly mentions
utilitarianism, these references to "utility" and to the interest, prosperity, or happiness of "the greater number" suggest that it is what he has in
mind.[18]

The reason why democracies will tend to promote the general interest is simply that the majority of citizens "may be mistaken but
cannot be in conflict of interest with themselves" (*DA*, p. 265). Although democratic officials "may often betray their trust and commit
grave errors, they will never *systematically* adopt a line hostile to the
majority" (*DA*, p. 267; my italics). In other words, no group or class
can expect a cumulative and sustained advantage from the workings of
democracy in the way elites in aristocratic societies can. Also, because
a democratic official generally "holds power for a shorter term" (*DA*,
p. 266) than officials in other regimes, there is less damage he can do.
Moreover, Tocqueville asserts that democracies are (contrary to what
he says in some of the passages I cited earlier) capable of *learning* from
their mistakes.

When one points such things [popular resistance to good legislation] out to
people in government, their only response is, "Let time do its work. When
people begin to feel the ill, it will enlighten them and make them aware of
their needs." This is often true: if democracy is more likely than a king
or body of nobles to make a mistake, it is also more likely to correct that
mistake once enlightenment arrives, because within democracy there are
generally no interests contrary to that of the majority and hostile to reason.
(*DA*, p. 258)

---

[18] One cannot, to be sure, identify majority rule with utilitarianism. If a large minority
has a strong preference for A over B while a small majority has a weak preference for B
over A, the majority choice of B is not the one that maximizes total utility. If asked,
Tocqueville might have answered that a strong preference will often be one that rests
on a *right* rather than on an *interest*, and as such will trump the majority interest (see
notably *AR* Part III, Ch. 6).

This statement is somewhat obscure, as it seems to imply – contrary to what he says elsewhere – that nondemocratic regimes have *more* severe cognitive deficiencies than democracy because of their "hostility to reason." The more important part of the argument is that because people in democracies have good values *and* are able to correct their false beliefs, they will in the long run also make good policy choices. The crucial condition is that they have enough *time* for the learning to take place: they must have "the faculty of committing errors that can be corrected" (*DA*, p. 258). The Americans have this enviable faculty because their geographical isolation ensures that they have no enemies who might exploit a momentary weakness (*DA*, pp. 192–93). "Democracy can discover truth only through experience, and many nations will perish before they have had an opportunity to learn from their mistakes" (*DA*, p. 258). Even when a regime is free of any tendency to make *systematic* mistakes, a single *large* mistake might, in a hostile environment, be enough to bring it down. An implication is that "in order for a democratic republic to survive easily in a European nation, all the other nations of Europe would have to establish democratic republics at the same time" (*DA*, p. 256).

PATHOLOGIES OF DEMOCRATIC GOVERNMENT

As I have noted repeatedly, *Democracy in America* is often a portrait of France. In particular, the sketch of the emergence of despotism out of equality is probably intended as a – possibly self-defeating – prophecy to his French readers and based on his observations of France. It may be worthwhile to summarize his analysis, as an instance of his grasp of multifactorial social causality. There are no fewer than *ten distinct paths* by which equality might lead to despotism, many of them mediated by industry, which is itself a natural result of equality (*DA*, p. 644).

1. Equality suggests the *idea* of a "single, uniform and powerful government" (*DA*, p. 796), because their delight "in simple and general ideas" inspired by equality easily causes individuals "to imagine a great nation whose citizens all conform to a single model and are directed by a single power" (*DA*, p. 789).
2. Equality also inspires a *taste* "for such a government" (*DA*, p. 789), because the hatred "which animates democratic peoples

against the most insignificant privileges, powerfully encourages the gradual concentration of all political rights in the hands of the sole representative of the state" (*DA*, p. 795). As noted in Chapter 4, the latter is too powerful to cause envy.

3. "On the one hand, the taste for well-being increases steadily, and on the other hand the state increasingly controls all the sources of well-being" (*DA*, p. 807 n. 3). The statement refers to the tendency for private savings associations to be replaced by the state.

4. At the same time, "the taste for well-being diverts them from participating in government" (*ibid.*), since "private life in democratic times is so active, so agitated, so filled with desires and labors that individuals have virtually no energy or leisure left for political life" (*DA*, p. 793). This is an instance of the satiation effect.

5. Industry "exposes [men] to great and sudden alternations of abundance and misery ... and [6] can also compromise the health and even the life of those who profit from or engage in it. Thus the industrial class needs to be regulated, supervised, and restrained more than other classes, and it is natural for the prerogatives of government to grow along with it" (*DA*, p. 809).

7. "As a nation becomes more industrial, it feels a proportionately greater need for roads, canals, ports and other works of a semi-public nature. . . . The obvious tendency for all sovereigns nowadays is to assume sole responsibility for undertakings of this kind, thereby constricting the independence of the populations they rule more and more each day" (*DA*, pp. 810–11).

8. The weakness of the individual citizen "causes him on occasion to feel the need of outside help, which he cannot expect to receive from any of [his equals] because they are all powerless and cold-hearted. In this extreme, he naturally turns his attention to the one immense being that alone stands out amid the universal abasement" (*DA*, p. 794).

9. As we saw in Chapter 3, each citizen is opposed to government support to industry, except in his particular case: he wants the government to help him but not others. The result is that "the sphere of the central power imperceptibly expands in every direction, even though each [man] wishes to restrict it" (*DA*, p. 794 n. 1).

10. In democratic societies, "all the citizens are constantly on the move and in a permanent state of transformation. Now, it is in the nature of every government to seek to expand its sphere continually. Hence in the long run it is unlikely that it will not succeed in doing so, since it acts with a fixed thought and constant will on men whose position, ideas, and desires vary from day to day" (*ibid.*).

Reading these gloomy analyses, one is tempted to say, "Come on! It can't be quite as bad as that." And indeed it can't. No state has acquired all these powers by nonviolent means. Yet except for the first and (perhaps more arguably) the second, the arguments show a remarkable understanding of the *growth of the public sector* in industrial societies. The state does indeed provide public goods, undertake countercyclical measures, and regulate workplace conditions. Citizens easily turn to the state for assistance, and firms for subsidies or protection. Retreat into private life and the ensuing political apathy are common phenomena. Social and geographical mobility can make it harder to organize for collective action against the expansionist tendencies of the government. To be sure, Tocqueville does not describe the interaction among these tendencies, nor does he say much about the countertendencies that have prevented the prophecy from coming true. Yet who, in the space of twenty-five pages, has done any better?

9

Revolution

INTRODUCTION

Tocqueville's life and work revolved around revolution. Had it not been for the 1830 revolution and the ambiguous situation it created for him, he would probably not have traveled to the United States. The 1789 revolution is the object of one of his two greatest works, and constantly present in the background of the other. His great-grandfather Malesherbes died under the guillotine, and his father, having narrowly escaped it, later wrote a book on the coming of the Revolution.[1] Tocqueville was also a participant-observer in and a memorialist of the 1848 revolution, with an existential absorption in the events. In March 1849, he complained to a friend that "now that properties and life are no longer at stake, I cannot interest myself in anything. This is the evil of revolutions, which, like gambling, create the habit of emotions and make us love them for their own sake, independently of the gain" (L, p. 649). He probably had a better understanding of the dynamics of revolution than anyone before or since. He grasped the *longue durée* in which the causes of a revolution can be traced back over centuries, as well as its tumultuous unfolding day-by-day and blow-by-blow.

In his discussion of the causes of the English revolution, Lawrence Stone distinguishes among preconditions (1529–1629), precipitants (1629–39) and triggers (1640–42). The preconditions "made some form

---

[1] Excerpted and translated in Palmer (1987).

of redistribution of political power almost inevitable . . . , but whether these changes would come about by peaceful evolution, political upheaval, or force of arms was altogether uncertain." Later, the "precipitants of the 1630s turned the prospects of a political breakdown from a possibility into a probability," whereas the trigger was provided by "a sequence of short-term, even fortuitous events which turned the probability into a certainty."[2]

Applying this scheme to *AR*, Book II of the published volume deals with preconditions (1439–1750) and Book III with the precipitants (1750–87). In Tocqueville's notes for the planned second volume, we find unsystematic but often striking comments on the triggering events that occurred between 1787 and 1789. In the *Recollections*, he focuses on the triggering of the revolution in February 1848 and on the subsequent struggles through June. Although he also has a few observations on the preconditions and precipitants of the 1848 revolution, these are lapidary compared to the profound analyses in *AR*. In a happy contrast, the *Recollections* offers observations on the psychology of revolutionary action that is found only in fragments in *AR*.

I noted in Chapter 4 that Tocqueville claimed that the revolutionaries of 1789 and 1848 were subject to the same social norm: you may kill and destroy but not steal. These observations occur in two separate writings, however, not as part of an explicit comparison. In the *Recollections*, the comparison of the two revolutions is very much present. Like Marx, who commented that the relation of 1848 to 1789 was that of a farce to a tragedy,[3] Tocqueville ridicules the actors of February 1848 when "the tepid passions of our day were expressed in the burning language of '93" (*R*, p. 74). Tocqueville genuinely admired many of the leaders of the French Revolution, but there seems hardly to be any political actor in 1848 that he did not feel contempt for.

The *Recollections* are indeed first and foremost satire and caricature. Only accidentally and occasionally do they offer analytical insights. By contrast, *AR* is wholly organized around a complex but coherent analytical structure that I try to spell out below. Although it is deeply original

---

[2] Stone (1986), pp. 127, 135.

[3] "Hegel remarks somewhere that all facts and personages of great importance in world history occur, as it were, twice. He forgot to add: the first time as tragedy, the second time as farce" (Marx 1852, p. 103).

and innovative, it may be worthwhile to note that it owes more to earlier writers than Tocqueville was willing to admit. He prided himself on reading primary documents only and avoiding secondary commentaries, even, he said, at the risk of occasionally reinventing the wheel (*L*, p. 1200). If we compare *AR* to the writings on the Revolution by Mme de Staël and Joseph Droz, however, it is hard to escape the conclusion that he had read them and been influenced by them.[4]

PRECONDITIONS: "ON NE S'APPUIE QUE SUR CE QUI RÉSISTE"

These words ("You can lean only against what offers resistance"), spoken to Napoleon by the poet François Andrieux, can be used to summarize a major strand in Tocqueville's argument in Book II of *AR*.[5] In a nutshell, he claimed that the successive French kings were so successful in reducing the nobility and the bourgeoisie to a state of political impotence that when Louis XVI needed their help to resist the Revolution, they had nothing to offer. Only in the west of France, where the nobles had resisted the summons of the king to come to the court, did they come to his assistance:

The letter of an *intendant* responding on this subject has survived. He complains that the nobles of his province are pleased to remain with their peasants rather than fulfill their obligations at court. It is worth noting that the province in question was Anjou, later known as the Vendée. The nobles who are said to have refused to do their duty toward the king were the only ones in France who would later take up arms in defense of the monarchy. (*AR*, pp. 155–56)

---

[4] I offer some documentation for this claim in Elster (2006), adding that "I have no direct evidence that would allow me to tell whether these instances reflect a direct influence of de Staël and Droz on Tocqueville, or whether the three writers simply expressed ideas that were in common circulation at the time." Yet some similarities are so striking and specific that a direct influence rather than a common cause is plausible.

[5] In fact, he makes a quite explicit (if grammatically somewhat opaque) statement to that effect in the notes for the second volume: "In the time of Henri IV, these princes, great lords, bishops, and wealthy bourgeois ... could ... limit the movement to which they gave rise and support the monarchy even when they might have resisted it. Under Louis XVI, these same classes . . . could still stir up the people, [but] they were incapable of leading it" (*O III*, pp. 467–68, amended in the light of marginal note (c) cited on p. 1134).

In fact, the administration had undermined *all* intermediary bodies, so that even in an ordinary crisis it could not enlist the assistance of anybody: "[I]n times of scarcity . . . the central government took fright at its isolation and weakness. It would have liked to revive for the occasion the individual influences and political associations it had destroyed. It called on them for help, but no one answered the call, and the government was regularly astonished to find dead those whom its own actions had deprived of life" (*AR*, pp. 163–64). In a major crisis, the regime collapsed like a house of cards: "Nothing had been left that could obstruct the government, nor anything that could shore it up" (*AR*, pp. 167–68). As we shall see, the bourgeoisie was fragmented and powerless, and the nobility reduced to a mere ornament.

The weakness of the nobility had several causes. As noted in earlier chapters, an important reason for the weakness of the nobles was their isolation from the bourgeoisie that followed from their tax exemption. Because they were not subject to the same taxes, the two classes had few common interests and few occasions to take concerted action. Although Tocqueville does not use the phrase "divide et impera," it is very clear from his analyses that this was the strategy he imputed to the kings: "Nearly all the unfortunate defects, errors, and prejudices I have just described owe either their origin, duration, or development to the skill that most of our kings have had in dividing men in order to govern them more absolutely" (*AR*, p. 167). In the notes for the second volume, we read that "kings were able to create this unchecked power only by dividing the classes and isolating each of them amid its own peculiar prejudices, jealousies, and hatreds so as never to have to deal with more than one at a time" (*O III*, p. 485). In his notes on England, he writes that in France, "those who worked most effectively to prevent landowners from becoming in this way members of a single body and forming an aristocracy rather than a caste were the kings who, for reasons of financial expediency dating back to the thirteenth century, conceived the idea of levying a special tax on commoners who owned fiefs" (*O III*, p. 342).

Yet as Georg Simmel argued in his analysis of "the triad," the fact that party C may benefit from a fallout between parties A and B is not by itself proof of intentional "divide et impera." There is always the possibility of an accidental (nonexplanatory) third-party benefit, "tertius gaudens."[6]

[6] Simmel (1908), pp. 82–94.

Does Tocqueville offer any proof in favor of the more intentional or Machiavellian thesis?

Tocqueville's interest in triadic structures, such as king-nobility-people, goes back to his early days. In a letter from 1828, he offers a more conventional idea of the relations among the three, asserting that the French kings first allied themselves with the people ("les communes") to destroy the nobility and then were in turn destroyed by the people in 1789.[7] The discussion in *AR* is subtler and, up to a point, convincing. The question remains, however: did Tocqueville show that the fragmentation was deliberately brought about by the kings and not simply an unintended by-product of actions undertaken for other purposes?

In addition to his analysis of the *effects* of tax exemption for the nobles, Tocqueville offers an account of the *origins* of the exemption, namely, that the nobility "cowardly" accepted tax exemption as a bribe to let the king impose new taxes without calling the Estates-General:

I dare to affirm that on the day the nation, tired of the interminable disorders that had accompanied the captivity of King John and the dementia of Charles VI, allowed kings to levy a general tax without its consent, and when the nobility was cowardly enough to allow the Third Estate to be taxed provided that it remained exempt – on that day the seed was sown of practically all the vices and abuses that ravaged the Ancien Régime for the remainder of its existence and ultimately led to its violent death. (*AR*, p. 136)

Before I pursue this point, let me signal the extraordinary causal importance that Tocqueville attached to the desire of the kings to avoid having to convoke the Estates-General. The venality of offices is also ascribed to this desire: "These institutions [the venality of offices] were established precisely in opposition to them [the estates]. They were born of the desire not to convoke them and of the need to hide from the French a tax that could not be shown in its true guise" (*AR*, p. 142). He explains the political importance of the *parlements* in the same way:

[7] The king "called the commons to his aid, joined forces with them, led them by the hand, enlisted their assistance to destroy feudalism, and was finally devoured when he found himself face-to-face with them in 1789" (*L*, p. 122).

The same desire to escape the tutelage of the estates led to the attribution to the parlements of most of their political prerogatives. This hobbled the judicial power in government in a way that was highly prejudicial to the orderly conduct of public business. There was a need to appear to provide new guarantees in place of those that had been eliminated, because the French, who had put up rather patiently with absolute power as long as it was not oppressive, never liked the sight of it, and it was always wise to raise some apparent barriers in front of it, barriers that could not stop it but nevertheless hid it a little. (*Ibid.*)

In each case, Tocqueville also invoked the king's need to hide from the French the nature and the extent of their real oppression. There is more than a hint of functionalism in this argument, as there was in his claim, discussed above, that the administration allowed criticism of religion as a "consolation" and (I shall now argue) in his claim that the tax exemption was a strategy of "divide et impera."

In functional explanation, one cites the beneficial consequences (for someone or something) of a behavioral pattern in order to *explain* that pattern, while neither showing that the pattern was created with the *intention* of providing those benefits nor pointing to a *feedback loop* whereby the consequences might sustain their causes.[8] When not supported in either of these two ways, the alleged explanation is spurious, since it does not exclude that the benefits could have arisen in some accidental way. A typical example is the explanation of conflict behavior in terms of third-party benefits. Strictly speaking, Tocqueville does not offer a functional explanation of the tax exemption, since he does impute a divide-and-conquer *intention* to the kings. Yet since he provides no evidence for this intention, it is hard not to conclude that he just *inferred* the ex ante intention to benefit from the factual ex post benefits, combining "post hoc ergo propter hoc" with "cui bono?" This is not exactly functionalism, but close enough to it.

Considering the issue in a broader perspective, it is not unusual that elite fragmentation benefits a third party. In Athens, extension of the suffrage was largely due to competition within the elite for the favor of the masses.[9]

---

[8] Elster (1983b), Ch. 2.

[9] "By the time of Cleisthenes, the elites recognized mass ambitions as a new weapon to use against each other. As a result, politically ambitious elites actively sponsored democratizing reforms. . . . Ironically, as the elites gained victories over their enemies by sponsoring democratic reforms, there were fewer and fewer institutions that they could control directly" (Ober 1989, p. 85).

It has been argued, although the claim is controversial, that in nineteenth-century Britain, Conservatives extended the suffrage in the expectation that the newly enfranchised would vote for them rather than for the Liberals.[10] Marx, commenting on how the struggle between Whigs and Tories over the Corn Laws benefited the working class, cites the English proverb "When thieves fall out, honest men come by their own."[11] In none of these cases, however, has it been argued that these intra-elite conflicts can be *explained* by their benefit to the non-elite party.[12] It is hard indeed to see how the weaker would be able to induce the stronger to fight each other. In the case of France, however, the elite fragmentation benefited the monarchy rather than the people. Yet – adopting the terminology of Chapter 5 – although the kings had both the opportunity (the power) and the desire to play the classes out against each other, it is more than doubtful that they had the cognitive capacity to anticipate that tax exemption for the nobles would have this effect. More important, Tocqueville offers no *evidence* to show that they were reasoning along those lines.

In fact, he also proposed a perfectly reputable intentional account that in no way relies on "divide et impera": the king offered the immunity as a bribe so that he would not have to call the Estates-General. As an additional explanatory factor, Tocqueville notes that when Charles VII first established the *taille* on a national basis, it would have been dangerous to impose it on the nobles: "When the king undertook for the first time to levy taxes on his own authority, he understood that he would have to begin by choosing a tax that did not appear to fall directly on the nobility, because nobles at the time constituted a class that was a rival and danger to the monarchy, and they would never have tolerated an innovation so prejudicial to themselves. He therefore chose a tax from which they were exempt: the *taille*" (*AR*, p. 137).

Moreover, one could hardly ask the nobles to pay a tax that was likely to be used against them. In his notes for the second volume, Tocqueville quotes Turgot: "Under Charles VII one began to mount

---

[10] In the *Recollections*, Tocqueville makes fun of the revolutionaries of 1848 who believed that the newly enfranchised groups would vote out of gratitude for the enfranchisers rather than out of interest (*R*, p. 97).

[11] Marx (1867), p. 830.

[12] One should perhaps make an exception for Marx. Given his general teleological outlook, he may have viewed this struggle as one of the ways in which History makes the ruling classes dig their own grave.

a permanent paid militia, and it was in this period that the *taille* was established on a permanent basis," and he adds that "since the purpose of the paid troops was to subdue the nobles or at least to circumvent them, it was quite natural that, in order to pave the way for the transition, they were not themselves asked to provide the money to be used against them" (*O III*, p. 413). Again, this is a reputable intentional explanation, but it does not support the story according to which the kings granted tax exemptions to the nobles in order to undermine their political power. In fact, to complicate matters, Tocqueville at one point reverses the causal chain by asserting that the exemptions were a "consolation" for the loss of power: "In the eighteenth century in England, it was the poor man who enjoyed the tax privilege; in France it was the rich man. There, the aristocracy took the heaviest public responsibilities on itself so that it would be allowed to govern; here it retained the tax exemption to the end to console itself for having lost the government" (*AR*, p. 135).

The exemption of the nobles from military service occurred at the same time as the establishment of the *taille* from which they were also exempt: "The original purpose of the *taille* was to enable the king to buy soldiers who would dispense nobles and their vassals of the need to perform military service" (*AR*, pp. 160–61).[13] The creation by Charles VII in 1439 of a national tax and of a national army financed by that tax was in a sense the beginning of modern France. Tocqueville emphasizes, however, the disastrous consequences of exempting the nobility from the obligation to pay taxes and from the responsibility to make up the king's army. In a capital passage (*AR*, p. 136) cited more fully above, Tocqueville affirms that on the day when the nobility cowardly allowed "the Third Estate to be taxed provided that it remained exempt ... the seed was sown of practically all the vices and abuses that ravaged the Ancien Régime."

Even before being exempt from the *taille*, the nobles had enjoyed tax immunities. The novel element was that they were also exempted from the duty to raise troops that had justified the tax exemption. They were "relieved of the very onerous obligation to make war at their own expense, yet their immunity from taxation had been maintained and

---

[13] From the account in Picot (1888), vol. I, pp. 321–31, it seems that the point of Charles VII's ordinance of 1439 was not so much to dispense the nobles from military service as to prohibit them from raising private armies.

in fact expanded considerably. In other words, they retained the indemnity while shedding the burden" (*AR*, p. 119). This amounted to a breach of an *implicit contract*. Without the obligation of public service, the nobility lost its energy and became a mere ornament: "One might say that the limbs gained at the expense of the body. The nobility enjoyed the right to command less and less, but nobles more and more claimed the exclusive prerogative of being the master's principal servants" (*AR*, p. 126). The double exemption from raising troops and from paying taxes was a poisoned gift – with the added twist that its long-term effect was to harm the donor as well as the recipient, for "on ne s'appuie que sur ce qui résiste."

Yet, to repeat, effects are not causes.[14] We are led to ask if Tocqueville did not needlessly complicate his explanation of the decline of the nobility. From Charles VII onward, the French kings were constantly trying to reduce the power of the nobles, *constrained at each step by the power they still retained*. Although in this process the kings certainly played the nobles off against one another, the idea that they offered them tax exemptions in order to play them off *against the bourgeoisie* is far-fetched and undocumented. More plausibly, as Tocqueville himself asserts, the kings made the nobles exempt from the tax because they were not strong enough to impose it on them. Later, this exemption may well have redounded to the kings' benefit, but if so the mechanism was that of "tertius gaudens," not "divide et impera."

The weakness of the bourgeoisie stemmed from its inability to act in concert with the nobility, from its internal fragmentation (Ch. 7), and from loss of its political freedoms. Whatever uncertainty there may be concerning the degree of intentionality in his account of the decline of the nobility, there is none whatsoever in his explanation of the decline of the towns: "Louis XI had curtailed municipal freedoms because he feared their democratic character. Louis XIV destroyed them though he did not fear them. Proof that this was the case can be seen in the fact that he sold these freedoms back to any town that could pay for them. In fact, his intention was not so much to abolish as to trade in them, and if he did abolish them, it was done as it were inadvertently, as a purely expedient fiscal policy" (*AR*, pp. 88–89). In other words, the king

[14] In a Marxist perspective, of course, it could be said that the kings were the unconscious tools of History in digging their own graves.

abolished municipal freedom by putting offices up for sale, but from his point of view the revenue he could raise from letting towns buy their freedom back was just as good. For the towns, the choice was between political decline and financial ruin (*AR*, p. 89).

The public service that the nobles had traditionally performed included not only the raising of armies for the king, but also the provision of public goods to the local peasantry, notably law, order, and famine relief. When they ceased to perform these tasks, they broke *a second implicit contract*, this time with the peasantry: "[I]f the French peasant had still been subject to the administration of his lord, feudal dues would have seemed far less unbearable to him" (*AR*, p. 78). Just as the royal militia replaced the nobles in their military function, so did the royal *intendant* and his *subdélégué* replace the *seigneur* in his administrative function. And just as the tax exemption fueled the envy of the bourgeois for the nobles, so did the withdrawal of the nobles from local administration fuel the hatred the peasantry felt for them. In Chapter 4, I emphasized that the hatred the peasant felt toward the seigneur was caused by tension between his status as a landowner and the daily frustrations he encountered. We now see a second and distinct source of resentment in the breach of the implicit contract: "Why, then, did these same feudal dues inspire in the hearts of the French a hatred so powerful that it outlived its object and thus seemed inextinguishable? The reason was in part that the French peasant had become a landowner and in part that he had been completely emancipated from the control of his lord" (*ibid.*).

The nobles, then, were the target both of the envy of the bourgeoisie and of the hatred of the peasantry. Given these powerful emotions, no wonder that the peasants burned their castles and that the third estate destroyed their privileges. In this respect, France was unique among the major European countries. Tocqueville argues that in Germany, the conditions for these emotions did not exist or existed only in attenuated form or in some communities. The German bourgeoisie may have felt envy toward the nobility because of unequal access to noble possessions, high office, or the court:

[T]he bourgeois could not in general purchase equestrian properties or obtain the highest posts in the civil service. Nor were they Hoffähig, which is to say, they could not appear at court.... As in France, this inferiority was all the more hurtful because this class grew more enlightened and influential with each passing day. . . . Irritation with the privileges of the nobility, which would contribute so much to the Revolution in our country, explains why the Revolution was initially received with approval in Germany. (*O III*, p. 249)

In Germany, inequality of tax burdens was not a factor, however. In fact, Tocqueville cites one of his German interlocutors to the effect that when the German nobles ceased to raise armies, they became subject to a new tax: "[O]nce they ceased to wage war at their own expense, a tax . . . was levied on them . . . for the specific purpose of replacing military service" (*O III*, p. 322).[15] Thus, the breeding ground for envy was less fertile.

Furthermore, because of the participation of the German nobility in local administration, the conditions for hatred were not present: "In the very parts of Germany where princes were most successful . . . in freeing themselves from noble oversight in general affairs of state, they allowed the nobles to retain much of their role as administrators of the countryside" (*AR*, p. 76). The only exception arose along the Rhine, where the "peasants in the late eighteenth century owned their own land and were almost as free as in France" (*AR*, p. 74). This was also where "the revolutionary passions of the French spread most rapidly and have always been strongest. By contrast, the parts of Germany that were for a long time most impervious to those passions were those in which nothing similar had yet been seen" (*ibid.*). Conjecturally, the fact that the nobles kept their contract with the peasantry attenuated the passions somewhat even in the parts of Germany where the peasants owned their land.

If we look to England, there is even less cause for envy and hatred: "In the eighteenth century in England, it was the poor man who enjoyed the tax privilege; in France it was the rich man" (*AR*, p. 135). At the same time, "England was administered as well as governed by the principal landowners" (*AR*, pp. 75–76).

---

[15] Elsewhere he remarks that a similar surcharge would have been appropriate in France: "Today the privilege of the tax, which was based on the fact that only nobles were obliged to serve, is combined with the privilege the nobles enjoy of not serving if they so wish, for nobles and even their valets are not subject to the laws governing the militia. Thus grounds for relief from the charge no longer exist, though a surcharge would be justified" (*O III*, p. 414).

There is one gap in this otherwise admirably tight argument: why, how, and when did the *intendant* (or his *subdélégué*) take the place of the seigneur in local administration? Virtually all references to the *intendant* in *AR* are to his functions in the eighteenth century, and there is no mention of the creation of the office in the sixteenth century. A divide-and-conquer explanation might be that the successive kings deliberately undermined the local power of the nobles by luring them to the court. Tocqueville, however, explicitly rejects this idea. He notes that "The nobility's abandonment of the countryside has often been attributed to the specific influence of certain kings and ministers, notably Louis XIV and Richelieu" (*AR*, p. 155), but then objects:

We must . . . beware of attributing the desertion of the countryside by what was then the leading class of the nation to the direct influence of some of our kings. The primary and persistent cause of this desertion was not the will of certain individuals but the slow and steady operation of certain institutions. Proof of this can be seen in the fact that when the government wanted to counter the evil in the eighteenth century, it could not even slow its progress. As nobles lost their political rights without acquiring others and local liberties disappeared, the emigration of nobles increased. There was no longer any need to lure them from their homes, because they no longer wished to stay in them. Country life had lost its appeal. (*AR*, p. 156)

The alleged "proof" is not one, of course, since the fact that the kings tried to reverse the trend later does not prove that the initiation of the trend was not due to their initiative. In fact, the phrase that "it was no longer necessary to lure them away" implies that it had been necessary at some point in the past. The details of the process remain obscure, however.

A final comment on the nature of the ancien régime may be in order. In his 1828 letter, Tocqueville asserted that in England the nobility joined forces with the third estate to check royal power (*L*, pp. 122–23). Although the nobility did not have that role in France, other institutions served, however imperfectly, the same end. The Estates-General early ceased to be an effective counterweight, but the two institutions that (according to Tocqueville) were introduced so that the kings would not have to convoke them took up their function. In his analysis, the venality of office and the parlements illustrated the *principle of the second-best*, namely, that "it is not true that a situation in which more, but not all, of the optimum conditions are fulfilled is necessarily, or is even likely to be, superior to a situation in which fewer are fulfilled."[16] Tocqueville offers two examples:

> The government, in its desire to turn everything into money, had put most public offices up for sale and thus deprived itself of the ability to grant and revoke them at will. One of its passions had thus seriously undermined the other, greed thwarting ambition. In order to act, it was thus repeatedly forced to rely on instruments it did not make and could not break. Thus it often saw its most absolute will sapped in execution. This bizarre and flawed constitution of public functions served as a substitute for any kind of political guarantee against the omnipotence of the central government. It was a haphazardly constructed dike that dispersed the government's force and blunted its impact.... The irregular intervention of the courts in government, which often disrupted the orderly dispatch of the public's affairs, thus served at times to safeguard liberty. It was a great evil that limited a still greater one. (*AR*, pp. 144, 150)

In *DA*, Tocqueville often argues that the ills of democracy are cured by democracy itself. Here, he claims the ancien régime similarly contained remedies for its own diseases. The analogy is imperfect, however, since in *DA* the argument does not always take the form of asserting that two negatives make a positive. When he asserts that the religion that is endogenous to democracies prevents citizens from engaging in the disorderly behavior that democracies allow, it is not a question of one ill limiting a greater one. By contrast, there is a perfect analogy with the claim that "the ill [newspapers] cause is . . . far less than the ill they heal" (*DA*, p. 600). As in the case of halfway-house arguments (Ch. 6), we may ask ourselves whether the use of second-best arguments in both of the major works is a self-conscious application of the same mental model. My inclination, once again, is to think that Tocqueville knew exactly what he was doing.

PRECIPITANTS: THE "TOCQUEVILLE PARADOX"

In the social sciences, the "Tocqueville paradox" (or the "Tocqueville effect") refers to the idea that subjective discontent (and hence the

---

[16] Lipsey and Lancaster (1956), pp. 11–12.

likelihood of revolution or rebellion) and objective grounds for discontent may be inversely related to each other.[17] In *AR*, Tocqueville offers two synchronic versions and one diachronic version of the paradox. At the beginning of Book II, he asks why the Revolution occurred in France rather than in Germany, given that feudal burdens were lighter in France. Somehow, "The yoke seemed most intolerable where in reality it was lightest" (*AR*, p. 71). The resolution of the paradox is, as we saw, that in Germany the nobles still performed the administrative functions that justified their appropriation of feudal benefits. In the absence of strong peasant hatred, mild bourgeois envy could not by itself trigger a revolution.

In Book III, Chapter iv, Tocqueville notes that another synchronic version of the paradox could be observed within France itself: "[T]he parts of France that were to become the principal center of that revolution were precisely those where progress was most evident" (*AR*, p. 201). The areas in Île-de-France where the Revolution would break out enjoyed greater personal freedom and lower taxes than the western lands that would be the bastion of the counterrevolution:

> If one studies what remains of the archives of the former généralité of the Île-de-France, it is easy to see that it was in the regions around Paris that the old regime reformed itself soonest and most profoundly. . . . Nowhere, by contrast, did the old regime maintain itself better than along the Loire, toward its mouth, in the marshes of Poitou and the moors of Brittany. It was precisely there that civil war flared up and spread and that the most durable and violent resistance to the Revolution occurred. Thus one might say that the better the situation of the French became, the more unbearable they found it. (*AR*, pp. 201–2)

The mechanism behind this synchronic paradox is not quite clear. As we saw, the nobles of Vendée were "pleased to remain with their peasants" and hence generated more loyalty than absentee landlords did. At the same time, the feudal burdens on the peasantry in these regions were heavier than in the Île-de-France (*AR*, p. 201). The net effect of these two mechanisms could presumably go either way. Yet I believe the reason why Tocqueville so unambiguously states that the

---

[17] For an elegant model, see Boudon (1986). In the terminology I explain below, his model aims at explaining the synchronic rather than the diachronic paradox.

better-off were more discontent is that he confused the synchronic and the diachronic paradoxes. In the continuation of the last-cited passage, he goes on to restate the paradox in one of the most famous statements in the whole work:

[It] is not always going from bad to worse that leads to revolution. What happens most often is that a people that put up with the most oppressive laws without complaint, as if they did not feel them, rejects those laws violently when the pressure is alleviated. The regime that a revolution destroys is almost always better than the one that immediately preceded it, and experience teaches that the most dangerous time for a bad government is usually when it begins to reform. (*AR*, p. 202)

This is obviously a diachronic statement, presented, misleadingly, as equivalent to the synchronic one that immediately precedes it. Let us focus, then, on the diachronic paradox, and first approach it as part of the larger question of how governments respond to an actual or predictable crisis. Broadly speaking, we may distinguish four responses: preemption, concession, moderate repression, and severe repression. In some cases, popular discontent has also been distracted by an external war, but this was not among the options in 1789.

Wisdom dictates preemption – meeting popular demands before they are formulated, or granting more than is demanded. Both Louis XV and Louis XVI were sorely lacking in this quality of mind. Concerning Louis XV, Tocqueville asserts that although he might have initiated a peaceful reform around 1750 and averted the revolution, it was not in his character to do so.[18] Concerning Louis XVI, Tocqueville makes fun of his blindness: "Decree of January 21, 1776, concerning the destruction of rabbits. . . . The preamble and body of this edict came from Louis XVI himself, who showed it to M. Turgot with the comment, 'Do you suppose I do no work of my own?' Poor and excellent king, who, on the eve of so great a Revolution, approached reform by way of rabbits, precisely seventeen years to the day before mounting the

---

[18] "We are assured that one of Louis XV's cleverest ministers, M. de Machault, anticipated this idea and pointed it out to his master. No one undertakes such a venture on the advice of another, however. One is apt to succeed in an enterprise of this kind only if capable of conceiving it" (*AR*, p. 192).

scaffold" (*O III*, p. 407).[19] Commenting on the calling of the Assemblée des Notables in 1787, Tocqueville cites as one of the "faults accumulated by Louis XVI" the fact that when "he assembles an assembly to ask its opinion about the state of the finances, he does not preempt (*ne vas pas au-devant de*) all the demands for information that it might request, and believes that it will help him to fill a deficit the size of which it is not told. Oh inexperience!" (*O III*, p. 1135).

Severe repression, for its part, requires a decisiveness that was also absent. Although Tocqueville does not mention the well-known aversion of Louis XVI for spilling the blood of his subjects, he does cite the more general tendency of the eighteenth-century monarchy to be *fortiter in modo, suaviter in re*: "[I]n the eighteenth-century monarchy, the forms of punishment were terrifying but the penalties were almost always moderate. One preferred to frighten rather than harm, or, rather, one was arbitrary and violent out of habit and indifference, and mild by temperament" (*AR*, p. 215). Although the comment refers to criminal justice, it also applies to the preference for moderate over severe repression. The administration was left, therefore, with the alternatives of concession and moderate repression.

As I argued in several places above, it is a fundamental Tocquevillian idea that *half-measures often work against their purpose.*[20] As with unstable halfway houses, when you try to get the best of both worlds you often get the worst of both:[21] "[A]t the beginning of a revolution

<hr>

[19] The best-known successful attempt to preempt revolution is perhaps the social insurance program of Bismarck. Workers, he said, "will think that if the state comes to any harm, I'll lose my pension" (Ritter 1983, p. 35). His contemporary Alexander II of Russia also perceived that "the only means of avoiding revolution – and what Louis XVI did not do – was to preempt [*devancer*] and prevent it" (Carrère d'Encausse 2008, p. 454). It may be worthwhile mentioning that Alexander provides a counterexample to Tocqueville's claim that servitude has virtually never been abolished by the master (*L*, pp. 466–67). As a final observation on these lines, we may cite Tocqueville's assertion to Lord Radnor from May 1848 that "the only way to attenuate and postpone [the] revolution is to do, *before one is forced to do it*, all that is possible to improve the situation of the people" (*L*, p. 630; my italics).

[20] The idea is stated as early as 1828 (*L*, p. 121), referring to Henri III who "irritated without subjugating."

[21] A recent instance occurred when Columbia University in New York City invited President Ahmadinejad of Iran to speak on campus, and the president of the university introduced him by a ten-minute diatribe against him. He managed to look both ridiculous in his own country (causing a Nobel Prize laureate to turn down an honorary degree from the university) and offensive in the Muslim world.

such measures always fail and merely inflame the people without satisfying them" (*AR*, p. 175). Or again, "[t]he half-measures that were
imposed on the enemies of the Church at that time did not diminish
their power but rather increased it.... Authors were persecuted just
enough to elicit complaint but not enough to provoke fear. They were
hobbled in a way that provoked resistance but not subjected to the
heavy yoke that might quell it" (*AR*, pp. 181–82).

Many passages in the notes for the second volume make the same point.
Tocqueville argues that in its struggle against the parlements, the government was "employing violence to the point of irritation but never pushing
it to the point of fear" (*O III*, p. 483). He also refers to the "attitude of
power mixed with incomplete violence and disdain" (*O III*, p. 569). Fa-
tally, "to raise hopes of voting by head [in the Estates-General] and yet not
authorize it was to spur the Third Estate to attack and allow the privileged
to resist" (*O III*, p. 546). As the king left the situation shrouded in uncertainty, each side could self-servingly and self-deceptively believe that it
would be resolved in its favor. After the attempt on June 23, 1789, by
Louis XVI to impose his will on the assembly, the latter "irritated and
aroused rather than demoralized by this mild pressure from the government, increasingly adopted the attitude of being in charge" (*O III*, p. 570).

The tendency of concessions to inflame rather than to appease the
population offers one explanation of the diachronic paradox. For each
demand that is granted, more will spring up until the capacity of the
system to absorb them is broken. Yet we have to ask: *why* does one
concession generate the demand for more? Generally speaking, it could
be because it induces a change in the *beliefs* of the citizens, in their
preferences, or in both.

On the one hand, the granting of a demand may provide new information about the resolve of the administration, and support the belief
that further demands will also be met with a positive response.[22] In
Chapter III.iv, Tocqueville does not appeal to this mechanism, although
he cites it elsewhere to argue why the recall of the *parlement* of Paris in
September 1788 was a point of no return for the monarchy: "The king ...
recalled Parlement and rescinded the stamp law and the territorial

---

[22] For a contemporary example, consider how the non-intervention by the USSR after
the first free elections in Poland in June 1989 signaled to the opposition in Hungary
that intervention was unlikely there as well.

tax. ... If the king wished to remain the king of the old monarchy, this was precisely what he should not have done. From that moment on, all sorts of concessions were indispensable" (*O III*, pp. 1141–42).[23]

On the other hand, reforms that satisfy a given desire may at the same time cause dormant or latent desires to appear on the horizon. This was Tocqueville's answer: "The evil that one endures patiently because it seems inevitable becomes unbearable the moment its elimination becomes conceivable. Then, every abuse that is eliminated seems only to reveal the others that remain and make their sting that much more painful. The ill has diminished, to be sure, but sensitivity to it has increased" (*AR*, p. 202). The key idea, already stated in the Introduction to *Democracy in America*, is that people do not resent the evils that appear to them as an inevitable part of the natural or social order: "The people, never having imagined a social condition other than their own and never expecting to become the equals of their leaders . . . loved their superiors when they were clement and just and submitted to their rigors without hardship or ignominy as if bowing to inevitable woes imposed by the hand of God" (*DA*, pp. 8–9). Once one such evil has been removed, similar evils will appear as removable and therefore as intolerable. A cognitive change (the evil is not inevitable) triggers a motivational change (it is intolerable). Although this argument would seem to apply to preemption as well as to concessions, we may note that preemptive measures do not signal lack of resolve. To make Tocqueville fully consistent with himself, we may speculate that the self-defeating consequences of concessive measures were due to a combination of signaling effects and the "release from adaptive preferences."

In this argument, *improvement causes discontent*. In another argument, improvement and discontent are *traced back to a common cause*, namely, increased economic activity. In the prerevolutionary period, "The number of people who did business with [the government], who had an interest in its loans, lived on its stipends, and speculated on its contracts, had increased prodigiously. Never had public and private fortunes been so intertwined" (*AR*, p. 204). Hence, the utter

---

[23] Ginkel and Smith (1999) argue that in a prerevolutionary situation, a rational government will not make concessions unless it believes that the calming effect of concessions on the masses will offset the weakness-signaling effect, thus making revolution on the whole a less likely outcome. The appropriate Tocquevillian response is that concessions may inflame the masses rather than calm them.

disorder of the public sector generated frustration in the increasing
number of individuals that had to deal with it:

In 1789 the state owed nearly 600 million to its creditors, nearly all of whom
were debtors themselves and who, as one financier said at the time, found in
their grievances against the government partners in all who suffered as they
did from the fecklessness of the state. As the number of malcontents of this
sort grew, moreover, so did their irritation, because the urge to speculate,
the passion to get rich, and the taste for comfort spread along with the
growth of business and made such evils seem unbearable to the very same
people who, thirty years earlier, would have endured them without complaint.
(*Ibid.*)[24]

Tocqueville claimed that the diachronic paradox arose with regard
to *three grievances*: liberty, money, and equality: "Men had developed
to the point where they had a clearer sense of what they lacked and
suffered more from it, even though the sum total of their suffering was
much smaller than before. Their sensitivity had grown far faster than
their relief.[25] This was true of the want of liberty and equality as well
as the want of money" (*O III*, p. 1073). So far I have dealt with the
paradoxes of liberty and money. The abolition of some abuses creates
more resentment, not less; increased prosperity generates more discontent, not less. Applying the logic of the paradox to the third grievance,
equality, we would expect him to assert that as society advances toward
equality, the greater is the discontent caused by inequality. As we saw in
Chapter 7, there are two ways of understanding this idea. In *DA* a central claim is that increased equality in one dimension causes inequality
in that dimension to appear as more and more intolerable. In addition,
there is the idea of *status inconsistency*, according to which increased
equality in one dimension causes inequality *in other dimensions* to

---

[24] This analysis of the relation between the individual investor or entrepreneur and the
state has some similarity with Tocqueville's discussion of the relation between the
peasant and his lord. The hatred of the peasant toward the lord and the irritation of
the entrepreneurs and financiers with the bureaucracy are generated by the frustrating
interaction with these authorities, rather than by the objective burden the latter
imposes on them.

[25] As an objection to a common interpretation of Tocqueville's theory of revolution (see
Ch. 5), it may be worthwhile noting that he is not here asserting that people's
expectations grew faster than their relief, only their *sensitivity*; see also the passage
from *AR*, p. 202, cited in the text.

appear as more and more intolerable. If status barriers to occupational choice remain constant or even become more rigid (as suggested in *O III*, p. 1110) while economic conditions are becoming more equal, rich commoners will feel increasingly frustrated.

Chapter v of Book III does not address the "Tocqueville paradox" as usually understood, but another paradoxical effect of the initiatives of the old regime. In that chapter, he discusses preemptive measures to alleviate the misery of the people in the years immediately before the Revolution. However wise the measures themselves may have been, the wisdom of the way they were proposed was highly questionable. The privileged classes publicly stated their own responsibility for the plight of the peasantry, as if their intention was to create disturbances rather than to prevent them: "This was to inflame each and every individual by enumerating his woes and pointing a finger of blame at those responsible, thereby emboldening the victims by revealing the small number of authors of their woes, piercing their hearts to the quick, and setting them aflame with greed, envy, and hatred" (*AR*, p. 210). Adding insult to the perception of injury, they also used contemptuous language when referring to the individuals they intended to help, as if the latter were unable to understand what they were saying (see the passage from *AR*, pp. 208–9, cited in Ch. 4). The precipitants of the Revolution included proactive no less than reactive attempts to improve the situation of the population.

TRIGGERS

Whether Tocqueville really pulled off the trick announced in the title of the final chapter of *AR* – "Comment la Révolution est sortie d'elle-même de ce qui précède" – is debatable. Maybe an argument could be made that given the preconditions and precipitants outlined in Books II and III, it would take so little to trigger the Revolution that by the laws of probability it was morally certain to occur. Tocqueville did not, however, want to limit himself to this kind of structuralist explanation. In the second volume, he intended to go beyond the argument that the revolution *had to* happen, in one way or another, to spell out the way in which it *did* happen. In the notes for the second volume of *AR*, Tocqueville covers events from the first *assemblée des notables* in 1787 to the end of

1789, with brief remarks on the summer of 1790. The tantalizing fragments offer elements of an explanation, but no "idée-mère."

In the French prerevolution (1787–88), two institutions from the
ancien régime played an important role in exposing the frailty of the
administration, the *assemblée des notables* and the *parlements*.[26] Even
when the government proposed measures that were in the interest of
the country, the people supported those who refused to ratify them. The
notables in the first assembly were applauded when they opposed
Calonne's proposal to abolish the corvée, tax exemption for the nobles
and internal tariffs: "All these measures were consistent with the spirit
of the time. All were opposed or delayed by notables. Yet it was the
government that was unpopular and the notables who had public opinion in their favor" (O III, p. 469). When in 1787 the king granted a very
democratic organization of the provincial assembly in the Dauphiné,
the regional parlement that refused to endorse it was glorified rather
than vilified by the people:

*Despite this huge concession, the king and ministers who made it were wildly
unpopular, while the Parlement, which opposed it, enjoyed the fanatical support of the people.* No less noteworthy is the fact that the minister who made . . .
this huge concession, which could not fail in short order to make the Third
Estate the absolute master of affairs, was execrated by the people, while the
Parlement, which opposed enforcing a law that was so democratic for the time,
received the people's fanatical ovation. (O III, p. 507; italics in original)

Tocqueville drew the conclusion that in politics, the approval or
disapproval of a proposer causes approval or disapproval of his
proposals rather than the other way around:

[I]n politics it is always wrong to judge the impression that a measure will
produce by its intrinsic value, whether for good or for ill. Its influence depends
primarily on the circumstances in which it is put forward and above all on
the person with whom it originates. That is why politics cannot be a science or
even an art. In politics one finds no fixed rules, not even the rule that in order to
please people one must do what they consider useful. When circumstances
conspire to make a government popular, one willingly suffers ill at its hands.
When it is unpopular, even its good deeds are painful. (O III, p. 1136)

---

[26] Egret (1962) is a superb study.

The idea may seem paradoxical, yet in this particular case at least it seems uncontroversially true.[27] It is related to the idea of the second-best: people may approve of an institution that by itself is harmful if it also has the effect of counteracting another that is perceived as even more dangerous. Once it ceases to have the latter effect, its popularity may crumble overnight, as was indeed the fate of the parlements after 1789 (*O III*, p. 490).

Among the triggers of the revolution, Tocqueville emphasized the enormous importance of events in the Dauphiné. As just noted, until it was squashed by the parlement, the proposed assembly of 1787 had an unusually democratic form. A year later, the immensely influential assembly in Vizille achieved an unprecedented unity of action among the three orders: "The assembly of Vizille was in a sense a material and visible sign to all that this new union had taken place and showed what effects it might have. This was the last time that an event in a remote corner of a tiny province in the Alps proved decisive for all of France. It brought to the attention of all what had been visible to only a few, showed everyone where power lay, and thus decided the victory in an instant" (*O III*, p. 484).[28]

An effect (or a sign) of their unity was the adoption of the system of "cross-voting" in electing deputies to the Estates-General.[29] In this system, deputies for a given order were chosen jointly by members of all three orders, just as once the Estates were assembled, the Third Estate demanded that the credentials of deputies from a given order be verified jointly by the three orders. Tocqueville asserts that the Estates-General might have found it easier to agree if this electoral system had been universally adopted: "If the vote in common had to be adopted, it is unfortunate that what was done in Dauphiné was not done everywhere, because there the deputies of all three orders were chosen by all three orders, and this might have favored an accord" (*O III*, p. 531). Elsewhere he notes that in *Qu'est-ce que le tiers état?*, Sieyès "*rejected the idea of having the orders elected by everyone. This idea, which was applied in the Dauphiné and which might be regarded*

---

[27] In addition to Egret (1962), one may cite the following rhetorical question from Droz (1860), vol. II, p. 10: "How did [the parlements] win popularity through actions that harmed popular interests?"

[28] The last sentence, not in the O edition, is taken from *AR II*, p. 78.

[29] For a description of the system and its effects, see Ch. 10 of Elster (2009).

as an acceptable bargain (*transaction*) that would inevitably lead quickly to an amalgamation of the entire nation in one common mass, was deliberately rejected by Sieyès" (*O III*, p. 541; italics in original).

The spearheading effect of the Dauphiné, although important, was blunted by the non-adoption of cross-voting in almost all other electoral districts. The explanation may lie in the fact that "In Dauphiné, the *taille* was real and not personal. Hence nobles were not as much at war with the Third Estate over this issue as they were in many other places and did not have to concede equality on as many points."[30] Cross-voting was less likely to be adopted where the *taille* was personal, as it was in most of France.

One reason the Revolution succeeded was indeed that the privileged classes did not begin to cooperate until it was too late. The *cahiers de doléance* display prominently what has been called "suicidal elite fragmentation."[31] After citing complaints by the clergy over the trespassing of the lords on the property of their tenants, Tocqueville adds that "several other cahiers [of the clergy were written] in the same spirit and with the same bitterness of peasants become curés. Later on we will see the clergy come in for similarly strong abuse from the nobility. The two orders had yet to learn to make common cause" (*O III*, p. 424). In his notes to himself, Tocqueville wrote that "When I come to the era of class warfare, show clearly how dizzying the disintegration was. It was not just the bourgeoisie that made war on the nobility but the lesser nobility that attacked the greater, the lower clergy the higher . . . until the Revolution simplified the division and established harmony among the various occupants of the same social compartment" (*O III*, p. 1147). Whereas previously the conflicts within and between the privileged orders had benefited the government, they now became so virulent as to bring it down: "Nothing serves more to . . . fuel despotism [than] the hatred [and] jealousy of the various classes. But with the proviso [that] this hatred and envy are nothing more than a bitter and tranquil emotion, just enough to prevent people from helping one another but not enough to spur them to fight. There is no

[30] This comment, not in the O edition, is taken from Tocqueville, *AR II*, p. 74. Real *taille* was assessed on property, personal *taille* on income. When the *taille* was real, both nobles and bourgeois could benefit from tax exemptions, depending on the status of the property in question.
[31] Shapiro and Markoff (1998), p. 284.

government that will not collapse once violent clashes between the classes have begun" (*O III*, p. 497).

Tocqueville is somewhat inconsistent in his treatment of the tension between the upper and lower clergy. He asserts that Necker's report to the king of December 27, 1788, was intended to create a split between the bishops and the parish priests, but adds that in the light of their later reunion the decision did not matter: "[T]his text also shows clearly that the electoral law promulgated in the wake of this report was deliberately designed to make curés the principal representatives of the clergy and to set off a disruptive internal battle between the bishops and their flock [*sic*]. This had no great consequences because the attacks on the clergy in general soon tightened this body's internal bonds" (*O III*, p. 546). Elsewhere he recognizes, however, the decisive role of the lower clergy in the struggle over the verification of credentials,[32] well before the reunion forged by the abolition of the tithe, the confiscation of the church goods, and the civil constitution of the clergy.

On the basis of the correspondence of the deputies from Anjou to their constituency, Tocqueville asserts that well before the meeting of the Estates-General, the bourgeoisie had formed a plan of action that anticipated what eventually took place:

The Tennis Court Oath in everyone's mind and anticipated six weeks before it took place. As early as May 9, the deputies of Anjou informed their principals that for a few days they would use "all means of conciliation capable of uniting the privileged orders with the Third, and after these means have been exhausted, we will constitute ourselves as a National Assembly." Thus it was not the heat of battle that drove the representatives beyond the point they wished to go. They intended beforehand to reach that point, and everybody [*sic*] was aware of it. (*O III*, p. 563, italics in the original)

This statement is clearly intended to refute the commonly held view that the six-week interval between the meeting of the Estates-General and their self-transformation into the National Assembly was crucial for that metamorphosis to occur. Apart from the fact that

---

[32] "Arrival of three curés from Poitou seeking authentication of their credentials. Speaking for the group, one said, 'We come, preceded by the torch of reason and guided by love of the public good, to take our places alongside our fellow citizens.' (Obviously these curés were more of their age than of their church.) Greeted with applause. This was the stone falling from the vault above" (*O III*, p. 567).

Tocqueville's very general claim can hardly be supported by this single source, it does not fit with his observation that as late as March 1789, "We find Mounier devoting a chapter to combating the fears of those who believed that even with the doubling of the Third and voting by head, the nobility and clergy would still dominate the assembly" (*O III*, p.550). In other words, Mounier took seriously the idea that even with double representation and vote by head, the privileged classes might well dominate the Third Estate. Had it not been for the six weeks of isolated deliberation that allowed the Third Estate to consolidate itself, the old habits of deference might very well have prevailed.

Tocqueville is eloquent on the disastrous consequences of the consolidation of the three estates in a single chamber. According to the "monarchiens," notably Mounier and Clermont-Tonnerre, a unicameral constituent assembly was necessary to make a clean break with the past.[33] Looking forward, they argued that it was also necessary to create something like the British system they admired. According to Clermont-Tonnerre, the "three-headed hydra" – king, first chamber, and second chamber – that the constitution should create could not itself create a constitution.[34]

Citing Mounier, Tocqueville chides him for his naïveté:

As if the unicameral assembly, whose dangers as a legislative body he demonstrates so clearly, would not be even more dangerous as a constituent body. It is true that only the violence of a single chamber, under the sway of a single passion, could operate reforms as radical and as destructive of the nobility and the clergy as everybody desired, even Mounier. The mistake was to imagine that in acting so rapidly, doing everything at the same time, dispensing with time and not respecting any established institutions, the very force that had helped you achieve all these things would not be your master, and that such changes could take place merely by discussion. (*O III*, pp. 607–8)[35]

---

[33] "Anarchy is a frightening but necessary transitional stage; the only moment in which a new order of things can be created. It is not in calm times that one can take uniform measures" (*AP*, vol. 9, p. 461, Clermont-Tonnerre).

[34] *AP*, vol. 8, p. 574.

[35] Elsewhere (*O III*, p. 549) he accuses Mounier of ignoring the fact that a unicameral assembly, while "excellent to make a revolution is not suited to stop it at will."

The idea of "being the absolute master for a certain period and thereafter admitting counterweights" (*O III*, p. 544) reflected the lack of practical political experience of the revolutionaries (*O III*, p. 549). As further discussed below, it amounted to an implausible belief in the possibility of *fine-tuning the revolution.*

Tocqueville also offers another explanation for the irresistibility of the popular movement that carried the Revolution, based on a purported psychological impossibility. He claims that one cannot at one and the same time be courageous against despotism and against anarchy. Having successfully resisted the king, the *constituante* could not also stand up to the people of Paris:

> Every assembly is obedient to the thought surrounding its creation. The Constituent Assembly of '89 was dispatched to fight aristocracy and despotism, and it was quite vigorous in opposing those enemies but [not] in opposing anarchy, which it was not prepared to combat. . . . It is rare for a man and almost impossible for an assembly to have the ability to alternately make violent efforts in two opposite directions. The energy that launched it violently in one direction impeded its progress in the other."(*O III*, p. 610; see also p. 604)

As Tocqueville notes, individuals may indeed be able to fight on two fronts. Elsewhere he observes that his maternal great-grandfather Malesherbes had defended Louis XVI against the people *and* the people against Louis XVI.[36] He might equally have cited Clermont-Tonnerre's words to the assembly on August 31, 1789: "You did not wish to obey armed despotism; will you now obey popular turmoil?"[37] Yet, he implies, the dynamics of an assembly makes it "almost impossible" to maintain a consistent attitude in the face of changing dangers.[38] Whether or not this idea can be defended as a generalization, it is clear

---

[36] Mélonio (1993), p. 9.

[37] *AP*, vol. 8, p. 513.

[38] Elsewhere he takes a moralizing attitude: qualifying the failure of the assembly in July 1789 to adopt Lally-Tolendal's resolution condemning popular violence as "the Constituent Assembly's greatest blunder, or one might say, its great crime," he adds that "from that day forward, it was destined to obey and not to command; the people of Paris became the sovereign. Power had passed briefly to the Assembly only to end with the people. . . . If [per impossibile!] it had sensed its power and influence, it would have stood up to both the monarchy and the people and retained leadership of the Revolution in its own hands" (*O III*, p. 576).

that the French revolutionaries of 1789 were indeed the victims of their own rhetoric.

1848: THE LAW OF UNINTENDED CONSEQUENCES

The *Recollections* is an amazing combination of narrative, first-person observations, character portraits, and political psychology. There is nothing else quite like them. They contain many observations worthy of discussion, but most of them are in the nature of scattered aperçus, rather than embedded in an overall theoretical framework. I shall limit myself to a few comments that bring out Tocqueville's ironic approach to politics as sound and fury, in which the most important consequences of action always turn out to be the unintended ones. *AR* also embodies this approach in the argument that the king made a mistake in offering a poisoned gift to the nobles and the nobles a mistake in accepting it. These were, however, processes that worked themselves out over centuries. In the analysis of the 1848 revolution, the time span is of the order of months or days, which enables us to nail down more precisely how the calculations came to naught.

Tocqueville had a mixed record of predictions. Most of the ones he makes in *DA* were either commonplace at the time, were so heavily hedged with conditions as to be empty, or turned out to be false.[39] One prediction that did come true, and in which he took justified pride, was his urgent warnings in a note from October 1847 and in a speech in parliament from January 1848, claiming that a socialist revolution was imminent. In the *Recollections*, he adds that while he "did see clearer than the next man the general causes that tilted the July monarchy towards its ruin," he "did not see the accidents that were to topple it over" (*R*, p. 17). The general causes were as follows:

The industrial revolution which . . . had brought in a flood of labourers now out of work . . . ; the passion for material pleasures, which, spurred on by the government, was getting a firmer and firmer hold over the whole of this

---

[39] His best effort was to predict that "within the next hundred years, I believe that the territory occupied or claimed by the United States will be filled with more than a hundred million people and divided into forty states" (*DA*, p. 436). The actual numbers are 123 million people and forty-eight states. He spoiled his record, however, by adding that the existence of these "forty distinct nations of unequal strength, would make the survival of the federal government no more than a lucky accident" (*ibid.*).

multitude, the democratic disease of envy silently at work; economic and political theories which . . . tended to encourage the belief that human wretchedness was due to the laws and not to providence and that poverty could be abolished by changing the system of society; the contempt felt for the ruling classes, especially its leaders – a contempt so deep and general that it paralyzed the resistance even of those who stood to lose most by the overthrow of authority; the centralization, thanks to which control of Paris . . . was all that was needed to complete a revolution; and lastly, the mobility of everything – institutions, ideas, mores and men – in a society on the move. (*R*, pp. 62–63)

Rather than reproducing his list of accidental causes, I shall present the analytic skeleton of the narrative. It is a story about the unintended and irreversible consequences of decisions taken largely under the sway of emotion. An important background fact is the existence of a law limiting the right to public assembly. As Tocqueville might have said, this was an unstable halfway house. Just as one can get around laws limiting freedom of the press by using indirect means (*DA*, p. 208), the opposition got around the law by organizing *banquets* that, while officially just dinners, were highly political. These banquets began in the countryside and were expected to culminate in Paris on February 22, 1848. They were, however, getting out of hand and the leaders of the opposition worried about the agitation they caused: "Certainly the decision to hold the final banquet was against their wishes; they were associated with it only under constraint, because the matter was already in progress and, especially, because their vanity was compromised" (*R*, p. 21). Under the influence of vanity, people may prefer to stick to an earlier decision even when it would be in their interest to cut their losses and give it up (see Ch. 4). Moreover, the actions of the government fueled the emotion: "by its defiance [it] pushed the opposition into this dangerous proceeding, hoping to lead it to destruction. Bravado and unwillingness to retreat carried the opposition forward, with the government urging and goading it on" (*ibid.*).

The fine grain of the story requires us to distinguish between the moderate and the radical opposition. The moderate opposition was "led by the heat of the argument to assert that the right of assembly at the banquets was one of the most assured and necessary of rights" (*R*, p. 24). As the government denied the existence of this right but was reluctant to use force to prevent the banquets, "it was tacitly agreed that the opposition should hold one last banquet, and that the authorities, without preventing its assembly, should prosecute the sponsors in the Courts, leaving them to decide" (R, p. 26). At this point the radical, mainly extraparliamentary opposition took the lead by publishing a program for the banquet that one "might have taken . . . for a decree of the Provisional Government, which was formed three days later" (R, pp. 26–27). As a result, the government "felt justified in changing course and officially announced that it forbade the banquet and would prevent it by force" (R, p. 27).

The subsequent events were driven by jockeying for position among the leaders of the opposition. The moderate Odilon Barrot, who was critical of the program, feared to offend those who until then had been his allies, yet "finding himself faced by civil war, retreated" (R, p. 27). To square the circle, "He withdrew from the dangerous demonstration; but while making this concession to moderate opinion, he allowed the extremists to impeach the Ministers. He accused the latter of violating the Constitution by forbidding the banquet, thus providing an excuse for those who were ready to take up arms in defense of the violated Constitution" (ibid.). This move triggered a chain reaction that culminated in the revolution of February 22:

Consequently the leaders of the radical party, who considered a revolution premature and did not want one yet, felt obliged, in order to make some distinction between themselves and their allies of the [moderate] opposition, to speak in revolutionary terms at the banquets and fan the flames of insurrection. The [moderate] opposition on its part, though it wanted no more banquets, was also forced to follow this unfortunate path in order not to appear to retreat before the government's threats. Finally, the mass of Conservatives, who thought that great concessions must be made and were ready to make them, were led by the violence of their adversaries and the passions of some of their leaders to deny even the right to assemble at private banquets. (R, pp. 27–28)

The effects of the successive decisions were *unintended*, since the actors did not consider how their actions might trigger other actors to take up more extreme positions, and *irreversible*, because their vanity would not allow them to retreat. Even the radicals did not welcome their triumph, "because, having a close view of their allies and knowing them well, they were afraid at this decisive moment of the victory, of what they would owe to them" (R, p. 24).

This theme – the fear of success, or the dangers of success – is a pervasive one in the *Recollections*.[40] In three separate arguments, Tocqueville asserts that an incomplete and partial success may be preferable to a total victory. Inverting the phrase that "We should have perished, had we not been so near to perishing" (R, p. 144), he asserts that "We would have been much stronger if we had been less successful" (R, p. 214), the reason being that "after victory one begins to have trouble with oneself, one's slackness, one's pride, and the rash security born of success" (*ibid.*).

A second example of this pattern occurs in the chapter on his tenure as foreign minister:

It was nothing but fear of the revolution that had driven the German princes into Frederick William's arms; as soon as, thanks to the Prussians, the revolution, suppressed everywhere, no longer made them afraid, the allies, whom one might almost call the new subjects of Prussia, aspired to regain their independence. The King of Prussia's enterprise was of the unhappy sort in which success itself makes ultimate triumph harder, and, comparing great things to small, his position was a little like our own, for, like us, he was fated to fail when he had re-established order and because he had re-established it. (R, p. 248)

Here, the dangers of too complete success do not stem from its impact on one's character, but from the desertion of one's allies. Hence, the position of Frederick William was indeed only "a little bit like" that of Tocqueville's.

In these two cases, the winners were not farsighted enough to pull their punches in order to retain the leverage that a residual danger would give them. In the third case, Tocqueville claimed that the poet-politician Lamartine attempted precisely this kind of fine-tuning: "He was ... striving to dominate the Mountain without overthrowing it and to damp down without quenching the revolutionary fires, so that the country would bless him for providing security, but would not feel safe enough to forget about him" (R, p. 110). Although Tocqueville claims that this was "the tortuous path that was ... soon to lead to his ruin"

---

[40] The following draws on an unpublished article on the *Recollections* by Stephen Holmes, "Saved by danger/destroyed by success," which also inspired my observations in Ch. 4 on the energizing effects of danger.

(*ibid.*), he adds that "it is possible that Lamartine's subterfuge and semi-connivance with the enemy, although they ruined him, saved us" (*R*, p. 112).

In his notes for the second volume of *AR* written a few years later, Tocqueville refers to another attempt at fine-tuning the strategy of revolution. He cites a letter written in July 1789 from the deputies from Anjou to their constituents, saying that "we must temper the movement of the violent passions without smothering a salutary fermentation," as an illustration of his claim that "the national assembly wanted to limit the fire and was afraid of extinguishing it" (*O III*, p. 575).[41] This balancing act, too, failed. Politicians are subject to the law of unintended consequences if they treat a revolutionary crowd as a force that can be turned on or off at will.

---

[41] It is useful to juxtapose the two French texts. The goal of Lamartine was to "dominer les Montagnards sans les abattre, et de ralentir le feu révolutionnaire sans l'éteindre." The assembly of 1789 "voulait circonscrire l'incendie et craignait d'éteindre le feu." The close verbal similarity suggests (but does not prove) that he had Lamartine in mind when writing about the 1789 assembly. Note also the affinity with the text by Marx cited in the Introduction.

Conclusion

In conclusion, I first want to make some general observations on the nature of Tocqueville's intellectual enterprise and then address some questions that arise from the – predictably controversial – title of the present work.

The methodology of social science is often characterized in terms of the relation between the micro-level and the macro-level. In some versions, this is a one-way relationship. In Thomas Schelling's wonderful *Micromotives and Macrobehavior,* the analysis moves from individual choices to their – often unintended – aggregate effects. Schelling does not deny that there is a reverse effect; he simply does not study it. In other versions, there is a one-way process in the opposite direction. In what has been called "the oversocialized conception of man," the motives and even actions of individuals are entirely shaped by their environment. Durkheim is perhaps the clearest exponent of this view. In *Le suicide* for example, he argued that in some societies the individual is so weak that "society can force some of its members to kill themselves."[1] The reverse effect is, implicitly, denied.

A complete analysis would have to take account of the obvious fact of two-way interactions. Many economic analyses do exactly that: prices (macro-facts) cause producers to make decentralized decisions about how much to produce in the next period (micro-facts) that, when

---

[1] Durkheim (1960), p. 237.

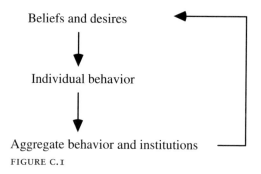

FIGURE C.I

aggregated, cause a new set of prices (macro-facts). These analyses are still incomplete, however, since they take the objectives (desires, preferences) of the agents as given. Perhaps the economist would answer that in competitive markets agents who do not maximize profits are eliminated, so that we can take it for granted that they will have this objective. Although I do not accept that rejoinder, the more important question is whether, assuming it to be true in this particular case, it can be generalized. It seems clear to me that it cannot. Values and social norms do not exist for efficiency reasons.[2]

Figure C.I presents a minimal model of two-way interaction. It leaves out emotions, the impact of desires on other desires (e.g., through the spillover effect) and on beliefs (through wishful thinking), and the impact of behavior on beliefs and desires (through the reduction of cognitive dissonance). It is mainly intended to embody the fact that the feedback from macro to micro does not shape behavior directly, as Durkheim thought, but only the mental states of the agents, leaving room for choice and change. It follows, I believe, that there is *no reason to expect this feedback process to represent a social equilibrium.* The desires and beliefs that shape the actions that determine aggregate outcomes are not necessarily the same as the desires and the beliefs that appear at the end of the process.

To pursue that issue, consider the more Tocquevillian Figure C.2, with opportunities substituted for beliefs. For the sake of simplicity, it ignores direct desire-opportunity interactions as well as the role of

---

[2] Elster (2007a).

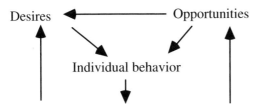

FIGURE C.2

capacities. In spite of these simplifications, the figure brings out the abstract logic of many Tocquevillian ideas.

In *AR*, Tocqueville describes a process of secular change in which the actors continuously make choices that modify the motives and the opportunities they will have some years later. In a stylized fashion, going somewhat beyond the text itself, the process could work as follows. At time 1, the king transfers part of the village administration from the seigneur to the Intendant. At time 2, the ties of the lord to the community are loosened, and the lure of the court enhanced. At time 3, as he spends more time at the court, the Intendant takes on more functions and the opportunities of the lord shrink accordingly. At time 4, life at the court has also eliminated any desire to take part in the government of the village. The transformation from seigneur to courtier is complete. A seigneur fallen in disgrace at the court will now complain of being "in exile on my estate" (*AR*, p. 163).

In *DA*, by contrast, the feedback does serve to maintain a social equilibrium. Envy – reinforced by conformism – is both the effect of equality and a factor that maintains it. It is a homeostatic mechanism. Political institutions, too, are part of this feedback process. One effect of equality is that it so degrades political life that outstanding individuals will not stand for office, thus denying citizens the opportunity to elect them and thereby perpetuating the degraded state. The role of religion also fits this model. Without religion, the citizens of a democracy would exploit many of the opportunities for disorderly behavior that democracy permits. As a result, the system would be destabilized and perhaps break down. However, in the presence of free institutions, citizens spontaneously adopt religion for their peace of mind, and thereby inadvertently stabilize the institutions as well. Social mobility has a similar stabilizing effect. On the one hand, it is part of the aggregate pattern of behavior that results from individual risk-taking and money-making. On the other hand, the weakening of classes that results from high mobility rates also leads to an attenuation of conflict and of the threat to the institutions. Finally, high rates of social mobility and risk-loving attitudes mutually reinforce one another. To use Marc Bloch's phrase in another brilliant work on social equilibrium (in medieval agriculture), Tocqueville's democracy constitutes "un admirable engrenage," a set of wonderfully interlocking parts.[3]

For contemporary readers, the question is not whether to accept or reject Tocqueville's specific analyses of the breakdown of the ancien régime, the self-perpetuation of democracy (in the United States), or its transformation into a tutelary despotism (in France). We can probably learn more about actual societies from *AR* than from *DA,* but that has not been my focus here. Instead I have tried both to bring out the individual mechanisms that embody the various arrows in Figure C.2 and – more importantly – to illustrate the value of the project as a whole. Even if the spillover effect turns out to be a marginal phenomenon or envy to be less important than Tocqueville thought it was, his work can still remain as an inspiration. It is important to understand what it would be an inspiration *for*: not for the construction of a general theory of the kind proposed by Talcott Parsons and his followers, but for the fine-grained analysis of a given society or regime.

Tocqueville's work is also exemplary because of the many, interconnected ways he considers the role of *time* in social life, taking account both of objective time as viewed by the observer and subjective time as experienced by the agents. Adopting this double perspective, he contrasted short-term and long-term effects of actions. For explanatory purposes, only subjective time counts. For the purpose of assessing the efficiency of a regime, objective time also matters, in that it allows us to identify opportunities that were missed because of motivational or cognitive flaws in the attitudes of the citizens toward the future.

More specifically, the fact that democratic citizens are in a hurry, "on the move" as Tocqueville says, has a number of implications. Because tastes and technology change in unpredictable ways, long-term investments often make little sense. Even when the consequences of an

---

[3] Bloch (1999), p. 99.

individual's choice are mainly under his own control, he does not have the time to form high-quality beliefs about them. Because democratic citizens have neither the time nor the capacity to anticipate the long-term consequences of alternative political choices, their votes will also be uninformed. The high turnover rate of politicians is an obstacle to the *learning* that might have been a remedy to this problem. The instability of the laws adds to the uncertainty of the economic environment, with the effect of truncating the time horizon of the citizens even more.

In the final analysis, *dynamic social mobility* and *high turnover of politicians* may be the most powerful explanatory features of democracies. A high rate of metabolism explains more and more important things than equality in the literal or static sense. Besides, as I noted, static equality is incompatible with dynamic equality. Unless citizens move in lockstep up and down the economic ladder – hardly a coherent idea – mobility will always generate inequality. If envy were as important as Tocqueville sometimes claims, it would have exercised a chilling effect on any attempt to break out and move up. "Whom do you take yourself for?" "Don't stick your neck out." These perennial expressions of small village mentalities are not consistent with a society in which *change is the norm.*

Tocqueville also identified what we might call the *benefits of myopia.* A short time horizon in itself is not conducive to progress, but the cause of myopia is. The restless energy in the political and the economic domains compensates for the shortsighted and ill-informed nature of the decisions that are made. Although – or because! – democratic citizens are "constantly changing course for fear of missing the shortest road to happiness" (*DA,* p. 626), they will, in the long run, be happier.

Throughout the two major works, Tocqueville was intensely preoccupied with the relations between equality and liberty. (Fraternity is not in his lexicon.) While often suggestive, his analyses are also elusive to a degree that explains why it is hard to grant him the stature of a great political theorist. The elusiveness has several sources. First, there is the pervasive confusion between static and dynamic equality. The idea of sacrificing liberty to equality makes little sense if equality is taken in its dynamic meaning; one might even argue that dynamic equality presupposes liberty. Second, Tocqueville leaves the reader in constant confusion as to which country he is referring to – equality-cum-liberty in America or equality below the despot in France under the two Napoleons. Occasionally, he even refers to China in order to bring out the nature of democracy.

There is also the British example of a liberal aristocracy that he clearly admired in many respects. We observe a clear evolution in Tocqueville's view about England from *DA* to *AR*. In the latter work, he praises England in phrases that are very close to those he used twenty years before about America, arguing that the vigor of British political life and the prosperity it imparts to society more than compensate for the bizarre imperfections of its administrative machinery (*AR*, p. 175). In the earlier work (*DA*, p. 661), he describes obstacles to upward mobility in England in words that are close to what he says about France in the later work. In *AR*, by contrast, he contrasts the openness of the British aristocracy with the caste-like character of the French nobility (*AR*, pp. 82–83). Reading this work, it is hard to avoid the impression that in England he had finally found a society that offered a viable compromise between his aristocratic values and his democratic ideas. This is not quite the same as an optimal compromise of equality and liberty.

The one political idea I want to retain as both clear and profound is the proposition that the material benefits of liberty are essentially by-products. To achieve them, one has to love liberty for its own sake. By definition, however, this observation has no practical implications. One cannot decide to love liberty for its own sake any more than one can decide to fall in love with a person. The love of liberty is a *character trait* that Tocqueville was immensely proud to possess, perhaps because it made him part of an aristocracy of the mind, but it has no *institutional* expression.

The title of the present work suggests several questions:

- Was Tocqueville a social scientist in our sense of the term?
- If he was a social scientist, was he the first one?
- If he was a social scientist, was he a good one?
- Should social scientists read Tocqueville today?

I hope that by now the reader will agree that his insights into causal mechanisms qualify Tocqueville as a social scientist. The question whether he was the first one is largely undecidable, since it turns on exactly how inclusively we understand that term. One might argue, for instance, that by virtue of his formulation of the Jury Theorem and his discovery of the Paradox of Voting, Condorcet should count as the first social scientist. While I would be prepared to say that he was the first to offer deductive models of social interaction, I view causal explanation as the more central part of social science. Although causal analysis may need deductive models to draw out the implications of the assumptions, they are, in my view, merely handmaidens to explanation. In the work of Condorcet, the deductive models were not harnessed to explanation. While the Jury Theorem may be understood as supporting democracy and the Paradox of Voting as undermining it, neither was intended to offer a causal account of existing democratic institutions.

In the Introduction, I cited Montesquieu, Hume, Adam Smith, and Bentham as other candidates for the distinction of being "the first social scientist." Once again, by understanding the idea of a social science in a sufficiently large sense, a good case could be made for any of these. Yet, as I also said, if we emphasize the criterion of *exportable causal mechanisms,* I think Tocqueville's claim is the stronger one. Now, a victory that occurs by means of a stipulative definition, however persuasive, is of course somewhat hollow. A more substantive question, therefore, is whether Tocqueville was a *good* social scientist. Responding to the comment of a reader who accused me of neglecting Whitehead's dictum that "A science that hesitates to forget its founder is lost," I shall also ask whether he still has something to teach us today.

One of the surprising experiences I had when writing this book was to discover how close Tocqueville came to formulating (but not to formalizing) basic insights of game theory. As I have observed a number of times, he was very much aware of the free-rider obstacle to collective action and of the fact that it is sometimes neutralized, sometimes not. As he notes, free-riding can be overcome by selective incentives (as in the American practice of rewarding informers), by social norms (as in the French practice of ostracizing nobles who engaged in trade), or by iterated interaction (as in the "convention" of mutual help in America). By contrast, because each firm seeks the help of the state while preferring it to remain passive with regard to other firms, "the sphere of the central power imperceptibly expands in every direction, even though each [man] wishes to restrict it" (*DA,* p. 794 n. 1).

As I believe I have shown, Tocqueville also identified the structure of an Assurance Game, which differs from the standard collective-action problem in that each agent prefers universal cooperation to free-riding. In fact, his pioneering analysis of pluralistic ignorance applies directly to this problem, suggesting a link between game theory and psychology that nobody (to my knowledge) has yet pointed out. If each individual has Assurance-Game preferences while falsely believing that others have Prisoner's-Dilemma preferences, they will all act in ways confirming that false belief.[4] These achievements count as social science of a high order. Although not as explicit as comparable statements by Hume, Tocqueville's analyses are, in my view, both deeper and broader in their implications.

Following Kenneth Arrow, we may view the problem of preference formation as an unsolved enigma for the social sciences. As we have seen, Tocqueville made a number of important contributions to that subject. His idea of spillover and compensation mechanisms is, I believe, especially valuable and worthy of further development today. Adding to the dueling example I cited in Chapter 1, let me offer three illustrations to show the fertility of the distinction that are, I believe, in the spirit of Tocqueville.

In his essay "How to profit from one's enemies," Plutarch first observes "that a man is farthest removed from envying the good fortune of his friends or the success of his relatives, if he has acquired the habit of commending his enemies." This is the spillover effect. Shortly after, he notes that "since all human nature bears its crop of contention, jealousy and envy . . . a man would profit in no moderate degree by venting these emotions upon his enemies, and turning the course of such discharges as far away from his associates and relatives." This is the compensation effect.

In an article on the organization of leisure, Harold Wilensky traces what he calls "the compensatory leisure hypothesis" and "the spillover leisure hypothesis" back to Engels's work *The Condition of the Working-Class in England in 1844.*[5] The first states that the worker who is alienated at work compensates by frenetic leisure activities, the second that "he develops a spillover leisure routine in which alienation from work becomes alienation from life."

---

[4] Bernheim (1984).
[5] Wilensky (1960).

In his *Socialist History of the French Revolution*, Jean Jaurès makes an acute comparison between the expected reactions of the French peasantry to the abolition of the tithe (without compensation) in August 1789 and their actual reactions:

Not only did the nobles think that the abolition of the tithe without compensation would increase their income from land, but they believed above all that this immediate satisfaction obtained at the expense of the clergy would make the peasantry less eager to pursue the abolition of the feudal dues: they hoped to divert the storm towards the goods of the church. What a poor calculation! Quite to the contrary, the peasants were all the more unlikely to accept the need for compensation with regard to the feudal dues as they had been dispensed with compensation for the tithe.[6]

The nobles, in other words, expected the compensation effect to operate; instead, one observed a spillover effect caused by the release from adaptive preferences (Ch. 9). These various examples substantiate, I hope, the claim that this pair of mechanisms merits a permanent place in the toolbox of the social scientist.

I also believe that the desire-opportunity-capacity scheme for explaining behavior is in some ways superior to standard choice models, not only by incorporating capacity as an independent variable, but also, and more important, by pointing to the covariation of these three factors. A given political or social system can offer individuals the opportunity to choose in certain ways while at the same blunting their desire to make these choices. Conversely, the system may stimulate the desires while blocking the means of satisfying them. The first effect can prevent social unrest, the second acerbate it. Once again, I believe these ideas are not only valuable but remain underexplored.

To my knowledge, the use of turnover rates in groups as independent variables in the explanation of individual behavior is relatively rare in the social sciences. As I argued in Chapter 7, this is perhaps the most important causal mechanism that Tocqueville deploys in *DA*. The absence or weakness of social norms, of class consciousness, and of class conflict can all be traced back to the high rates of social mobility that characterize American society. The high rate of metabolism of the political and legal system also serves as an important explanatory

[6] Jaurès (1968), p. 469.

variable. In addition to considering these aggregate facts as dependent variables and explaining them in terms of individual psychology, Tocqueville closed the explanatory loop, as I argued earlier, by also analyzing their impact on individual beliefs and motivations.

Tocqueville had an acutely developed sense of *irony in history,* to the point where it can sometimes seem as if irony substitutes for analysis. As I suggested in Chapter 9, in some cases the paradoxical or perverse consequences of institutions or of choices somehow seem to enter into their explanation. Yet his sense of irony also led him to valuable analytical insights. His remarks in the two major works on the *instability of halfway houses* offer both ironical comments on the futile desire to have the best of both worlds and a causal explanation of why it is indeed futile. Similarly, his remarks in the two works on *second-best institutions* – curing one ill by means of another – constitute both an ironical response to naïve wishes for improvement and a causal account of why they are in fact naïve.

As a further observation, let me suggest how Tocqueville can help us sort out puzzles and paradoxes of social causality. Suppose we observe that new pedagogical methods have great effects where they are first introduced but have less of an impact when they are generalized. Tocqueville would have said that new methods attract teachers that are more strongly motivated than the average teacher, but that not everybody can be above average. Or consider the "Hawthorne effect" – the accidental discovery that productivity in a factory increased both when illumination was brightened and when it was dimmed. Tocqueville would have said that these were transitional effects, not equilibrium effects. The same distinction clarifies the puzzling fact that couples who experiment with living together before they marry often find that the good behavior during the "trial period" does not persist afterward. There is, I believe, a *Tocquevillian mind-set* that is consistently helpful in thinking about such issues.

These questions are to some extent the bread and butter of contemporary social scientists when they worry about selection bias, endogeneity, and the like. I do not believe, though, that they have incorporated all of Tocqueville's insights. In the literature on the recent transitions in Eastern Europe, for instance, I have not come across any analyses that take account simultaneously of the distinction between short-term and long-term effects *and* the distinction between transitional effects and equilibrium effects. The Tocquevillian methodology I set out in

Chapter 6 deserves a more central place in contemporary social science than it currently has.

Finally, Tocqueville's writings on the ancien régime and the revolution may constitute the most theoretically informed historical analyses ever written.[7] Among the themes of this work are the "Tocqueville paradox," pluralistic ignorance, the dangers of concession or moderate repression and the superiority of preemptive measures, the causes and the effects of emotions such as envy and hate, and the inevitable and inevitably futile attempt to harness revolutionary forces to partisan ends. These are all exportable causal mechanisms that can serve to justify the title of this book.

[7] Veyne (1976) is the only other contender.

References

Adman, P. (2008), "Does workplace experience enhance political participation?" *Political Behavior* 30, 115–38.

Adorno, T. W., et al. (1950), *The Authoritarian Personality*, New York: Harper.

AP = *Archives Parlementaires. Série I: 1789–1799*, Paris 1875–88.

Aron, R. (1962), *Les étapes de la pensée sociologique*, Paris: Gallimard.

Aronson, E. (2003), *The Social Animal*, New York: Freeman.

Arrow, K. (1971), "Political and economic evaluation of social effects and externalities," in **M. Intriligator** (ed.), *Frontiers of quantitative economics*, pp. 3–25, Amsterdam: North-Holland.

Arrow, K. (2006), "Questions about a paradox," in **B. Weingast** and **D. Wittman** (eds.), *The Oxford Handbook of Political Economy*, Oxford University Press, pp. 971–79.

Banfield, E. (1958), *The Moral Basis of a Backward Society*, New York: The Free Press.

Bernheim, D. (1984), "Rationalizable strategic behavior," *Econometrica* 52, 1007–28.

Billacois, F. (1990), *The Duel*, New Haven, Conn.: Yale University Press.

Bloch M. (1961), *Les rois thaumaturges*, Paris: Armand Colin.

Bloch, M. (1999), *Les caractères originaux de l'histoire rurale française*, Paris: Armand Colin.

Boudon, R. (1986), "The logic of relative frustration," in **J. Elster** (ed.), *Rational Choice*, Oxford: Blackwell, pp. 171–96.

Bryce, J. (1901), "The constitution of the United States as seen in the past," in his *Studies in History and Jurisprudence*, **vol.** 1, Oxford University Press.

Camerer, C. (2003), *Behavioral Game Theory*, New York: Russell Sage.

Caplan, B. (2007), *The Myth of the Rational Voter*, Princeton University Press.

Carrère d'Encausse, H. (2008), *Alexandre II*, Paris: Fayard.

Chapman, G. (1996), "Temporal discounting and utility for health and money," *Journal of Experimental Psychology: Learning, Memory, and Cognition* 22, 771–91.

Cooray, L. J. M. (1979), *Conventions: The Australian Constitution and the Future*, Sydney: Legal Books.

Cukierman, A. (1992), *Central Bank Strategy, Credibility, and Independence: Theory and Evidence*, Cambridge, Mass.: M.I.T. Press.

Descartes, R. (1978), *Descartes: His Moral Philosophy and Psychology*, tr. J. Blom, Hassocks, Sussex: Harvester.

Dicey, A. V. (1915), *Introduction to the Study of the Law and the Constitution*, reprinted in Liberty Classics, Indianapolis, Ind., 1982.

Doganis, C. (2007), *Aux origines de la corruption*, Paris: Presses Universitaires de la France.

Doris, J. (2002), *Lack of character*, Cambridge Univesity Press.

Droz, J. (1860), *Histoire du régime de Louis XVI*, Paris: Renouard.

Duquesnoy, A. (1894), *Journal sur l'assemblée constituante*, Paris: Alphonse Picard.

Durkheim, E. (1960), *Le suicide*, Paris: Presses Universitaires de France.

Egret, J. (1962), *La pré-révolution française*, Paris: Presses Universitaires de France.

Elster, J. (1978), *Logic and Society*, Chichester: Wiley.

Elster, J. (1983a), *Sour Grapes*, Cambridge University Press.

Elster, J. (1983b), *Explaining Technical Change*, Cambridge University Press.

Elster, J. (1984), *Ulysses and the Sirens*, rev. ed., Cambridge University Press.

Elster, J. (1985), *Making Sense of Marx*, Cambridge University Press.

Elster, J. (1989), *The Cement of Society*, Cambridge University Press.

Elster, J. (1993), *Political Psychology*, Cambridge University Press.

Elster, J. (1995), "Transition, constitution-making and separation in Czechoslovakia," *Archives Européennes de Sociologie* 36, 105–34.

Elster, J. (1999), *Alchemies of the Mind*, Cambridge University Press.

Elster, J. (2000), *Ulysses Unbound*, Cambridge University Press.

Elster, J. (2004), "Mimicking impartiality," in Keith Dowding et al. (eds.), *Justice and Democracy*, Cambridge University Press.

Elster, J. (2006), "Tocqueville on 1789," in C. B. Welch (ed.), *The Cambridge Companion to Tocqueville*, Cambridge University Press.

Elster, J. (2007a), *Explaining Social Behavior*, Cambridge University Press.

Elster, J. (2007b), "The night of August 4 1789," *Revue Européenne des Sciences Sociales* 45, 71–94.

Elster, J. (2009), *Le désintéressement*, Paris: Seuil.

Feller, W. (1968), *An Introduction to Probability Theory and Its Applications*, vol. 1, 3d ed., New York: Wiley.

Foster, G. (1972), "The anatomy of envy," *Current Anthropology* 13, 165–86.

Gilovich, T., D. Griffin, and D. Kahneman, eds. (2002), *Heuristics and Biases: The Psychology of Intuitive Judgment*, Cambridge University Press.

Ginkel, J., and A. Smith, (1999), "So you say you want a revolution: A game-theoretic explanation of revolution in repressive regimes," *Journal of Conflict Resolution* 43, 291–316.

Hansen, M. H. (1991), *The Athenian Democracy in the Age of Demosthenes*, Oxford: Blackwell.

Hume, D. (1978), *A Treatise of Human Nature*, Oxford University Press.

Jackson, J. (2003), *France: The Dark Years, 1940–1944*, Oxford University Press.

Jaurès, J. (1968), *Histoire socialiste de la Révolution Française*, Paris: Editions Sociales.

Jouanna, A. (1998), Le temps des guerres de religion en France, in A. Jouanna et al. (eds.), *Histoire et dictionnaire des guerres de religion*, Paris: Robert Laffont.

Knei-Paz, B. (1977), *The Social and Political Thought of Leon Trotsky*, Oxford University Press.

Kolm, S. (1984), *La bonne économie*, Paris: Presses Universitaires de France.

Kunda, Z. (1990), "The case for motivated reasoning," *Psychological Bulletin* 108, 480–98.

Kuran. T. (1995), *Private Truths, Public Lies*, Cambridge, Mass.: Harvard University Press.

Lefebvre, G. (1988), *La grande peur*, Paris: Armand Colin.

Leibniz, G. W. (1875–90), *Gesammelte Schriften*, Hildesheim: Olms.

Levenson, J. (1968), *Confucian China and Its Modern Fate*, Berkeley: University of California Press.

Lévi-Strauss, C. (1960), *La pensée sauvage*, Paris: Plon.

Lichtenstein, S., and P. Slovic, eds. (2006), *The Construction of Preference*, Cambridge University Press.

Lipsey, R. G., and K. Lancaster (1956), "The general theory of the second best," *Review of Economic Studies* 24, 11–32.

List, C. (2006), "The discursive dilemma and public reason," *Ethics* 116, 362–402.

Marx, K. (1845–46), *The German Ideology*, in K. Marx and F. Engels, *Collected Works*, vol. 5, London: Lawrence and Wishart 1987.

Marx, K. (1852), *The Eighteenth Brumaire of Louis Napoleon*, in K. Marx and F. Engels, *Collected Works*, vol. 11, London: Lawrence and Wishart 1979.

Marx, K. (1867) *Capital*, vol. 1, London: Penguin Classics.

Mélonio, F. (1993), *Tocqueville et les Français*, Paris: Aubier.

Miller, D. T. (1999), "The norm of self-interest," *American Psychologist* 54, 1053–60.

Mischel, W. (1968), *Personality and Assessment*, New York: Wiley.

Monroe, K., M. C. Barton, and U. Klingemann (1990), "Altruism and the theory of rational action: Rescuers of Jews in Nazi Europe," *Ethics* 101, 103–22.

Montaigne, M. de (1991), *The Complete Essays*, tr. M. A. Screech, Harmondsworth: Penguin.

Mousnier, R. (1974), *Les institutions de la France sous la monarchie absolue*, Paris: Presses Universitaires de France.

Netanyahu, B. (1995), *The Origins of the Inquisition*, New York: Random House.

Nicolas, J. (2008), *La rebellion française 1661–1789*, Paris: Gallimard.

Ober, J. (1989), *Mass and Elite in Democratic Athens*, Princeton University Press.

Page, S. (2006), *The Difference*, Princeton University Press.

Palmer, R. R. (1987), *The Two Tocquevilles*, Princeton University Press.

Picot, G. (1888), *Histoire des États Généraux*, vols. I–V, reprint New York: Burt Franklin 1963.

Posner, E. (2000), *Law and Social Norms*, Cambridge, Mass.: Harvard University Press.

Rachman, B. (2006), "How community institutions create economic advantage: Jewish diamond merchants in New York," *Law and Social Inquiry* 31, 384–420.

Ritter, G. (1983), *Social Welfare in Germany and Britain: Origins and Development*, Leamington Spa and New York: Berg.

Ross, L., and **R. Nisbett** (1991), *The Person and the Situation*, Philadelphia: Temple University Press.

Schelling, T. (1960), *The Strategy of Conflict*, Cambridge, Mass.: Harvard University Press.

Schelling, T. (1978), *Micromotives and Macrobehavior*, New York: Norton.

Schneider, J. (1978), "Peacocks and penguins: The political economy of European cloth and colors," *American Ethnologist* 5, 443–78.

Schumpeter, J. (1955), *Imperialism and Social Classes*, New York: Kelley.

Schumpeter, J. (1961), *Capitalism, Socialism and Democracy*, London: Allen and Unwin.

Shapiro, G., and **J. Markoff,** (1998), *Revolutionary Demands*, Stanford University Press.

Shiller, R., M. Boycko, and **V. Korobov** (1991), "Popular attitudes towards free markets," *American Economic Review* 81, 385–400.

Shugart, M., and **J. Carey,** (1992), *Presidents and Assemblies*, Cambridge University Press.

Simmel, G. (1908), *Soziologie*, Berlin: Duncker und Humblot.

Smith, A. (1976), *An Inquiry into the Nature and Causes of the Wealth of Nations*, Oxford University Press.

Stone, L. (1986), *The Causes of the English Revolution 1529–1642*, London: Routledge.

Taillandier, S. R. (1853), *Etudes sur la Revolution en Allemagne*, Paris: Franck.

Taylor, G. (1982), "Pluralistic ignorance and the spiral of silence," *Public Opinion Quarterly* 46, 311–35.

Varese, F., and **M. Yaish** (2000), "The importance of being asked: The rescue of Jews in Nazi Europe," *Rationality and Society* 12, 307–24.

Veyne, P. (1976), *Le pain et le cirque*, Paris: Seuil.

Walcot, P. (1978), *Envy and the Greeks*, Warminster: Aris and Phillips.

Weil, E. (1971), "Tradition et traditionalisme," in his *Essais et conférences*, vol. II, Paris: Plon.

White, M. (1987), *Philosophy, The Federalist, and the Constitution*, Cambridge, Mass.: Harvard University Press.

Wilensky, H. (1960), "Work, careers, and social integration," *International Social Science Journal* 12, 543–60.

Wilson, J. G. W. (1992), "American constitutional conventions," *Buffalo Law Review* 40, 645–738.

Wood, G. (1972), *The Creation of the American Republic*, New York: Norton.

Wood, G. (1987), "Interest and disinterestedness in the making of the constitution," in R. Beeman, S. Botein, and E. Carter II (eds.), *Beyond Confederation: Origins of the Constitution and American National Identity*, University of North Carolina Press, pp. 69–109.

Index

adultery, 23
Ahmadinejad, Mahmoud, 165 n. 21
Alexander II of Russia, 165 n.19
altruism, 12, 24
Andersen, Hans Christian, 40
Andrieux, François, 152
anomie, 86–89
Arrow, Kenneth, 11, 76 n. 23, 189
associations, 19, 23, 109–10
Assurance Game, 58, 188
Athens, 119 n. 4, 137, 139, 155
authority, 13
    in belief formation, 29–30
    in religion, 21

bankruptcies, 15, 127
Barrot, Odilon, 178
belief formation, 27–28
    conformism in, 38–42
    and envy, 71
    and interests, 42–43
    fallacies in, 94–95
    and freedom of the press, 35–38
    heuristics and biases in, 28
    ideological, 28, 44–46
    motivated, 27–28
    rational, 27, 30–33
Bentham, Jeremy, 10
bicameralism, 140
Billacois, François, 19
Bismarck, Otto von, 165 n. 19
Blake, William, 23

Bloch, Marc, 34 n. 8, 184
bourgeoisie, 67 n. 12, 69 n. 15,
    74–75, 118, 123–25, 129,
    158–60, 173–74
Bruyère, Jean de la, 47, 48, 49
Bryce, James, 4
by-products, 18, 106–7, 186

caste, 122
Catholicism, 45–46, 112–13
checks and balances, 139–44
Chou En-lai, 100
class consciousness, 78, 126, 129
classes, 125–32; *see also* bourgeoisie;
    nobility; peasantry; workers
class struggle, 128
Clermont-Tonnerre, Comte de, 174–75
Coleman, James, 2
compensation effect, 13, 19–22, 60, 188–
    89
concessions, 166–67
Condorcet, Marquis de, 10, 29, 187
conformism, 29, 36, 38–42
    cognitive versus motivational, 29–30, 38
    inner versus outer, 38
conspicuous consumption, 65 n. 9
contempt, 75
contradictions (in Tocqueville's writings),
    2, 4–5, 29, 36, 42, 50, 86, 96–98, 130
    n. 24
cooperation, 50–56
coordination, 51

cross-voting, 171–72
crowds, 77–78, 180

danger, 74
decentralization, 107–8
democratic government
  deficiencies of, 133–34, 144–45
  pathologies of, 147–49
  turnover in, 135–37, 185
  virtues of, 19, 134–35, 145–47
Descartes, René, 53–54
desires and capacities, 80–81
desires and opportunities, 81–93
despotism, 21, 33, 98, 105, 109, 120,
  147–49, 175
Dicey, Albert Venn, 9, 141 n. 5
disinterestedness, 25
Droz, Joseph, 152
duels, 19–20, 76
Durkheim, Émile, 2, 6, 86 n. 7, 181

egoism, 48–49
Elisabeth of Bohemia, 53
England, 160, 186
envy, 60, 61–71, 80, 148, 159–60, 163,
  183
  alleviation of, 70
  avoidance of, 70
  black versus white, 62–63
  causes of, 68–70
  enjoyment of, 71
  effects of, 70–71
  and hatred, 3, 71–73
  neighborhood, 69–70
  preemption of, 70
  provocation of, 71
equality, 33, 44–45, 68, 115 n. 2, 119,
  133–34, 147–49, 168
  dynamic, 115
    effects of, 116, 127–28, 189–90
  political, 120–22
  static, 114, 126
    effects of, 115–16, 128
  versus equalization, 66–67, 82–83,
    101–3
  versus liberty, 57, 63–64, 80–81, 185–
    86
equilibrium, 6, 54, 95–106, 182–84
Estates-General, 154, 162
  of 1789, 173–76
ethical individualism, 7, 95

fallacies, 94–95, 110–11
fatalism, 34
fear, 67, 74
freedom of the press, 35–36, 101, 177
free riding, 6, 75, 124, 128–29, 139,
  187
Freud, Sigmund, 28
functional explanation, 7, 15 n. 12, 76,
  118, 155

Gambetta, Léon, 144 n. 15
game theory, 187
general ideas, 31–35
geographical mobility, 128
Genovese, Eugene, 84 n. 6
Germany, 7–8, 159–60

half-measures, 165–66
halfway houses, 43, 73–74, 112–13, 141,
  177, 190
hatred, 72, 101, 159–60, 163
Hegel, Georg Wilhelm Friedrich, 6, 8, 33,
  36–37, 84 n. 6
historians, 32–33
holism, 6
Holmes, Stephen, vii, 94 n. 1,
  179 n. 40
honor, 24, 41–42, 75–77
Hume, David, 10, 51–52

individualism, 56–58
individuality, 48 n. 3
interest, 47, 59; *see also* self-interest
  and passion, 59–64
  short-term versus short-lived, 60 n. 1

Jaurès, Jean, 189
judicial review, 141–43
juries, 106, 135

Lamartine, Alphonse de, 179–80
learning, 135, 146–47
Leibniz, Gottfried Wilhelm, 104
liberty, 21, 106, 120, 168, 186; *see also*
  equality
  costs and benefits of, 80–81, 105–6
  neutralized by interest, 90–91
  neutralized by religion, 21
  neutralizes individualism, 57
literature, 22, 103–4

Louis XV, 164
Louis XVI, 164–67

Madison, James, 59
majority, 29–30, 38, 55–56, 81, 109, 140,
    145–46
Malesherbes, Guillaume-Chrétien de
    Lamoignon de, 150, 175
Marx, Karl, 2, 6, 7–8, 46, 94, 126, 131,
    151, 156, 180 n. 41
master-servant relationsm 103, 132
mechanisms, 2, 5, 14, 38, 74 n. 22
    concatenation of, 22, 23
mediocrity, 70, 95
military service, 67
Mill, John Stuart, 1, 4 n. 6
mobility, *see* geographical mobility; social
    mobility
mores, 6, 96–98
Montaigne, Michel de, 36, 42, 77 n. 26
Montesquieu, Baron de, 10, 24–25
Mounier, Jean-Joseph, 174

Necker, Jacques, 173
nobility, 69 n. 15, 72–73, 76, 77 n. 26, 78,
    116–18, 122, 124–25,
    128–29, 152–58, 159–61

organicism, 6–7
ostracism, 39, 41, 187

parlements, 154–55, 161–62, 170
Pascal, Blaise, 36
passion, 47, 59; *see also* contempt; envy;
    fear; hatred; vanity
    and interest, 59–64
    and social norms, 75–78
peasantry, 65, 67 n. 12, 71, 72–73, 118,
    121–24, 125–26, 159–60, 163,
    169
pluralistic ignorance, 2, 39–40, 58,
    188
preemption, 164–65
preference formation, 11, 73–75; *see also*
    compensation effect; satiation effect;
    spillover effect
    adaptive, 91, 167
    motivated, 23–25
president (American), 85, 135, 143
    election of, 143–44

Prisoner's Dilemma, 51, 188
privilege, 62 n. 5, 66–68, 73, 112, 114,
    117–20, 157, 161 n. 15
Protestantism, 45–46, 113
pseudo-science, 4, 44
punishment, 109

rational choice, 79
rationality, 49
Rawls, John, 1
religion, 7, 17, 20–22, 25, 41 n. 18, 45–46,
    60, 90, 102, 106–7, 183; *see also*
    Catholicism; Protestantism
repression, 73–74, 165–66
resignation, 92
responses to crisis, 164; *see also*
    concessions; preemption; repression
revolution, 77–78, 86–88, 99–101, 150
    of 1789, 152–76
        precipitants of, 162–79
        preconditions for, 152–62
        triggers of, 169–76
    of 1830, 150
    of 1848, 74–75, 77, 156 n. 10,
        176–80
        dynamics of, 177–80
        general causes of, 176–77
risk attitudes, 11, 15–16, 127
Rochefoucauld, Duc de la, 47 n. 1

safety valve, 99, 124
satiation effect, 13, 22–23, 148
Schelling, Thomas, vii, 181
Schumpeter, Joseph, 104, 125
second-best, 120, 162, 171, 190
self-interest, 24–26, 47–49, 107,
    138–39
    enlightened, 24–25, 49–50, 52–56, 59,
        64
Simmel, Georg, 153
slavery, 30 n. 6, 84, 89, 91, 97, 98,
    112
Smith, Adam, 10, 130
socialization, 88 n. 9
social mobility, 41, 77, 87, 89, 115, 137,
    189
    in the ancien régime, 122–25
social norms, 7, 41, 75–78, 129
Spencer, Herbert, 6

spillover effect, 13, 17–19, 22, 31, 35, 98,
    105, 106, 188–89
Staël, Mme de, 152
status (in)consistency, 73, 119, 168
Stendhal, 5, 87
Stone, Lawrence, 150
suffrage, 68, 109–10, 112, 114, 119–20,
    155–56

taxation, 117–18, 123, 153–58
teleology, 7, 33
time preferences, 11, 12, 16–18, 54–58, 80
Tocqueville paradox, 40, 162–69
Turgot, Anne-Robert-Jacques, 59, 157
Turner, Frederic Jackson, 99

uncertainty, 55–56
utilitarianism, 133, 146

vanity, 61, 177
Veblen, Thorstein, 65 n. 9
venality of office, 154, 161–62
Veyne, Paul, vii, 28, 91 n. 12, 92 n. 15,
    129, 191 n. 7

Washington, George, 59
Weber, Max, 2
Wilde, Oscar, 22
wishful thinking, 42
women (American), 91, 110–11
workers, 74–75, 131–32

Franklin Pierce University

00179691